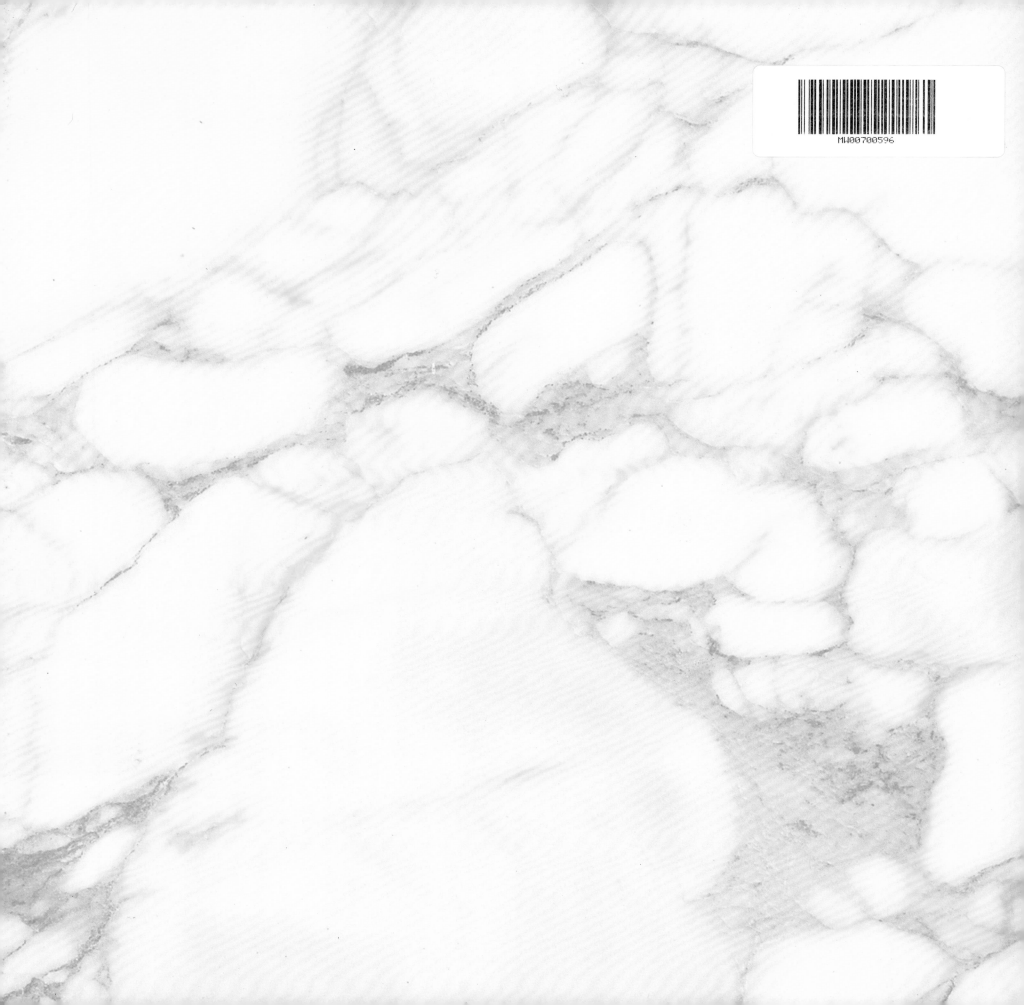

The *Hermitage*
at
ONE HUNDRED

··· RIDLEY WILLS II ···

The *Hermitage* at ONE HUNDRED

NASHVILLE'S FIRST MILLION-DOLLAR HOTEL

Providence House Publishers
WWW.PROVIDENCEHOUSE.COM
FRANKLIN, TENNESSEE

Printed in South Korea.

13   12   11   10   09   1   2   3   4   5

Library of Congress Control Number: 2009932725

ISBN: 978-1-57736-422-1

Cover illustration by David Wright Photography
Cover and page design by LeAnna Massingille

PROVIDENCE HOUSE PUBLISHERS
a HILLSBORO PRESS book
238 Seaboard Lane • Franklin, Tennessee 37067
www.providencehouse.com
800-321-5692

This book is dedicated to all those Nashvillians who cherish The Hermitage Hotel and have nostalgic memories of special occasions there. This includes those who met their spouses at the hotel, spent honeymoons there, attended dances in the ballroom, celebrated meaningful wedding and anniversary parties there, or made business deals in the dining room.

HOTEL
HERMITAGE
NASHVILLE
Will Appreciate Your Business
HOWARD BAUGHMAN, MGR.
DECEMBER

POST CARD

...ACE CAN BE USED FOR A WRITTEN MESSAGE,
USING ONE-CENT STAMP

FOREWORD

We take great honor and pride in being the caretakers of the glorious tradition of The Hermitage Hotel. It has remained a fixture in downtown Nashville, surviving ups and downs as the world changed around it. At the dawn of its second century, thanks to the deep and long-term commitment of its owners, its past has been preserved and its future assured.

The grandeur of the original hotel has been carefully restored along with a reinterpretation of luxury for a modern era. Because of the respectful and loving treatment of this hotel's history and importance, hope exists for other landmark properties facing closure or demolition. Today's Hermitage embodies historic spaces with modern luxury.

None of this could have been accomplished without the commitment, dedication, and pride of our employee associates. Their unique, personal, and respectful service distinguishes the hotel as much as the many architectural features do and helps create our high rate of return guests. World travelers, heads of major corporations and heads of state, renowned celebrities, musicians, and even cherished family pets find a home at the Hermitage. The hotel's prestige also contributes to Nashville's prominence as a world-class city, and we are grateful to the residents, government, and especially the downtown business community for their support through the years.

We invite you to enjoy this book, and welcome you to come and be a part of the Hermitage story as new chapters are written in the history of this grand hotel.

Greg Sligh
Managing Director

ACKNOWLEDGMENTS

I n 2006, Tom Vickstrom, controller of The Hermitage Hotel, contacted me in regard to my collection of Hermitage Hotel postcards that he was interested in making copies of for the hotel's one-hundredth birthday in 2010. David Andrews, a concierge at the Hermitage, had told Tom about the fact that I was a local historian and that I had a large Tennessee postcard collection. Thanks, David. When Tom told me that they were looking for an author to write the centennial history of the Hermitage, I told him that I might be interested in doing so, having already given a paper on the subject in the hotel, and being intrigued with its rich history. I gave Tom a copy of the paper I wrote and the titles of several books that I had authored on local history. Tom got back with me and suggested that he and Greg Sligh, the managing director of the Hermitage, meet with me in my home. We had a nice visit and I was able to show them a number of the books I had written, as well as a portion of my collection of Nashville maps, drawings, and photographs. Shortly thereafter, Greg and Tom asked me to write the one-hundred-year history of the hotel, a task that I have thoroughly enjoyed.

I got off the starting block quickly as I already had a file of newspaper clippings accumulated over the years about The Hermitage Hotel. Tom helped immensely by going to the Nashville Public Library on his lunch hours and finding an even larger number of archival newspaper articles about the Hermitage, all carefully dated. I am grateful to him for that and for the many other things he did to open avenues of investigation for me and make my task easier. Without Tom's enormous help, manifested often in identifying people to whom I should talk, writing this book would have been more difficult and less interesting. Another reason this project has been so pleasant is that Greg and Tom are both gentlemen who care deeply about the hotel that has been entrusted to their stewardship. They introduced me to other members of their management team, including John Powers, director of engineering, whose knowledge of the building is impressive, whose interest in it is obvious, and who generously gave of his time to take me on an extensive tour, starting on the roof and going all the way to the basement. On several occasions, Tom and John joined me for lunch in the hotel dining room when I invited people there to be interviewed. Janet Kurtz, director of sales and marketing for the Hermitage, graciously allowed me to sit in her department's tight offices more than once to scan stacks of trade magazines that mentioned the hotel.

I spent most of my research time either in my office at home, calling various people with knowledge of the hotel; in the Nashville Room at the Nashville Public Library; or at the Tennessee State Library and Archives. At both libraries, the staff was uniformly helpful. Meredith Haddock, director of the Tennessee State Library and Archives, assisted willingly by providing me with copies of all Hermitage Hotel photographs in the State Library and Archives' collection. Helping him accomplish this were Susan Gordon and Dara Brock, both of his

staff. I am grateful for their collective help and that of James A. Hoobler, senior curator of arts and architecture at the Tennessee State Museum.

Grace Hall, the widow of longtime general manager Richard "Dick" Hall, and a friend of mine, read a portion of the book and gave me insightful suggestions. Thanks, Gracie. I had a number of phone calls with Lannie Neal, another friend, who worked at the front desk after school in the 1950s and still remembers details of interesting events that took place on his watch. Although I spoke with Bob Pardue, who worked in guest services at the Hermitage during the 1930s and 1940s, the fact that he wrote down his memories of the hotel during that period and was willing to share them with me was extremely helpful.

One of my most enjoyable interviews was with Patrick Franzone, then general manager of the Millennium Maxwell House Hotel and a former general manager of the Hermitage. His appreciation and fondness for the Hermitage came through loud and clear. Those same feelings were expressed by another former general manager, Doug Vandenberg, general manager of the Holiday Inn Express in Nashville, who told me his years at the Hermitage were the best in his hotel career.

In 2008, Tom Vickstrom brought in Beth Odle, an experienced and well-recommended photo researcher in Nashville, to come up with the images for the book. Beth did a comprehensive and first-rate job. Not only did she find lots of excellent photographs, she also uncovered a number of interesting articles from the *Nashville Banner* collection at the Nashville Public Library

that I used in the book. Early in 2009, I asked Pace Cooper, president of Cooper Hotels in Memphis, to read a portion of the book. He did so and made several good suggestions. Another person who helped was Wanda Davis, who did valuable research late in the project including the material on Robert Meyer, and found images of Gilbert Gaul's paintings.

Fiona Soltes, a gifted writer, editor, and researcher did a wonderful job in editing my text, including the moving of particularly interesting stories to eye-catching sidebars.

I would also like to thank Andrew Miller and his staff at Providence House Publishers for their tireless efforts to make this book a treasure for those who read it: Melissa Istre, Holly Jones, Maren Kurek, Mary Lawson, and LeAnna Massingille.

To all the people I've mentioned and to the others I interviewed or spoke with, many of whom are credited in the book, I am appreciative of your help and your affection for Nashville's "Grand Old Hotel."

The *Hermitage* at
ONE HUNDRED

Chapter One

GRAND BEGINNINGS

In downtown Nashville, at the corner of Sixth Avenue and Union, time stands still.

Amid Italian marble, rich fabrics, and soaring archways, it matters not whether the faces in the vaulted ceiling's painted glass look down on this century or last. For one hundred years, each who pass below, each who enter the lobby of The Hermitage Hotel, has been treated with luxurious attention.

There is a sense here, even today, of memories being made and history being told. It is a tale of famous faces and grand occasions, but also of personalities, passion, a dedicated staff, and a clear vision of what the hotel—and its home city— could be.

And it was high time. Back when the 1900 census figures were published, Nashville Board of Trade members, city officials, and civic leaders were chagrined. Since the 1890 census,

Nashville had been passed in population by Memphis and Atlanta; civic pride had taken a big hit. Fortunately, there was some positive news. The massive Union Station, with its Romanesque tower 221 feet tall, opened in 1900 as an important community icon. Dan Buntin's handsome Arcade, patterned after one in Milan, Italy, came on the scene three years later. In 1904, it was announced that First National Bank would build a twelve-story skyscraper on the corner of Fourth and Church. A year later, E. B. Stahlman's Mecklenburg Realty Company announced plans to build another skyscraper, named the Stahlman Building, on the corner of Third and Union.

A Beaux Arts–style public library opened in September 1904, thanks to the generosity of Scottish philanthropist Andrew Carnegie. Two months later, young attorney Pat Mann led a progressive effort to change the sometimes-confusing names of the city streets running north and south from the river thirty blocks west to First through Thirtieth avenues, north and south. The mayor and city council did their parts by annexing seven square miles to increase the city's size from twenty-two square miles to twenty-nine. The city's leadership also took consolation in the fact that Nashville was still the fifth largest city in the South.[1]

Still, a group of community movers and shakers, many of whom had been involved in one or more of the above mentioned projects, were determined to do more to enhance the quality of life in Nashville. Their idea was to build Nashville's first million-dollar hotel. They would name it the Hermitage Hotel in honor of Andrew Jackson's home. It didn't hurt that the name "Hermitage" was derived from a Russian word meaning "place of rest," either.

With a growing city, the investors felt the Hermitage would compete effectively with Nashville's other major hotels: the Duncan, the Maxwell House, and the Tulane. The original investors also were motivated because there was a

well-known shortage of first-class hotels in the city, particularly during holidays and state fair week.

And so on June 5, 1908, nineteen businessmen incorporated the Hermitage Hotel Company with capital of $350,000. Of this amount, $100,000 came from the architect James Edwin Ruthven (J. E. R.) Carpenter. They had already identified two homes on Sixth Avenue North that could be purchased and demolished to make way for the hotel; it would stand on the corner of Sixth Avenue North and Union Street and back up to Capitol Alley.[2] This was the same site where former governor William Carroll once lived. Even earlier, the site was part of Lot 112 in the original plan of Nashville drawn by Thomas Malley in 1784.[3]

The Details of the Work

The ambitious construction schedule called for receiving bids to demolish the Thomas Tobias and Tom Fite houses by early July; beginning

Above, left: This 1908 Nashville Plat Map shows the location of the two houses that were purchased and demolished to build the hotel. NPL-SC

Above, right: The book Art Work of Nashville, 1894–1901 *includes this photo which shows the view from the east side of North High Street (later renamed Sixth Avenue) looking toward the Capitol grounds. In 1903 the second building from the right became the Elks Club, the demise of which can be seen in the photos on page 150. NPL-SC*

excavating work on August 5; having steel girders on the site by early September to ensure that they would be on hand when needed; and opening the new hotel in September 1909. That would coincide with the opening of the Tennessee State Fair, a time when hotel rooms in the city were historically filled to overflowing. The first priority of the incorporators was to call a meeting of stockholders, and the gathering took place on June 9, 1908. Its stated purpose was to elect a board of directors and officers, and appoint special committees to "take charge of the details of the work." At the meeting, Robert L. Burch was elected president and William S. Bransford was appointed chairman of the executive committee. The New York architectural firm Carpenter and Blair was named architect. J. E. R. Carpenter, a native Tennessean, would draw the plans and was on hand to meet with the stockholders.[4]

The Beaux Arts Style

Carpenter was said to be the first native Tennessean to be formally trained in architecture. He graduated from the Massachusetts Institute of Technology and joined a New York firm which specialized in the Beaux Arts style. He soon returned to Tennessee, however, following the death of his father, and set up shop in his hometown of Columbia. He designed several buildings in middle Tennessee in the late 1800s. In 1900, Carpenter moved to France for further training in the academic classical architectural style taught at the École des Beaux-Arts in Paris, the official French state school that opened in 1819. Here Beaux Arts education for artists was a combination of history of all art movements with ancient Roman, Renaissance, and Baroque styles being the most emphasized.[5]

The Beaux Arts style influenced U.S. architecture from 1885 until 1920. Famous American architects who trained at the École des Beaux-Arts before Carpenter arrived included Richard M. Hunt, the nation's most venerable architect; Charles McKim of McKim, Mead, and White; and Boston's Henry H. Richardson and Robert Peabody. Hunt, McKim, and Peabody were architects for the World's Columbian Exposition in Chicago in 1893.[6] Hunt also was the architect for George Vanderbilt's mansion, Biltmore, in Asheville, North Carolina, as well as many mansions along the east coast and New York City's Fifth Avenue. Richardson developed a style of architecture known as "Richardson Romanesque." His name was familiar to Nashvillians because his Allegheny County Courthouse in Pittsburgh was the model for Union Station.[7]

Beaux Arts was at its most spectacular in large public commissions, such as the major pavilions at the World's Columbian Exposition and the Exposition Universelle of 1900 in Paris. Because it is a flamboyant style, Beaux Arts was popular with America's industrial barons of the late nineteenth century who were interested in displaying their wealth in increasingly ornate and costly homes. The Vanderbilt mansion in Newport, Rhode Island, is an excellent example. The style also can be found in the Manhattan apartments that Carpenter would later design, in London department stores, and in the recently restored Union Station in Washington, D.C.

On the main façades, "monumentality is conveyed by colossal orders and paired columns, dynamism by marked wall projections and decorative details in high relief, such as swags, garlands and medallions."[8] The decorative motifs are used for theatrical effect. Typically, walls are masonry and façades are often made of light-colored stone. Roofs vary from flat to low pitched, hipped, or mansard. Windows receive a variety of treatments, but

Opposite page, top left: An August 1909 view of the steel skeleton of the Hermitage Hotel. NB

Opposite page, top right: This state fair ad appeared in the Nashville Banner *on September 17, 1910, the same day that the Hotel Hermitage opened for business.* NB

Opposite page, bottom: Steel workers on the top girders of the Hermitage Hotel in August of 1909. The view looks northeast, showing the Stahlman Building on the left and the First National Bank on the right. NB

Below: Tennessee native J. E. R. Carpenter designed the Hermitage as one of his last Tennessee projects. He went on to great acclaim as one of New York City's premier luxury apartment designers. AA

Sizing Up the Competition

OTHER LEADING HOTELS IN THE AREA

MAXWELL HOUSE, NASHVILLE, TENN.

The Hermitage Hotel was far from Nashville's first. The Maxwell House, for example, at the corner of Church Street and Fourth Avenue North, opened as a hotel in 1869. For the next three decades, it was the site of important political gatherings, and a preferred hotel for governors such as Robert Love Taylor; U.S. presidents such as Teddy Roosevelt and Woodrow Wilson; and other celebrities. The Maxwell House was also famous for its cuisine, its handsome rotunda, grand promenade, and the twelve brass cuspidors in the lobby. The hotel's men's bar served Jack Daniel's whiskey, and its Christmas menus were legendary.[9] So was the coffee. Maxwell House Coffee, named for the hotel, was first served there. By the first decade of the twentieth century, however, the luster of the Maxwell House was beginning to fade. Some—including investors of the Hermitage Hotel—felt that the Maxwell House was on a downhill slide.

As for the Tulane, at the northeast corner of Eighth Avenue and Church Street, it was built in the early 1890s. The hotel had one hundred sixty rooms on six floors and featured an exterior of brick, terra cotta, and cut stone. Like the Maxwell House, it had its own season of being home to politicians, political parties, state officials, vaudeville stars, Southern League baseball teams, and college football teams in town to play Vanderbilt University.[10] Governors Benton McMillan, James B. Frazier, and John Cox all boarded there. But the Tulane's location, two blocks away from the business district, was a negative on which the Hermitage owners felt they could capitalize.

Finally, The Duncan Hotel stood the southwest corner of Fourth Avenue North and Cedar Street. Built around 1890, the four-story brick and stone-trimmed building was noted for its pink and white marble staircase in a handsomely furnished lobby, as well as a 75-by-100-foot ballroom with large fireplaces and mirrors on the second floor. The Duncan was host to numerous receptions, cotillions, and dinners.[11] Its location, however, ended up being its downfall, just as the Hermitage investors had predicted. It closed in 1916.

The Tulane Hotel, Nashville, Tenn.

Duncan Hotel, Nashville, Tenn.

The Hermitage Hotel's ornate ceilings and columns are modeled after the then-popular Beaux Arts style. PP

are usually embellished with window crowns and surrounds. The use of roofline balustrades and window balconies with balustrades are common.

In Paris, Carpenter embraced the Beaux Arts style. He loved its classicism, symmetrical elements, luxurious details, and flamboyance. At the École des Beaux-Arts, Carpenter is thought to have met and formed a friendship with Walter D. Blair, who had previously attended Richmond College, the University of Virginia, and the University of Pennsylvania. Upon completion of their studies in Paris, Carpenter and Blair moved to New York City where, in 1905, they formed an architectural firm, Carpenter and Blair. Another young American architect, who studied at the École des Beaux-Arts in 1908, was Russell Eason Hart. After six months working in private studios in Paris in 1909, he returned to New York where he had worked earlier and spent a year doing drafting and design work for Carpenter and Blair. Sometime after Carpenter got the contract to design the Hermitage Hotel, he invited Hart to move to Nashville to serve as resident architect during the construction of the hotel. Hart accepted and moved with his family to Nashville in 1910. By that time, Hart had already been working on the project for a year from the New York office. As soon as the Hermitage Hotel project was completed, Hart established his own architectural practice in Nashville. He designed many prominent homes in Nashville, including the Governor's Mansion which was originally a private residence known as Far Hills. In 1921, Hart would join with F. E. Freeland and Martin S. Roberts to form the first architectural/engineering firm in the state of Tennessee.[12] Since 1928, that firm has been known as Hart Freeland Roberts, Inc.[13]

Carpenter's Nashville masterpiece, then called Hotel Hermitage, would front approximately one hundred feet on Sixth Avenue and have a depth of approximately one hundred forty feet to the alley. Carpenter's plans called for a building of ten floors, although there was some discussion of raising an additional $50,000 and building two additional floors where some of Nashville's wealthiest citizens would take apartments. The Hermitage would, like the Stahlman Building, be a modern, steel and concrete structure. Both buildings had steel-riveted columns encased with 12-by-12 brick and clay tiles four inches thick. The handsome exterior would feature a stone and light grayish-yellow brick and white terra cotta finish, in the Italian renaissance style of architecture. The owners' intent was for the hotel to be equal to the finest in the country. The fireproof structure would contain two hundred fifty rooms, and a large ballroom with vaulted ceiling the entire wing of the ninth floor facing Sixth Avenue North.[14]

Russell Hart, a colleague of Hermitage architect J. E. R. Carpenter, was chosen as the new hotel's onsite architect, overseeing the day-to-day construction. He was later selected to reconstruct the Parthenon building in Nashville's Centennial Park, a project that lasted from 1920–31. Hart traveled to Athens, Greece, to study the original Parthenon and meticulously searched out the exact details to replicate both the exterior and interior. NPL-SC

Above: Businesses attempted to capitalize on the excitement surrounding the opening of the Hermitage and placed newspaper ads proclaiming their involvement in the project. These ads appeared in The Nashville American *and* The Nashville Tennessean *in September 1910. TN*

Opposite page: The Commercial History of Tennessee 1910 *featured the architecture of the Hermitage.* EWF

Among the contractors were: Braid Electric Co. (electrical work); Cain-Sloan Co. (linens, towels, sheets, pillow cases, mats, quilts, and comforts); E&N Manufacturing Co. (cabinet work); Foster-Creighton-Gould (structural steel); Foy-Proctor Co. (concrete work); Keith, Simmons & Co. (hardware); Model Laundry (laundry work); T. J. Mooney Co. (plumbing and heating); Nashville Bridge Company (steel); H. E. Parmer Co. (tiles); and B. F. Stief Jewelry Co. (silver). Because most of these contractors were local firms, the economic impact of their successful bids was considerable. For example, Model Laundry built a $40,000 addition to its plant to meet the anticipated demand for its services. At the time, the electrical contract awarded Braid Electric was one of the largest commercial lighting contracts ever let in Nashville.[15]

Progress Continues

The excavation work for the Hermitage went slowly as the workers were digging the foundation by hand. The contractor knew in advance that this would be the case. Three years earlier when the foundation was dug for the nearby Stahlman Building, the workers had to dig through solid limestone.

Progress continued, however, and the citizens took note. As the Hermitage's steel girders rose into the sky, neighbors in the aging but still exclusive residential areas along Park Place, Sixth, and Seventh Avenues North looked up each morning to check for the new developments. The new hotel would, they understood, be modern in every respect with each room equipped with a private bath, cold and hot running water, electric fans and lights, and telephones with long distance capabilities. It was rumored that

Every room in the Hermitage will be equipped with private bath, running hot, cold and ice water, local and long distance telephones, electric lights and fans, and other strictly modern conveniences and comforts. The furnishings will be thoroughly in keeping with the elaborate architecture and equipment of the building. The decorative effects will be artistic and pleasing.

Grill Room, Hotel Hermitage.

The lobby and all the public rooms on the first floor will be finished in the finest grade of Italian marble, with marbled floors, etc. The main dining room will be finished in Circassian walnut, panelled to the ceiling. The ceiling decorations will be handsome and elaborate and in harmony with the purposes of the room. The grill room is unique; the ceiling being a series of domes, carried on columns, as shown in the accompanying illustration.

The name chosen for this new hostelry has an historical significance, especially appropriate to Ten-

nessee and Nashville. Situated near Nashville is the old homestead of Andrew Jackson, Tennessee's first president of the United States. This he called the "Hermitage." It is still preserved and is one of the historic points about Nashville. Located on the grounds is the Tennessee home for Confederate soldiers. As a tribute to the memory of "Old Hickory" the Hermitage Hotel is named.

Street Entrance to Grill Room, Hotel Hermitage.

Main Entrance, Hotel Hermitage.

the general manager was someone with long experience in some of the best New York hotels; that the hotel would serve only distilled water to prevent typhoid fever; and that, because of its concrete floors, the building was dust-proof, fireproof, and noise-proof. Pretty impressive, to be sure.

In the meantime, as the steel work on the Hermitage reached the top floor, the Nashville City Council passed, in August 1909, a Capitol Boulevard Ordinance to widen the ten-foot wide alley running from the Vendome Theater on Church Street to the Capitol by thirty-five feet on each side. Fortunately, the city council did not force the Hermitage owners and their architect J. E. R. Carpenter to make structural changes to the hotel.

Conversely, the Nashville YMCA had to change its plans for a new building to be bound by Capitol Boulevard on the east, Union Street on the north, and Seventh Avenue North on the west.[16] The construction of the YMCA and YWCA buildings facing each other on Seventh Avenue North

Making an Investment
PROMINENT BUSINESSMEN MAKE MARK

The incorporators and directors of the forthcoming Hermitage Hotel represented a crosssection of Nashville business:

- Edward B. Stahlman, railroad executive, newspaper publisher;
- William S. Bransford, vice president of Realty Savings Bank and Trust Company;
- Robert L. Burch, editor, merchant, and manufacturer;
- Edgar W. Foster, business manager of the *Nashville Banner* and president of the Merchants Delivery Company;
- Joseph Frank, president of Joseph Frank & Son, Clothiers and Men's Furnishings, and a director of the Merchant's Bank;
- Edward A. Lindsey, second vice president of First National Bank; and
- John H. Carpenter, business partner and brother of architect J. E. R. Carpenter.

Other stockholders in the Hermitage Hotel Company included: James E. R. Carpenter; Claude C. Christopher; Whiteford R. Cole; Pat Mann Estes; John W. Love; Charles S. Martin; Byrd Murray; James O. Palmer; John B. Ransom; Eugene S. Shannon; George A. Washington; and R. M. Wilson.[17]

Above: The ballroom's ornate coffered ceiling features original craftsmanship. The chandelier fixtures are the 1910 originals and are still in use today. JA

Previous pages: This 1913 postcard shows the Hermitage Hotel from Sixth Avenue North, looking south. The Watkins Institute tower can been seen in the background. RW II

and the Hermitage Hotel, only a block away, could have made competition particularly keen for the limited number of steel workers in the city. Fortunately, the Hermitage was well along when steel work began on the YWCA and YMCA buildings in late 1909 and early 1910. The time it took to hand-dig the excavation, plus the lack of skilled iron workers in Nashville, may well have contributed to the later-than-originally-hoped-for opening in September 1909.

That year, a magazine article furnished more details on the new hotel:

The decorative effects will be artistic and pleasing. The lobby and all the public rooms on the first floor will be finished in the finest grade of Italian marble, with marbled floors, etc. The main dining room walls will be finished in Circassian walnut paneling. The ceiling decorations will be handsome and elaborate and in harmony with purposes of the room. The Grill Room is unique; the ceiling being a series of domes, carried on columns.[18]

It must have gratified the owners of the hotel to later learn that the handsome Circassian walnut paneling in the Hermitage dining room was cut in the same style and design as the paneling in the *Titanic* ballroom. The *Titanic*, which sank on its maiden voyage in 1912, was considered the most opulent and luxurious ocean liner ever built.

Opening Night Arrives

The Hermitage, "Nashville's magnificent $1,000,000 hostelry," opened its doors to the public at 6 PM on Saturday, September 17, 1910, even though the work had not been completely finished.[19] The marble in the high-vaulted and magnificent lobby was still being installed; the Grill Room would not open until later; and the exterior lacked some finishing touches. All the same, early that evening, hundreds of sightseers entered through the main entrance on Sixth Avenue North, crossed the marble foyer, climbed the steps, and strolled through the exquisite lobby on Persian rugs below a large painted glass skylight. Beneath the rug in the center of the lobby, which was painted in antique silver and gold, was a compass fashioned from Tennessee marble. (The marble compass can be seen in the photo on page 80.) There was no fireplace on the west wall as there is today; instead, there was a cigar stand. To the left of that stand was a door to the two service elevators and the Capitol Boulevard service entrance. To the right was a glass door opening into the dining room. The check-in desk was on the north side, where it remains today.

Hotel staff enjoyed hearing visitors discuss the rich draperies, the handsome furniture upholstered in velvet, the Persian rugs, and the glittering,

THE HERMITAGE HOTEL

A caption from the September 18, 1910, edition of The Nashville Tennessean *reads: "This magnificent new hostelry was opened to the public Saturday night at 6 o'clock. Although all the fixtures have not been installed, the lobby, parlors, and dining room are completed in the most modern and elegant style. In every particular it will rank as one of the leading and most perfectly furnished hotels in the entire country. Every detail has been worked out for the satisfaction of the most fastidious. The service is par excellence." TN*

Opposite page: Circa 1911 postcards feature the new hotel's lobby and exterior. Note the lobby seating draped in linens to preserve the longevity of the upholstery prior to air conditioning. RW II
Below: This advertisement from the Social Directory of 1911–1915 features the name of the hotel's first manager, Timothy Murphy. Advertised room rates were quickly revised to $2.00 and up. RW II

cut-glass chandeliers. Bellmen dressed in spotless white tried to be inconspicuous and yet ready, at a second's notice, to be helpful with luggage. The bellmen and all other hotel employees, except for the black waiters in the dining room, were white, recruited primarily from Nashville.[20]

On opening night, Nashville's own Frank Davis, chief clerk, was everywhere, seeing old friends and making all the visitors feel welcome and special. The hotel's directors were on hand with their wives, proud of what they had accomplished and confident that the hotel would not only be a success, but would also propel Nashville back to the very top tier of southern cities. Architect Carpenter accepted countless congratulations on the splendid building.

Nearly four hundred guests, the cream of Nashville society, were served dinner in the main dining room that night. Among those there were Mr. and Mrs. Robert Burch, whose guests were Mr. and Mrs. E. A. Lindsey; Mr. and Mrs. James Palmer and their guests Mr. and Mrs. Alton Wade; Mr. and Mrs. W. S. Bransford, with Mr. and Mrs. Clark Kirkman; Mr. and Mrs. Eugene Shannon who had with them Dr. and Mrs. Al Harris; Mr. and Mrs. Joel O. Cheek with six guests; and Mr. and Mrs. John Carpenter, who had a dinner party of six. The guests sat at tables covered with snowy damask linen and with centerpieces of pink roses and maidenhair ferns. The exquisite murals on the walls were enhanced by stands of superb American Beauty roses, ascension lilies, Killarney roses, and stands of ferns.[21]

W. C. Williams, the headwaiter, was naturally solicitous of the distinguished guests and made sure that the forty waiters under his command were attentive to their every need. Williams had, for four years, been at the famous Plaza Hotel in Asbury Park.[22] A four-piece orchestra made up of musicians from the Waldorf-Astoria played for the occasion. And every room that was finished was occupied.[23]

HOTEL HERMITAGE

Complete in all Details. Inspection Invited

RATES, $1.50 AND UPWARD

Special attention given to Five O'clock Teas, After Theatre Suppers, Banquets and all other social functions.

TIMOTHY MURPHY, Manager

On Monday, throngs of people watched a giant parade of automobiles headed to Cumberland Park for the opening of Tennessee's fifth annual State Fair. The favorite topic of conversation at the weeklong fair was the Saturday night opening of the Hermitage.

A short time later, a Nashville newspaper gave an extravagant description of Nashville's newest hotel. It stated,

The Hotel Hermitage is one of the South's leading hotels, in fact one of America's noted hostelries. It is the only absolute fireproof hotel in the city and occupies one of the most desirable corners. There is no hotel in the country more magnificently fitted, appointed, and furnished. The magnificent lobby is brilliant in its conception, being elegantly appointed with works of the latest art, and carpeted with the finest weaves of oriental design and the very finest of upholstered furniture is arranged in the most pleasing manner. The walls, columns, etc. are Venetian, Grecian, and Italian marble, while the floors, wainscoting, etc. are of the finest Tennessee marble. The mezzanine is on the second floor and La Marquise and the Loggia are situated over the Sixth Avenue entrance. Four rapidly moving elevators give rapid service to every floor. There are 250 rooms in the hotel and every one is equipped with private bath, circulating hot, cold, and ice water, telephones, and electric devices showing when mail is in the box.[24]

The rooms did not, however, have showers. If a gentleman guest wished to take a shower, he had to use one in the men's restroom in the basement.

On the same level, the Grill Room, adjoining the Oak Bar, was originally planned as a rathskeller. Built by a craftsman brought from Germany, the Grill Room became a private club for men only for many

Rotunda of Hotel Hermitage, Nashville, Tenn.

Shots Fired

WAR OF WORDS TURNS DEADLY

Even in the days when the foundation of the Hermitage Hotel was still being laid, stories abounded. Consider the tale of Col. Duncan Cooper and his twenty-seven-year-old attorney son, Robin Cooper. In late 1908, the men passed by the construction site with former Nashville sheriff John Sharp. Colonel Cooper lingered to watch the workmen building the foundation, being careful not to lean too heavily on the plank fence that surrounded the gaping hole.

Meanwhile, the younger Cooper and Sharp continued on up the hill to the intersection of Union Street and Seventh Avenue North. They stopped and waited for Colonel Cooper to catch up, but then the son saw his father's hated political enemy, Edward Ward Carmack (pictured above), editor of *The Nashville Tennessean*, walking up from Church Street. Earlier that day, Colonel Cooper had been enraged over Carmack's

editorial in *The Nashville Tennessean* titled "The Diplomat of the Zweibund." The editorial accused Cooper of corruption. Also stung by previous editorials, Cooper had allegedly said that if his name appeared again in *The Nashville Tennessean*, either he or Senator Carmack "must die." Having heard this threat, Carmack borrowed "a blue-steel pistol, a five-shooter loaded all around" from Major William O. Vertrees, a friend and lawyer. The Coopers also were armed.

Just before Colonel Cooper caught up to his son, the younger Cooper warned Sharp to keep "Papa" from seeing his rival. He then grabbed his father's left elbow and tried to turn him away from Carmack. The old man knew something was amiss and turned and said, "Is that Carmack?" Before Cooper's son could reply, Colonel Cooper broke away from his son's grasp. At that moment, Carmack had stopped to speak to Mrs. Charles Eastman, who was walking down Seventh Avenue, arm in arm with an infirm male relative. When she heard Colonel Cooper angrily shouting at Carmack, she instinctively bolted to the right, pulling her relative through the front gate of a nearby home. Thinking he was being ambushed, Carmack dashed behind two telephone poles, raised his pistol, and fired at the young Cooper. His first shot hit the man in the shoulder, and the next passed through the left sleeve of his coat without touching him. Robin Cooper returned the fire, hitting Carmack three times, twice in the heart and once in the neck. Carmack died instantly, still holding a smoldering cigar in his left hand.[25] *The Nashville Tennessean* charged the next morning that the Coopers ambushed and murdered Carmack while *The Nashville American* claimed that the encounter was accidental, and that the Coopers were defending themselves. At the ensuing trial, a jury found Sharp innocent and the two Coopers guilty of second-degree murder.

The Coopers were sentenced to twenty years in prison. After a motion for a new trial was denied, the case went to the State Supreme Court. While the court was sitting, Gov. Malcolm Patterson, who had defeated Carmack in a bitter 1906 Democratic primary, pardoned Colonel Cooper, his closest political advisor. The court upheld the conviction of Duncan Cooper although he did not fire a shot. A week after pardoning Cooper, Patterson announced his candidacy for a third term as governor. The Republicans ran Ben W. Hooper, a Newport lawyer, against him. In September 1909, realizing that he would be beaten, Patterson withdrew from the race. Democrat Bob Taylor took his place and was defeated by Hooper, who became the state's second Republican governor since Reconstruction. Earlier, the Supreme Court reversed Robin Cooper's conviction "for jury instruction errors and remanded for retrial." At his second trial, Robin's conviction was overturned and he was released. Though a free man, Colonel Cooper was shunned by many Tennesseans. Patterson also suffered. The pardoning of the Coopers ended his political career.[26]

CARMACK SHOT DEAD IN STREET

Ex-Senator Killed in Nashville Son of Col. Duncan Cooper, R senting Newspaper Attacks

VICTIM FIRED TWO SHO

Cooper's Friends Insist That mack Fired First and Poi to Wounds as Evidence.

WOMAN FRIEND SEES KILL

Mr. Carmack Was Talking t When Coopers Came Up Excitement in t

Special to T

Grill Room,
Hotel Hermitage,
Nashville, Tenn.

Above: The Grill Room was featured on this postcard, circa 1913. Note the electric fans in use. The rathskeller concept was a popular hotel feature of the day. Its origins and name are German, meaning "restaurant in city hall basement." RW II
Opposite page: The Capitol Grille today. MEN

years.[27] It was entered by steps slightly to the north of the present steps and was separated from the Oak Bar by a glass door slightly to the north to the present entrance.

The glass porch, or loggia, a feature entirely new in hotels, was designed to be open as its tile floor was slanted slightly so that water could flow to drains on the balconies. In the winter, the loggia was enclosed with glass. Soon, the glass enclosure was made permanent. The loggia stretched the full length of the hotel overlooking Sixth Avenue to the east and the hotel lobby to the west, and featured wicker armchairs, tables, and desks; ferns; brass spittoons; and a handsome rug. The loggia was also for men only.

At that time, the ninth floor had a convention hall with a fifteen-foot vaulted ceiling; it seated two hundred people. When the Southern Agricultural Workers met at the Hermitage thirteen months after the hotel opened, the attendees would convene in the hall where Gov. Ben W. Hooper would welcome them.[28]

A banquet was held in the Hermitage Hotel ballroom on February 23, 1911, in honor of Tennessee's Luke Lea, newly elected to the United States Senate. Lea is believed to be the tall man standing in the center, at the flag. RML

That's not all. The lobby featured a beautiful cut-glass ceiling designed by an Italian artist. When the Grill Room opened, it featured a vaulted ceiling and red oak paneling from Russia.[29]

Decades after the opening, Clara Hieronymus, art and theater columnist for *The Tennessean*, praised Carpenter for having adhered to the ornate style in which he had been trained. He gave the Hermitage, Hieronymus wrote, "a well-unified style in the mode of Beaux Arts classicism, employing arched openings between coupled columns, a five-level composition, and extravagant detailing influenced by the French Renaissance style."[30]

Upon its completion, the owners of the Hermitage leased space to John H. Carpenter, a brother of James E. R. Carpenter and the president of the Nashville Interurban Railroad.[31] Carpenter would maintain his residence in the Hermitage for the first two years before moving to Louise Avenue, and then, in 1913, to Lynnmeade, the home that James designed for him on Harding Pike.

Above, left: Circa 1913 postcard of the hotel's loggia. The May 23, 1908, issue of the Nashville Banner *reported this description from the 1908 prospectus: "In balmy weather the loggia will give all the comforts of the old southern porch and in winter it will be enclosed in glass and converted into a pleasant resort for tea drinkers and afternoon loungers."* RW II
Above, right: The veranda sky ceiling today. MC

The West Wall

THEN AND NOW

Today, visitors to The Hermitage Hotel lobby are drawn toward a warm and inviting fireplace flanked by overstuffed chairs. Originally, that same west wall was home to a cigar stand with a long glass case in front and three cabinets against the wall. From 1913 until 1918, the Best and Russell Cigar Company operated the stand, and customers could buy cigarettes, cigars, local and out-of-town newspapers, pipes, smoking tobacco, post-cards, and popular magazines such as *Harper's Weekly* (until 1916) and *Collier's Weekly*. Managers of the cigar stand included Charles J. Ransom (1913); H. S. Edwards (1914); and William L. Smith (1916).[32]

Designing Dreams

J. E. R. CARPENTER RISES TO THE TOP

When James Edwin Ruthven Carpenter designed the Hermitage Hotel in 1908, he was well known in Tennessee architectural circles. But his talent would eventually take him to heights never before seen. In New York City, he would carve out a legacy that has stood the test of time.

Carpenter was born in the tiny town of Mount Pleasant, Tennessee, in 1867. His father, J. E. R. Carpenter, was a prominent local merchant and iron manufacturer who was also mayor of Columbia in 1884. Carpenter's mother, Jane Wilson Carpenter, was from an old Maury County family that once owned Blythewood, one of the county's most cherished antebellum landmarks. She was educated at the Columbia Institute.

Carpenter attended local schools before entering the University of Tennessee in 1885. Shortly afterward, he transferred to the Massachusetts Institute of Technology to study architecture. In Boston, he studied under the renowned Boston architect Henry H. Richardson, said to have been the most original and talented American architect of the era. This schooling took place at Richardson's home, not at the school. Carpenter is credited with being the first native-born Tennessean to receive formal training in architecture.

After he graduated, Carpenter's talent won him a job with one of the country's most prestigious architectural firms in America: McKim, Mead, and White. The New York City company specialized in the Beaux Arts style.

Carpenter was well on his way to establishing a national career, but following the death of his father, he returned to Tennessee to help his family. His first job after coming home was as draftsman for the Columbia arsenal that later became Columbia Military Academy. After practicing draftsmanship in Columbia a short time, Carpenter moved to Nashville. He appeared in the Nashville City Directory in 1890, and from 1891 until 1892, practiced architecture with Baxter Hodge and Hodge's son, James A. Hodge, in a firm known as Hodge & Carpenter. In 1892, Carpenter published a book called *Artistic Homes for City and Suburb*. The book contains descriptions, floor plans, and sketches for fourteen homes suited to the South.[1] He also designed a number of homes, including one in Columbia at 207 West Eighth Street for J. Rosenthal, a prosperous merchant;[2] and Lynnmeade, a home built for his brother, John H. Carpenter, and his wife, Mary.

In 1892, Carpenter moved to Norfolk, Virginia, where he opened an architectural practice with fellow former

Nashvillian John Kevan Peeples. The firm specialized in designing business and commercial buildings, churches, homes, and hotels across the state. They designed the Fayerweather Gymnasium at the University of Virginia and the Monticello Hotel in Norfolk. They also entered a design for the Jefferson

Hotel in Richmond, a commission ultimately awarded to Carrère and Hastings of New York. The hotel owner, Major Lewis Ginter, recorded that "the design submitted by Messrs. Carpenter and Peeples was easily second."[3]

Carpenter married Marion Stires on February 9, 1899. They had one daughter, Marion.

Around 1900, Carpenter traveled to France to study at the École des Beaux-Arts in Paris. The Beaux Arts style was to influence Carpenter's design greatly, seen in his early work at the Hermitage Hotel, but also in his later apartment designs.

In the Beaux Arts style, the rooms are generally arranged so that the least important spaces are entered first and most important spaces are arrived at last. This also carried through in the various architectural elements: the least important visual elements occur at the lower levels, gradually moving upward to the most important elements at the top. Also important is the idea of symmetry, where elements occur evenly on each half of the room or building.

Upon his return to America, Carpenter collaborated to design a number of important buildings in Tennessee: St. Thomas Hospital (1903); Maury County Courthouse (1905); the rebuilt Main Building at Vanderbilt University (1906); and the Stahlman Building. After designing the Hermitage Hotel, Carpenter and Blair also did work in other southern cities. They designed the sixteen-story Empire Building (1909) and the Ridgely Apartments (1914), both in Birmingham, Alabama; the American National Bank Building in Pensacola, Florida; and the eighteen-story Hurt Building in Atlanta (1913).[4]

It was the work on the Stahlman Building that gave Carpenter the edge when architects were being considered for Nashville's first million-dollar hotel, the Hotel Hermitage, in 1909–10. Stahlman was an incorporator and influential member of the committee. Carpenter submitted a design for a grand hotel in the Beaux Arts style, and was selected.

Main Building. Vanderbilt University.
Nashville, Tenn.

A New Style of Living

Carpenter moved to New York City in 1910, after being hired to design an apartment building in Manhattan. He arrived just as societal changes made apartment living more desirable. His plan for the nine-story apartment building at 116 East 58th Street was simple, yet revolutionary. The arrangement of rooms would pivot around a central foyer. In a book about Carpenter, Andrew Alpern described it:

> It was this novel feature that distinguished Carpenter's planning approach and set him apart from earlier designers. For them, the parlor, library, and dining room were what matter, with everything else in the apartment subservient. For Carpenter, the starting point was the functional effectiveness of the entire suite of rooms, and the circulation patterns were critical to the result.[5]

The building was christened the Fullerton, and Carpenter made one of the apartments his own home. Following this well-received venture, Carpenter designed several more apartment buildings, including buildings on Park and Fifth avenues, some of the priciest real estate in the world. He has been called the father of modern apartment design in New York City, pioneering the high-rise luxury apartments that replaced the mansion home. In all, over the course of twenty-plus years, Carpenter designed forty-four buildings; forty-one are still in use today.[6]

One of Carpenter's last designs was for the Lincoln Building, a fifty-two-story office building, which was completed in 1930. It is noted as a significant marker of mid-Manhattan. Unfortunately for Carpenter, he was an investor in the project, and he had a large debt obligation as a result of the stock market crash. He died suddenly of a heart attack on June 11, 1932.[7]

The Fullerton

THE WORLD'S NEW YORK APARTMENT HOUSE ALBUM

TYPICAL FLOOR PLAN OF THE FULLERTON.

THE FULLERTON APARTMENTS

No. 116 East Fifty-eighth Street

7896. St. Thomas Hospital, Nashville, Tenn.

Chapter Two

WAR AND SUFFRAGE

"NASHVILLE OFFERS OPPORTU

NOTICE

ETTERS MAILED IN HOTEL ENVELOPES
T TO THE DEAD LETTER OFFIC
DDRESS.

HOTEL HERMITAGE

MEYER HOTEL CO., PROPRIETORS
HOMER WILSON, MANAGER
NASHVILLE, TENN.

Positioned within full view of the Tennessee State Capitol, the Hermitage Hotel has long been a mainstay for powerful meetings between powerful people. Even today, amid more casual guests, it's not uncommon to spot legislators and lobbyists gathering to discuss issues. Previous years have brought landmark battles and U.S. presidents, as well.

On November 9, 1911, William Howard Taft became the first such president to visit the Hermitage. That night, he was entertained in the hotel's main dining room. *The Nashville Tennessean* described the banquet as the most elaborate one ever given in the city, complete with a $7-per-person extravagant meal, music by the Royal Hungarian Orchestra, and a menu handsomely engraved with the seal of the City of Nashville and the Tennessee and American flags. Jacob McGavock Dickinson, former secretary of war in Taft's cabinet and a good friend, presided. In addition to the

Nashville Banner.

TENNESSEE   KENTUCKY

VOLUME XXXVI, NO. 184   SIXTEEN PAGES   NASHVILLE BANNER, FRIDAY EVENING, NOVEMBER 10, 1911.   5 O'CLOCK EDITION   TWO CENTS

CITY OF NASHVILLE GIVES GRAND OVATION TO LEADING CITIZEN OF THE AMERICAN UNION

WILLIAM HOWARD TAFT CITY'S HONORED GUEST

Thousands Greet Him at Station, Other Thousands Along Line of March, And Auditorium Overflowing.

Great Banquet at Hotel Hermitage—Old Confederate Soldiers in Uniform of Lost Cause Escort President, and Sit With Their Banner Upon Speakers Stand.

AT THE BANQUET TABLE AT HERMITAGE HOTEL

CHINESE OFFICIALS FLEE AND FIGHTING CONTINUES

Heavy Losses Reported to Have Been Suffered on Both Sides in the Battle Being Fought at Foo Chow.

Situation at Tien Tain Grows More Serious, Minister to Japan Deserts Post in Order to Avoid Meeting Students — Incendiaries Put to Death by Revolutionists.

---

expected speeches, several rousing Yale College songs were sung by a quartet of Vanderbilt University students. That wasn't all that was special; ladies who attended were part of the banquet rather than seated in a separate gallery.[1]

It was an interesting time. Coming years would challenge the place of those women, especially in regard to the right to vote. In 1911, however, unescorted ladies still entered the hotel through a separate entrance on Union Street. From there, they could climb three or four steps to reach the dining room to the right, go directly to the lobby without climbing any steps, walk down a grand stairway to the Grill Room, or turn left and climb seven or eight steps to reach the ladies' reception and tea rooms. As they were not allowed in the men's loggia or the Oak Bar until after World War I, they would normally have a waiter take their drinks to the tea or reception rooms, the restaurant, or the Grill Room. As an alternative, ladies could order their drinks through a small opening to the left of the entrance to the Oak Bar. In those days, women had to either be accompanied by another lady or a gentleman to even ride the elevators.

By 1914, women's rights were an increasing topic of conversation, and not just in the hotel's gentlemen-only loggia. That year, the hotel would be host to the suffragists' 1914 national convention. Many were still opposed to the idea of women's suffrage, a movement that had little success until 1869 when the Utah Territory gave women the right to vote.

The first suffragist organization in Nashville surfaced in 1890 and lasted only about six months due to prejudice and criticism. Nevertheless, by 1900 there were suffragist organizations in every southern state.[2] The Nashville

---

SPECIAL FOR TO-DAY.

Rockaway Oysters in Half Shell 30—Cocktail 35
Blue Point Oysters on Half Shell 25—Cocktail 30
Grape Fruit with Maraschino 25
Canape of Caviar 50
Queen or Ripe Olives 20
Chow-Chow 20

Oysters and Relishes
Marinated Herring, Wine Sauce 30
Imported Sardines in Oil 30
Antipasto, Special 25   Mixed Sweet Pickles 15
Celery 30   Chicken Okra 25—40

Soup
Cream of Asparagus, au Croutons 25—40   Consomme Alexandra 25—40
Mulligatawny Soup 25—40   Oyster Stew 25—40

Entrees
Broiled Spring Chicken on Toast and Potato in Cream 65—1.25
Baked Tenderloin of Beef with Vegetables, Bourgeoise 60—1.00
Calf Sweetbreads in Chafing Dish, a la King 65—1.25
Broiled Loin of Veal and Potato O'Brien 60
Broiled Jumbo Squab on Toast with Bacon 80
Turkey Croquette, Cream Sauce and Asparagus Tips 50—90
Leg of Lamb, Mint Sauce 50—90

Roast
Ribs of Beef 50—90   Potato Salad 50—90
Ribs of Beef, Potato Salad 50—90
Pickled Lamb Tongue and Beets 45—80

Cold
Cold Tennessee Ham and Slaw 50—90
Sliced Turkey and Tomato Surprise 75—1.50
Drawn Butter 50—90   Corn 25
California   Beets 25
Stuffed Sweet Pepper 25   Spinach and Egg 25

Vegetables
June Peas 25   Mashed 15
Fried or Candied Sweet Potatoes 25   French Fried 20
Potatoes Baked 15   Boiled New Burmuda 20
Hashed Brown 20   Au Gratin 30   O'Brien 30
Asparagus 40   Tomato Stuffed with Chicken Salad 40
Combination 35   Chicken 60—1.00

Salads
Lobster 60   Watercress and Egg 25
Waldorf 50   with Tomato 35   10c per person
Head Lettuce 30—with Tomato 35
Roquefort Cheese or Thousand Islands Dressing 10c per person
Charlotte Russe 30
Apple Pie 15

Entremets
French Pastry 15   Cherry Tart 20   Pie, a la Mode 35
Pear Pie 15   Vanilla and Chocolate Eclair 15   Tutti Frutti Ice 25
Strawberry Short Cake 20
Chocolate 25   Frozen Biscuit, Tortoni 30
Vanilla 25   Mixed in fancy form 30   Orange Sherbet 20

Ice Cream
Strawberry Melba 40   Swiss 20
Peach Parfait 30   American 20

Cheese
Imported Roquefort or Camembert 25
Neufchatel Cheese and Imported Jelly 25   Orange Pekoe 15

Coffee, Tea and Milk
Tea: English Breakfast, Russian, Oolong, Ceylon, Orange Pekoe 15
Coffee, pot for one 15   Bottle Milk 15   Butter Milk 10
Chocolate or Cocoa, pot for one 15—with Whipped Cream 20

Half Portion served for one only; served for two 25c extra charge.
Please call for and examine check before paying. All prices must be stamped on check.

Do not pay Check unless totaled in Red Ink

Friday, November 21, 1913

Hotel Hermitage, Nashville

SEE THE OTHER SPECIAL BILL OF FARE FOR FISH.

Equal Suffrage League was organized in 1911, and at its second meeting, Anne Dallas Dudley was unanimously elected president. Although prejudice, indifference, and ignorance were formidable adversaries, some people realized woman suffrage was no longer a joke. In 1911, a *Nashville Tennessean* editorial stated, "However much men may object to the practical application of woman's suffrage, the movement is so strong that it can not be laughed down and it is only a question of a little while when the matter will have to be fought out in all the states."[3]

While in Nashville, the National American Woman Suffrage Association convention gave stylish young Anne Dallas Dudley, wife of Guilford Dudley, president of Nashville's Life and Casualty Insurance Company, an opportunity to shine. She overlooked no detail in planning the meeting. Yellow banners and streamers hung throughout the Hermitage, demonstrating the movement's colors.

Pennants, Bunting, and Streamers

Sadie Warner Frazer, the twenty-nine-year-old wife of George Augustine Frazer, was one of the young Nashville matrons who helped make the 1914 national convention run smoothly. She was transportation chairman. Before the convention, Frazer spent many hours on the telephone asking her friends for the use of their automobiles for part of the day. The response was wonderful, and she soon had cars lined up for every hour of the entire week. Frazer spent each day of the convention in the Nashville chapter headquarters, located in the previously vacant corner store of the Hermitage Hotel.

At that time, nearly all cars in Nashville were driven by chauffeurs; Frazer lined up those she had borrowed on Union Street, holding them there until she

Above, left: Nashville taxicab ad from the Nashville Banner, September 17, 1910. NB
Above, right: Circa 1914 postcard showing the hotel's exterior. RW II
Opposite page, top: The hotel quickly became the center of attention when a banquet honoring President William Howard Taft was held on November 9, 1911. Taft is pictured sixth from the right. NB
Opposite page, bottom: This circa 1913 menu was discovered during the 2002 renovation, in a restaurant wall. HH

gave the signal from the ladies' entrance of the hotel. The chauffeur would bring the car, jump out, and come around with cap in hand to deliver people to the Capitol. On the last day of the convention, Frazer and her volunteer friends wanted to hear Dr. Anna Howard Shaw, president of the national association, address the legislature. However, the lobby was humming and they were besieged with requests from delegates who wanted to be driven to the Capitol early so they could get good seats. Suddenly, Shaw emerged from the hotel's elevator. She walked directly to Frazer's desk, announcing that she was ready to be driven to the Capitol. The car that was to take her was not expected for another hour. Frazer had to improvise in a hurry as she could tell that Shaw was getting impatient.

Leaving Shaw with one of her committee members, Frazer ran across the lobby and out the ladies' entrance. She stood there for a moment, knowing that Shaw was not far behind. Before long, she recognized a friend, Alvin Graham, drive up Union Street in a fancy sports car. She hailed him in no uncertain terms. Graham, who was wearing hunting clothes, immediately pulled to the curb, somewhat surprised at her boldness. Frazer said, "Mr. Graham, I want you to do me a great favor. I want you to take Dr. Shaw to the Capitol." Just then, Shaw came through the door. Frazer made the introductions and said, "Dr. Shaw, Mr. Graham is going to have the honor of driving you to the Capitol." Graham and Shaw both beamed, and Frazer was wreathed in smiles of relief. He opened the door, and Shaw, dressed in black, stepped in and took her seat beside him, his three hunting dogs and all of his hunting gear. Later, Shaw told Frazer how much she enjoyed her ride to the Capitol "with that delightful young man." The near crisis had a happy ending.[4]

Dudley, in the meantime, felt that the convention marked the turning point in the suffrage movement in Tennessee. She and other suffrage

leaders were increasingly confident that their time would soon come. Little did they suspect that the crucial fight would take place in the very hotel in which they stayed.

Frazer, granddaughter of the late John Berrien Lindsley, chancellor of the University of Nashville, was one of an estimated 2,000 Middle Tennessee women who took part in the first suffragist parade ever held in a southern city. It happened on Saturday, May 2, 1914 in downtown Nashville, and the more than one hundred automobiles were covered with "suffrage pennants, bunting, and streamers." Along the way to Centennial Park, the women on foot handed out suffragist literature. Sometimes they were heartened by enthusiastic applause, but at other times, they were viewed with grim disapproval. Many were dressed in white dresses with yellow sashes that read

Above: Suffragists marched in Centennial Park. TSLA

Jackson Day Balls
LADIES CELEBRATE OLD HICKORY

The Hermitage Hotel has long been the place for grand affairs, and the Ladies' Hermitage Association Jackson Day Balls were no exception. The twenty-third annual ball took place at the Hermitage on Monday, January 9, 1911. The year before, the ball had been held at the Tulane Hotel. The purpose of the annual event, held at the Hermitage for many years after, was "to revive the memory of General Andrew Jackson and to keep alive in the hearts of all true Americans the spirit of those who made this great country possible." Large crowds of the most prominent people from the city and state attended, and the decorations featured hundreds of white snowballs entwined with garlands of Jackson vine that draped the windows, arches, doorways, and mantels of the hotel's public area as well as the rotunda balcony. In the ballroom, the central point of interest was a portrait of Andrew Jackson by Ralph E. W. Earl. It was draped with the national colors and garlanded with sprays of vines and white chrysanthemums lit by twin branches of tiny electric lights. The same treatment was given to the room's sidelights, windows, mantels, and doors.[5]

Louise Lindsley, the LHA regent, received the guests on the mezzanine during a reception that lasted from 9 to 10 PM. According to the newspaper society pages, this was followed by a grand march led by four "exquisitely dressed" little girls wearing white chiffon, silk, and lace gowns. Next came a flower dance, performed by the season's debutantes and their escorts. They danced a square dance, followed by the Virginia reel, and then all the other guests joined in. Dinner tables were adorned with low bowls and vases filled with white flowers and fringed with ferns, and an elaborate

Ace Photography

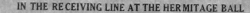

Reading from Left to Right: Mrs. Maggie L. Hicks, Mrs. Bettie M. Donelson, Mrs. B. W. Hooper, Mrs. Robert A. Henry, Miss Louise Lindsley, Mrs. B. F. Wilson, Regent, Miss Carrie Sims, Mrs. Mary C. Dorris.

menu was served until long after midnight. In the ballroom, the dancers, who stayed until the early hours of the morning, were accompanied by an orchestra screened by palms and ferns.[6]

A year later, in the midst of the suffragist goings-on at the hotel, many of the ladies who participated in a 1914 march from downtown to Centennial Park were on hand for the Jackson Day events on January 8, 1915. That year marked the one-hundredth anniversary of the Battle of New Orleans, and thousands attended the ensuing parade complete with a police detail, a company of uniformed Confederate veterans, and two companies of the Tennessee National Guard. That evening, following a men's banquet at the Maxwell House, the Ladies' Hermitage Association (LHA) held the one-hundredth anniversary ball at the Hermitage. This one was said to surpass "in interest and brilliance" any of the previous twenty-six balls sponsored by the LHA. The theme was patriotic, with a wealth of Jackson vine and cotton balls. Historic rifles and swords and hundreds of American flags were grouped effectively in public areas. The spacious dining hall was used as the ballroom.

Suspended from the draperies at the entrance were the figures "100" fashioned in cotton. Inscrolled on the wall to the side of the entrance were the dates "1815–1915" made of cotton bolls. The decorations on the south wall consisted of the coats of arms of Louisiana, Tennessee and the United States. In the center an American eagle was placed with the motto "E. Pluribus Unum." To the right and left were the state flags of Tennessee and Louisiana. On the opposite wall hung the portrait of the hero of 1815, Gen. Andrew Jackson, the property of the Ladies' Hermitage Association.

The decorations in the loggia were of particular interest to the gentlemen. Stands represented Jackson's principal battles: Horseshoe, Talladega, Emuckfaw, Mobile, and New Orleans. Much of the success of the evening was due to the tireless efforts of the efficient regent, Mrs. B. F. Wilson. She accomplished this despite having recently lost her beautiful Harding Pike home, Wilson Manor, to a fire. The grand march featured eighteen of Nashville's most beautiful "society belles," each representing one of the states in the Union at the time of the Battle of New Orleans.[7]

"Votes for Women,"[8] and once they reached the park, they heard Dudley give the first open-air speech ever delivered by a woman in Tennessee.

Another suffragist who walked in the parade was twenty-year-old Frances Bond, daughter of prominent Nashville attorney Frank P. Bond and future wife of Joe C. Davis. When the elder Bond, who was opposed to women's suffrage, learned that his daughter marched in the parade, he just laughed. He later spoke at a mass meeting of anti-suffragists at the Ryman Auditorium while Frances Bond was outside on Fifth Avenue North walking in a suffragist picket line.[9]

By 1916, momentum seemed to be slowly swinging toward the enfranchisement of women in Tennessee. The anti-suffragists realized that they needed to be more aggressive in their opposition, and the organization of the Tennessee chapter of the National Association Opposed to Woman Suffrage followed suit. Their unanimous opinion was that "woman's moral influence in public affairs was greater out of politics, and that doubling the electorate could confer no benefit on the state."[10]

The anti-suffragists were not the only folks making a stir in town—or at the hotel. The construction of a powder plant in nearby Old Hickory in early 1918, as well as the emergence of other substantial war-related enterprises, brought many people downtown. To prepare for the anticipated influx of visitors, Homer Wilson, the Hermitage's manager, re-carpeted practically the entire hotel and installed more than $10,000 worth of handsome furniture. On February 28, 1918, he announced that all the single rooms in the Hermitage would have double beds installed, thereby enabling the hotel to accommodate one hundred twenty additional guests.[11]

At the same time, the challenges of the war were real, and management responded accordingly. In July 1918, the Hermitage hosted the Tennessee Hotel Association, during which time the convention resolved that "hereafter hotels shall only furnish one and one-half teaspoons of sugar for iced tea, cereals and fruits, and two lumps for coffee; also that they remove sugar bowls from their tables."[12]

Just 36 States

The Nashville Woman Suffrage Association held annual meetings in both 1918 and 1919. At the latter gathering, held in the hotel's assembly room January 23–24, the local group listened attentively as Florence Lee Brown Cotnam, a member of the national board from Arkansas, spoke. Local leaders included Dudley, by then a member of the national board, and Kate Burch

Above: Welcome home ad appearing in The Nashville Tennessean, *March 1919.* NT
Opposite Page: Members of the 114th and 115th Field Artillery 30th Infantry Division were honored in victory parades on March 31, 1919, and April 5, 1919. The parade routes ran through Capitol Boulevard toward the Capitol. This picture was taken during the April 5 parade; the Hermitage Hotel can be seen in the background. TSLA

Above: Today, the grand ballroom continues as a splendid setting for business and social events. DWP
Opposite page: Looking south from the steps of the Capitol, this is a view of the Hermitage Hotel and the YMCA Building circa 1920. TSLA

Warner, president of the Tennessee Woman Suffrage Association, also spoke.[13]

The suffragist movement had deliberately slowed its activities during World War I, as all Americans focused their energies on defeating the Germans. But time passed. Soldiers came home. The 114th Field Artillery, for example, arrived by train on March 30, 1919. The troops were commanded by Col. Luke Lea, one of the earliest supporters of the Hermitage Hotel, and some 1,200 citizens including Gov. A. H. Roberts turned out to greet them. The following day, a crowd estimated at between 100,000 and a quarter of a million people lined the streets along which a parade would travel.[14] Equally enthusiastic crowds gathered to welcome home Col. Harry Berry's 115th Field Artillery with another parade the following Saturday.[15]

Civil War on Display

GILBERT GAUL PAINTINGS IN THE LOBBY

One Tennessean who especially appreciated the beauty of the Hermitage Hotel was artist Gilbert Gaul. It's not that he was known for hanging around the hotel lobby, but his paintings certainly were. Around the time of the hotel opening, Gaul was in Knoxville exhibiting a series of Civil War paintings at the Appalachian Exposition; he won a gold medal. But Nashville easily figured into the story. Gaul lived

in the city from 1905 until 1910, only a block from the Hermitage. He moved to Charleston, South Carolina, and then back to his native New Jersey, but before leaving Nashville, sold his original paintings and thousands of color prints at auction to a couple of Nashville men. Later, Henry Sperry, also of Nashville, became a third owner. When one of the first owners moved to Baltimore, he took two of the Gaul paintings with him, left six on loan to the Hermitage for display in the lobby, and stored four—along with the thousands of unsold reproductions—in the basement of the Carnegie Library downtown.[16] Regardless of Gaul's lack of success at the time, he has since been described as the first important Tennessee artist who was not a portrait painter. His works also included Native American Indian paintings.

In 1925, six years after Gaul's death, Robert R. Meyer bought all of the artist's Civil War paintings and the right to reproduce them for $1,400. The paintings would continue to be displayed in the Hermitage lobby until the late 1960s when they were moved to the Tennessee State Museum for safekeeping. Meyer sold "exquisite reproductions" that were smaller than the originals at the Hermitage newsstand. The price in the early days was one dollar per reproduction. Meyer's family later donated the paintings to the Birmingham Museum of Art. They include *Leaving Home*, *Holding the Line at All Hazards*, and *Glorious Fighting*.[17]

Anne Dallas Dudley with her children Trevania and Guilford. She founded the Nashville Equal Suffrage League in 1911 and was a prominent activist in the women's suffrage movement in the U.S. She is especially noted for her efforts to see the nineteenth amendment ratified in her home state of Tennessee. TSLA

Celebrations continued. On April 8, an impressive banquet was held at the Hermitage in honor of Admiral Albert Gleaves, a native Nashvillian who had been responsible for transporting U.S. troops across the Atlantic to France. Some 1.7 million American servicemen made the trip safely; Admiral Gleaves commanded 44,000 officers and 83 ships.[18]

Just a couple of months later, on June 4, 1919, the 66th U.S. Congress passed the nineteenth amendment to the Constitution, giving women the right to vote. It had taken seventy years of petitioning, lobbying, and, in recent years, picketing, to achieve this. Twenty-one successive Congresses had previously rejected what was known as the Susan B. Anthony Amendment.[19] But the battle still wasn't over. To become law, the amendment had to be ratified by three-quarters of the then forty-eight states. The well-heeled anti-suffragist forces only had to persuade thirteen state legislatures to reject the amendment, seemingly a much easier task than the suffragists faced. Cynics predicted that it would take twenty years to gain the votes of thirty-six states. But they underestimated the tenacity of sixty-year-old Carrie Chapman Catt, a veteran of more than thirty years in the suffrage movement and the president of the National American Woman Suffrage Association (NAWSA). She sent telegrams to the governors of all states whose legislatures had adjourned, beseeching them to call special sessions to vote on the ratification. She also encouraged suffrage organizations in all forty-eight states to put their long-planned campaigns into high gear. So far, so good; six ratifications came in eight days. But conservatives fought back, arguing in statehouses across the country that ratification was the first step toward socialism, free love, and the destruction of the home.[20]

Only Eight Left

By New Year's Day 1920, the suffragists had won twenty-two ratifications. More came quickly. On February 27, Oklahoma became the thirty-third state to ratify. When the state of Washington voted to ratify on March 22, there were only eight states left, but four of them—Florida, Louisiana, North Carolina, and Tennessee—were in the South, the part of the country most opposed to women's suffrage.

In New England, neither Connecticut nor Vermont was likely to be supportive, as each had an influential anti-suffrage governor. But the suffragists had a fighting chance in Delaware and Tennessee. Following a bitter fight in the Republican-dominated Delaware legislature, suffragists lost that state in June. Ironically, in 1787, Delaware had been the first state to ratify the Constitution. The failure in Delaware left Tennessee as the crucial test.[21]

In Tennessee, Governor Roberts, a Democrat, was committed to the suffragist cause. Already during his administration, women had been granted the right to vote for municipal offices and for president and vice-president of the United States. The suffragists pressed him to call a special session of the legislature to consider ratification. Conversely, anti-suffragists from across the state threatened to defeat him in the August Democratic primary if he dared to convene a special session. To diffuse the issue, he called for the special session four days after the primary.[22] Roberts had another problem. Abby Crawford Milton, the state president of the League of Women Voters was married to George Fort Milton, the publisher of the *Chattanooga Times*, a newspaper that supported ratification but opposed his re-election and attacked him editorially.

The Hermitage Hotel served as the anti-ratification headquarters during the fight for women's suffrage. Pictured in August 1920 are Mrs. James S. Pinckard, president-general of the Southern Women's League for the Rejection of the Susan B. Anthony Amendment; a Confederate veteran "who fought and bled for Tennessee's states rights"; and Josephine A. Pearson, president of the Tennessee Association Opposed to Woman Suffrage. TSLA

Consequently, Roberts refused to work with Milton or the equally energetic Catherine Kenny, the Tennessee League of Women Voters' chairman of ratification. To avoid dealing with them, the governor named Kate Burch Warner, immediate past president of the League, as his own ratification committee chairman. Warner, the wife of Leslie Warner and a Vassar College graduate, opened her headquarters at Nashville's newest and finest hotel: the Hermitage. Warner realized that her committee was expected to replace Kenny's. But she could not resign for fear of offending the governor, lest he change his mind about calling the special session of the legislature. Carrie Chapman Catt urged Milton not to fight the governor regarding the appointment; instead, she suggested that both committees work together, and that a Republican Ratification Committee be named to keep from getting in each other's way. Catt also communicated with Dudley, NAWSA's national vice-president and one of Tennessee's most influential suffragists, to offer advice.[23]

Because Tennessee's ratification was crucial, Catt came to Nashville by train on July 17 and registered at the Hermitage Hotel. There she settled in Suite 309. Although she had expected to be in Tennessee only for a few days, Catt remained there for six weeks through what her biographer, Mary Gray Peck, would write was "the last and most harrowing six weeks of the whole 72 years that women had to fight for the ballot in these 'free and equal' United States."[24] One of Catt's first steps was to persuade Col. Luke Lea, publisher of the anti-Roberts *Nashville Tennessean*, to lay off attacking the governor for the good of the cause. She also convinced Governor Roberts to recognize Kenny's committee as well as Warner's. These were no small achievements.

The Temperature Rises

Catt's Nashville presence galvanized the anti-suffragist forces into action. Josephine Anderson Pearson, president of the Tennessee Association Opposed to Woman Suffrage, immediately came to Nashville from her home in Monteagle, Tennessee. Before the death of her mother in 1915, Pearson had promised her that, should the Susan B. Anthony Amendment ever come to the Tennessee legislature, she would fight it. Upon her arrival in Nashville, she checked into the Hermitage Hotel, having requested the least expensive room. She also reserved rooms on the mezzanine level for the anti-suffragist campaign headquarters. When national leaders of the anti-suffragist organization arrived the next day, Pearson was moved to a larger space. Not only that, but it was cooler, too; the night before she had been unable to sleep in her small third-floor room thanks to one of the hottest Augusts in Nashville history. Better yet, the new corner room had a view of the Capitol two blocks away.[25]

Anti-ratification group in Hermitage Hotel meeting room, August 1920. TSLA

One of the anti-suffragists' first moves was to order stationery printed with the state organization's new name: The Southern Women's League for the Rejection of the Susan B. Anthony Amendment. Using the stationery, Pearson wrote her supporters across the state seeking financial and moral assistance. She cited three evils of the nineteenth amendment: loss of state rights; Negro women's suffrage; and racial equality. Her forces also printed and circulated handbills in the hotel lobby that read, "Beware men of the South, heed not the song of the suffrage siren."[26]

As the summer heat beat down on the Volunteer state, both sides diligently tracked down legislators in their home communities to secure support. Each side also brought in leaders from other states to work the crowds and denounce the other side. The suffragists sarcastically called the antis the "Home, Heaven, and Mother Crowd." The antis, meanwhile, held a mass meeting at the Ryman

The Place to Be

From the early days on, the Hermitage Hotel claimed its share of convention business. In October 1911, for example, the Southern Agricultural Workers held its thirteenth annual meeting there. Delegates came from eleven southern states, the District of Columbia, and England. The convention was important enough that Gov. Ben W. Hooper gave the welcoming address.[27]

On Feb. 24, 1912, the Woodrow Wilson Club held a noon reception at the Hermitage for the leading Democratic presidential candidate. Woodrow Wilson, then governor of New Jersey, gave a brief speech. His brother, Joe Wilson, worked for the *Nashville Banner*, and their father, Dr. Joseph R. Wilson, had lived in nearby Clarksville, Tennessee, from 1885 to 1892 while he was a professor of theology at Southwestern Presbyterian University. Wilson was in town for the dedication of the new YMCA building at Seventh and Union.[28]

As for the Fifty Years in Business Club, the group held its first convention at the Hermitage in June 1912. Charles C. Gilbert, assistant secretary of the Nashville Board of Trade and club founder, welcomed delegates from sixteen southern and border states in addition to prominent Nashvillians.[29]

A couple of years later, in February 1914, the International Association of Rotary Clubs issued a charter for the Rotary Club of Nashville. It was the 94th rotary club organized in the world, composed of nearly one hundred local businessmen.

The Rotarians met each Tuesday at the Hermitage to discuss "matters of interest to the club and its members." James H. Allison, managing editor of *The Nashville Tennessean* and *The Nashville American*, was president. The Rotary Club hosted numerous conferences at the hotel, including one for the Rotary Clubs of Kentucky and Tennessee on February 10 and 11, 1919.[30] By 1921, however, rotary offices and meetings had moved to the Chamber of Commerce Building on Fourth Avenue North.

Then there was the American Institute of Architects, which held its annual meeting at the Hermitage in 1919. On April 30 of that year, 169 of the leading architects in the country convened for the 52nd annual event. It was the third time the group had met in Nashville, each time because of the architects' appreciation for William Strickland, the architect of the Tennessee State Capitol. They must also have enjoyed staying in J. E. R. Carpenter's handsome Beaux Arts hotel.[31]

The year following, the National Exchange Club, a service organization, chartered a Nashville arm. Just like the Nashville Rotary, the Exchange Club of Nashville chose to hold its weekly meetings at the hotel. In 1921, the club created its annual "Sunshine Special" for the children in area orphanages, a program that was later adopted as a nationwide project. It offered fun events for underprivileged kids.[32]

'50 Years in Business Club' Held First Convention in 1912

Many prominent business leaders of Nashville took part in the first convention of the Fifty Years in Business Club. The picture above was posed in front of the Hermitage Hotel where the delegates from sixteen Southern States gathered in June, 1912. Front row, left to right: the late S. W. Berger, Sr., the late H. W. Buttorff, the late E. S. Shannon, the late J. H. Meeks, the late D. Loveman, the late Miss Carrie Neatherly with a convention poster; William Meyer of Goodlettsville, George H. Armistead, Sr., then editor and publisher of the Franklin, Tenn., Review-Appeal and now editor-in-chief of The Banner, the late W. C. Kendrick, and the late James B. Carr. Back row: Charles C. Gilbert, founder of the Fifty Years in Business Club; Charles S. Mitchell, Ernest Jungerman, now of Florence, Ala., the late C. Levy, F. B. Hollenberg, the late M. S. Combs, the late W. E. Meyer, the late Robert Burch, the late Ben Cornelius, John M. Gray, Jr., the late J. Taylor Stratton, the late Ed Thompson, the late George M. Jackson, and the late Samuel Douglas.

Homer Wilson is noted as manager of the Hermitage Hotel in this ad taken from the Ward-Belmont College yearbook Milestones 1918. NPL-SC

Auditorium in hopes of "saving" the South from the amendment.

The Center of the Fight

On August 6, 1920, Tennesseans learned that Governor Roberts had won the Democratic primary. He would face Republican Alfred A. Taylor in the general election for the state's next governor. True to his word, Roberts issued a proclamation calling the 61st Tennessee General Assembly into extraordinary session at noon on the following Monday, August 9. Each side marshaled its forces. U.S. Senator Kenneth McKellar came from Washington, D.C., bringing the support of the Woodrow Wilson administration for the pro-ratification side. Charl Ormond Williams, vice-chairman of the Democratic National Committee, came up from Memphis to lend her considerable administrative skills to the suffragist cause. On the other side, Anne Ector Pleasant, wife of former Louisiana Gov. Ruffin G. Pleasant, arrived. A press release from Pearson's headquarters at the Hermitage reminded Tennesseans that Pleasant's father, Maj. Gen. Matthew Duncan Ector, Confederate States Army, had three horses shot out from beneath him at the Battle of Lookout Mountain and a leg amputated in the Atlanta Campaign. The antis also were delighted to publicize the presence of Kate Gordon of New Orleans and Laura Clay of Kentucky, two former national officers of the NAWSA who had broken with the organization when it embraced the federal amendment. They were in favor of suffrage, but only if it was approved through state actions.[33]

And so, on Saturday, August 7, the Hermitage lobby became the center of the fight; men, women, suffragists, anti-suffragists, politicians, house members, state senators, Democrats, and Republicans all milled around in suffocating numbers under the hotel skylight. Scuffles broke out among the men. Late that afternoon, the anti group moved to a reception on the mezzanine level. There, ladies from Nashville's fashionable areas thanked legislators in advance for protecting southern womanhood from the evils of enfranchisement.

In the evening, the antis treated legislators to free liquor from a suite on the eighth floor. Few people on that floor got any sleep before the wee hours of the morning, as tipsy legislators roamed the halls singing the anti-suffrage theme song, "Keep the Home Fires Burning"—or anything else that popped into their somewhat clouded minds.[34]

On Sunday, powerful Nashville attorney and Speaker of the House Seth Walker informed the governor that he had changed his mind about supporting ratification and, therefore, would not introduce the nineteenth amendment resolution in the House as he had promised to do. He urged Governor Roberts to reconsider his position and oppose the measure if he valued his political future. The governor was not about to do so. However, he and Albert Williams, his liaison with the legislature, worried about how many votes Walker was taking with him. Others had already defected. Although the suffragists earlier thought they had the commitment of 62 House members (12 more than they needed), those numbers had dropped to 55 in favor and 44 against. One pro-ratification supporter, Betty Gram, confronted Walker and asked him if the Louisville and Nashville Railroad had anything to do with his sudden reversal. He was insulted and walked away.[35]

When the Tennessee legislature convened at noon on Monday, the galleries were packed with women, the antis wearing red roses and the suffragists wearing yellow. Corridors in the Capitol also were draped with bunting, predominantly yellow. The first test of strength came on Wednesday when the antis made a resolution to delay the ratification vote until "the will of the

This picture appeared in the 1911 book Pen and Sunlight Sketches of Nashville: The Most Progressive Metropolis of the South. *Originally painted with a striking effect of silver and gold, the lobby was a classic men's domain.* NPL-SC

SENATE CHAMBER AT THE MOMENT THE VOTE WAS BEING COUNTED BY THE CLERK

Suffrage Scene At The Capitol Wh The Senate Ratifie Aug. 13th.

ANDREW L. TODD, SPEAKER OF THE SENATE AND MISS CHARL O. WILLIAMS, LEADER OF THE WOMEN'S FORCES, SMILING AFTER VICTORY

MISS JOS PEARSO MONTEAGLE, OF THE ANTI-SU

MRS. JAMES S. BEASLEY AND MRS. CLAUDE D. SULLIVAN, REPUBLICAN AND DEMOCRATIC SISTERS AND FRIENDS IN VICTORY.

WILLIAMS AND MRS. ASLEY, DEMOCRATIC CAN LEADERS OF HAKE HANDS AND SMILE

A G SEN SUFF AND REA HOME THE HOW VICT IN TH

MRS. GUILFORD O. DUDLEY

people can be heard" in county conventions. By a vote of 50 to 37, the resolution was tabled.

In the meantime, back at the Hermitage, Catt's suite was the site for evening meetings of suffragist leaders mapping out strategy. Pearson's brain trust did the same in her own suite. On Friday, the State Senate passed a resolution of ratification with 25 yes votes, 4 no votes, and 2 not voting. This was by a wider margin than the suffragists thought possible. They were thrilled.[36]

The "Suffs," as the suffragists were called, had each been assigned a ratification-inclined legislator. Over the weekend, they kept close tabs on their charges.[37] Tensions were high; rumors and unsubstantiated charges were rife. Seth Walker got a call from President Woodrow Wilson encouraging him to support ratification. Mrs. Catt was convinced her telephone was tapped. Sue Shelton White and Anita Pollitzer agreed to eavesdrop on the goings on in the Hermitage's so-called Jack Daniel's suite. The *Chattanooga Times* got wind of what they had done and ran a front-page story under the headline, "Two women spies caught in hotel."

On Monday, as lobbyists feverishly worked the legislators, no one was certain where people stood.[38] Consequently, neither side was sufficiently confident to force a vote. Harry "Baby" Burn, a young legislator from McMinn County, wore a red rose, but told Anita Pollitzer, "My vote will never hurt you."[39]

On day seven, Tuesday, a motion was made that the House concur in the Senate's adoption of the resolution ratifying the nineteenth amendment. While debate ensued, Walker moved to adjourn until the next morning. His motion carried 52 to 44. Because suffragists were being summoned to go home by fake messages, the suffragist leaders set up patrols of the Hermitage corridors that night to prevent kidnappings. Carrie Chapman Catt told her associates that all they could do was pray.[40]

On Wednesday morning, the suffragettes wore white dresses with yellow sashes. The antis came too, wearing red roses. That morning, a nervous Harry

Early Leaders Make Their Mark

FAMED TENOR AMONG NOTABLE GUESTS

With the Hermitage Hotel having quickly established itself as one of the South's leading hotels, original manager Timothy Murphy felt he had accomplished what he had been charged to do. He was proud of the Hermitage and its ambience. The ladies' tea and reception rooms were features that brought compliments from Nashville matrons who enjoyed them after days of shopping downtown. The fact that Woodrow Wilson had stayed at the Hermitage rather than the Maxwell House proved that the Hermitage had eclipsed its older rival. Nevertheless, Murphy was not a Nashville native. Having previously been manager of the Homestead in Hot Springs, Virginia, and the Royal Poinciana Hotel in Palm Beach, Florida, he simply felt more comfortable working in a more cosmopolitan environment. Consequently, he resigned in 1912 and soon left the city. Hugh F. Galvin replaced him as the hotel's second manager.

During Galvin's two years as general manager, the hotel orchestra played after-theater music in the Grill (it was then spelled without the "e") on Friday nights. Specials at the time included Blue Point Oysters on the half shell at 25 cents; ribs of beef between 50 and 90 cents; leg of lamb with mint sauce for 50 to 90 cents; lobster salad at 60 cents; and, for dessert, strawberry Melba for 40 cents a serving.[41]

After Galvin left the Hermitage in 1914, Homer Wilson became the third general manager. He and his wife, Grace, boarded at the hotel until his death in 1918. During his years at the Hermitage, Wilson worked for Meyer Hotels Company under the leadership of President Robert R. Meyer. The Birmingham company began leasing the hotel the year Wilson came, and would continue doing so for twenty-five years.[42]

Also of note was the hotel's next manager, Robert E. Hyde, who found himself in the papers after a supposed flap with Italian opera singer Enrico Caruso. Caruso, who had been the lead tenor at the Metropolitan Opera for fifteen years, came for a performance at the Ryman Auditorium. A Nashville newspaper article stated that the forty-six-year-old Caruso was only offered one mattress on his bed at the Hermitage. Caruso termed the tale "utterly silly," and Hyde told a reporter the story was "absolutely and wholly untrue. I never thought of saying any such thing. Caruso could have had sixteen mattresses at the Hermitage if he had wanted them."

Hyde's biggest concern that week was finding rooms for everyone. With a large convention and Caruso in town at the same time, all the hotels were full, forcing some visitors to stay in boarding houses.[43]

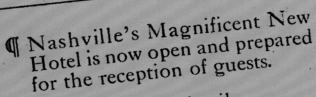

HOTEL HERMITAGE
BATH IN ALL ROOMS

¶ Nashville's Magnificent New Hotel is now open and prepared for the reception of guests.

¶ Complete in all details.

¶ Modern in all conveniences.

¶ In furnishing and decorations it has no equal in all the South.

Rates $2.00 Per Day and Up

TIMOTHY MURPHY, Manager.

Mail orders for Caruso Concert for NASHVILLE and out-of-town on sale now. Mail your check for tickets.

CARUSO
IN CONCERT
Ryman Auditorium
April 29th.

Mail orders now being filled. Prices—$3.50, $5.00, $6.00

More Than Two Thirds of the House Already Sold

If you want tickets you had better hurry. For tickets mail check payable to CARUSO CONCERT FUND, care O. K. HOUCK PIANO CO., Nashville, at once.

Benefit Florence Crittenden Home

MR. CARUSO USES THE

Burn still wore his red rose. He had, earlier in the morning, received a letter from his mother in Niota, Tennessee, urging him to "be a good boy and help Mrs. Catt put the 'rat' in ratification." Mrs. Burn, a widow with a college education, didn't understand why she could not vote when an illiterate tenant on her farm could. Even though many in McMinn County were fiercely anti-suffrage, Burn, only twenty-four years old, was wavering. The suffragist leadership, unaware of his uncertainty, was not counting on him. They figured they had forty-seven votes, two short of the forty-nine they needed.[44]

"Second the Motion"

When Speaker Walker pounded his gavel at 10:30 AM to start the meeting, the sergeant-at-arms had to clear suffragettes, antis, and a mob of lobbyists from the floor. Fierce debate ensued. At one point, Walker relinquished his gavel and asked to speak. When recognized, he stated that the antis had forty-nine sure votes, a majority of the ninety-six present. He then dramatically said, "The hour has come. The battle has been fought and won, and I move you, Mr. Speaker, that the motion to concur in the Senate action goes where it belongs—to the table." Figuring that hesitant antis would feel more comfortable tabling a motion than killing it outright, he could effectively kill the proposition. There were shouts of "second the motion" from the anti legislators. In the ensuing roll call, Harry Burn voted in favor of tabling. Others voted as expected until legislator Banks Turner's name was called. Suffragists gasped with joy when Turner, known to be on the anti side, voted against the motion to table. That morning, before the legislature met, Turner had been in the governor's office where he heard Ohio Gov. James M. Cox, the Democratic presidential nominee, plea by telephone for support of the amendment. At that moment, Turner became a suffragist. As the remainder of the roll call brought predictable votes, his conversion resulted in a tie vote—48 to 48. The motion to table was defeated.[45]

Walker, a close friend of Turner's, was shocked. He instantly called for a recount. With this granted, Walker walked to Turner's desk, sat down and put his arm around him. As the clerk methodically went through the roll call, Walker used every argument he could think of to get Turner to change his mind. When the clerk called Turner's name, everyone was silent and all eyes were on him. Turner pushed aside Walker's arm, arose, and voted "nay." The roll call was over. The motion to table had been twice defeated and the suffragists let out a long cheer. It now was apparent that the original motion to concur in the Senate's ratification of the nineteenth amendment would pass.

Running out of options, Walker reluctantly called for the vote. The suspense was still heavy as the clerk droned through the roll call. Harry Burn was the seventh legislator to vote. At that point there were two "ayes" and four "nays," all predictable. Burn's "aye" came so quickly that it caught many in the chamber off guard. Some thought he was confused. Others were dumfounded. The suffragettes were amazed and thrilled as this meant, if they could hold Turner's vote, they would win. When his time came, Turner shouted "aye." The resolution carried 49 to 47. Before the clerk announced the result, Seth Walker pulled out his last parliamentary maneuver. He rose to his feet and shouted, "I change my vote from "nay" to "yea." Veteran legislators knew what he was trying to do. Only a legislator voting on the winning side could legally bring up a motion to reconsider. If that happened, as was the case on that day, that member could control the measure for seventy-two hours and only he could call for a revote during that period. Maybe, during that time, Walker could convince Burn or Turner to change their minds. Walker's maneuver caused such uproar that few heard the clerk's announcement that the ratification of the nineteenth amendment had passed by a vote of 50 to 46, with 2 abstentions, one cast by the noncommittal Lon McFarland. The suffragists were beside

In 1997 artist Alan LeQuire created 19th Amendment Woman Suffrage, *a bas-relief in honor of the suffrage fight. Note the Hermitage Hotel in the background.* AL

themselves with joy. They hugged each other, threw their yellow boutonnieres in the air, and sang and cried as yellow flower petals floated down from the galleries. The jubilation spread throughout the Capitol and to the Capitol grounds. Even at the Hermitage Hotel, where Carrie Chapman Catt nervously waited in her suite, she could hear the cheers and realize that they had won and Tennessee had become "the perfect 36."[46]

The reaction of the antis was disbelief followed by rumors and charges that Harry Burn had been bribed and even that Seth Walker had only pretended to be anti when, in truth, he was for ratification all along. On Thursday, the day after the vote, Harry Burn, the youngest member of the legislature, rose in the House Chamber and explained why he voted as he did. He said, "I know that a mother's advice is always safest for her boy to follow, and my mother wanted me to vote for ratification."[47]

As the legislators, lobbyists, antis, and suffragists waited for Seth Walker's motion to reconsider to play out, the antis held rallies across the state. When the legislators reassembled on Saturday, all forty-nine who voted "yea" on Wednesday showed up. However, only nine antis were on hand. The others had taken the train to Decatur, Alabama where they gathered in a hotel lobby, hoping to prevent the assembling of a quorum in the statehouse and, thereby, prevent action on the ratification. The "Sterling 49" who voted for ratification couldn't have cared less about the missing antis because they had a quorum. After listening to the House chaplain open the proceedings that morning with a prayer in which he asked that "God's richest blessings be granted to our absent ones" and waiting for the noon deadline to come, they called up Walker's motion and voted it down.

On Tuesday, August 24, 1920, Governor Roberts signed, sealed, and mailed, by special delivery registered mail, Tennessee's ratification to Secretary of State Bainbridge Colby.[48] Votes for women had become the law of the land. Tennessee was "the perfect 36" and one of only three southern states to ratify

Signature Clinches Suffrage Act

VOTES FOR WOMEN

On August 18, 1920, Tennessee became the 36th state to ratify the 19th Amendment to the U. S. Constitution, thereby giving all American women the right to vote. After weeks of intense lobbying by national leaders, Tennessee passed the measure by one vote. The headquarters for both suffragists, wearing yellow roses, and anti-suffragists, wearing red roses, were in the Hermitage Hotel.

DONATED IN MEMORY OF CARLEEN S. WALLER
THE HISTORICAL COMMISSION OF METROPOLITAN NASHVILLE AND DAVIDSON COUNTY
NO. 54   ERECTED 1986

WAR MEMORIAL PLAZA

the nineteenth amendment. Much of the tumultuous politicking, strategizing, and drinking during the bitter fight for ratification in the Tennessee statehouse took place at the Hermitage, Nashville's finest and newest hotel. Many consider the successful suffragist fight at the Hermitage Hotel and the Capitol to be the most important event in Nashville during the twentieth century.

Interestingly, Governor Roberts did not benefit from his staunch ratification stance. In the November general election, he lost to Republican Alfred A. Taylor, the oldest governor to occupy the governor's chair, by more than 40,000 votes.

Above, left: This photo from the front page of The Nashville Tennessean *on August 26, 1920, shows Governor A. H. Roberts signing the amendment as suffrage leader Charl Williams looks on.* NT

Above, right: Commemorative marker outside the Tennessee State Capitol. JA

Chapter Three

A RISING PRESTIGE

Though the Hermitage Hotel has been home to countless meetings, special events, and historically important moments, it's always been about the people. That doesn't just count the staff who still works tirelessly behind the scenes to deliver an experience like no other; it's also about the literally millions of guests—some famous, some just not yet.

About 1922, Thomas E. Dewey of Owosso, Michigan, stayed at the Hermitage while in Nashville for a nationwide opera competition. Dewey, a young baritone singer, lost. In disgust, he decided to attend law school, and graduated from the Law School at Columbia University in 1925. Five years later, he launched his government career as chief assistant to the U.S. Attorney for the southern district of New York. Elected district attorney in 1937, he unsuccessfully ran for governor in 1938, but persevered and gained the governorship in 1942. Dewey

HOTEL HERMITAGE · NASHVILLE, TENN.

HOWARD E. BAUGHMAN, Manager

Good Enough for a Gangster
CAPONE STAYS AT THE HERMITAGE

In the mid-1920s, the North and South were finally connected by the first major thoroughfare. The Dixie Highway, as it was called, was complete with a well-surfaced section over Monteagle Mountain. Travelers could now go comfortably from Chicago to Miami, and one who often took the route was notorious Chicago gangster Al Capone. Capone came south each winter to take advantage of Florida's sun, sea, and sand, and would usually spend the night at the Hermitage on his way to and from another hotel in St. Petersburg, Florida.[1] He also frequently stopped in Monteagle, Tennessee, where he allegedly built a handsome stone home for a girlfriend. In 1928, Capone, who made his treks south in an armor-plated Cadillac with bulletproof glass and run-flat tires, bought a fourteen-room villa on Palm Island, Florida, where he spent the winters until his conviction on income tax evasion in 1931.[2]

was elected for three successive terms, gaining a reputation for political moderation and administrative efficiency. As Republican nominee for U.S. president in 1944, Dewey lost to Franklin D. Roosevelt. He ran again in 1948, but was once again defeated, this time by Democratic candidate Harry S. Truman.[3]

Fun with Frat Dances

During the 1920s, high school fraternities and sororities were important in Nashville, and their dances were highlights of the December social scene in particular. Affairs were usually held at the Belle Meade or Richland country clubs or at the Hermitage Hotel. On December 22, 1924, the Alpha Sigma Lambda fraternity had a dance at the Hermitage. Among those who attended was Sam Fleming, a freshman at Vanderbilt University who later became CEO of Third National Bank.

A dozen years later, high school dances at the hotel were still in vogue. In December 1936, David Proctor, a Montgomery Bell Academy senior and officer of Alpha Chi, took his girlfriend, Elizabeth Craig, to a fraternity dance there. Craig didn't have her pocketbook and had to borrow 15 cents from her date to enter the pay stall in the ladies' room. On another occasion—in the very same ladies' room—Craig had to scramble under the door for lack of the 15 cents.[4]

College fraternal organizations also held dances at the Hermitage. Vanderbilt's Phi Kappa Psi fraternity, for example, held one on Friday night, January 17, 1919, with four alumni and their wives serving as chaperones.

In the meantime, the Hermitage placed regular ads in The Vanderbilt University annual, *The Commodore*. One quarter-page advertisement identified the Hermitage as "Nashville's New Million Dollar Hotel. Fireproof, strictly modern in every appointment. 250 rooms-250 baths. Beautiful dining room, Grill Room, and ball room. Rates: $2 and upward. Robert R. Meyer, President; Robert E. Hyde, Manager." Considerable business came from Vanderbilt alumni and parents.

Let the Battles Begin

But competition was on its way. The Hermitage, which had reigned supreme in Nashville almost since its opening in 1910, gained a fierce new rival in September 1925 when the twelve-story Andrew Jackson Hotel opened on the corner of Sixth Avenue North and Deaderick Street. Owned by Charles L. Loridan, a hotel and tobacco mogul from Atlanta, the hotel had four hundred rooms. It was easily the largest hotel in Nashville, though still smaller than the 625-room Peabody Hotel that opened in Memphis the same year. Loridan leased the Andrew Jackson to the Dinkler Hotel Company of Atlanta. Other hotels owned or leased by the Dinkler Hotel Company were the Ansley in Atlanta; the Tutwiler in Birmingham, Alabama; the St. Charles in New Orleans; and the Jefferson Davis in Montgomery, Alabama.[5]

Chattanooga and Knoxville also received modern, fireproof hotels in the 1920s. The Read House, a massive red brick ten-story hotel with four hundred rooms, opened in Chattanooga in 1926, while the seventeen-story Andrew Johnson Hotel, with three hundred fifty rooms, opened in Knoxville several years later.

The competition wasn't just among the hotels themselves; the year 1926 brought the first big political campaign to be waged from Nashville's two modern hotels, the Hermitage and the Andrew Jackson. It was a gubernatorial contest between Hill McAlister and incumbent Austin Peay. McAlister's headquarters were at the Hermitage, while Peay set up his campaign office at the Andrew Jackson. Peay won, but so did the Hermitage. Later campaigns would bring the likes of Burgin Dossett, Prentice Cooper, Jim Nance McCord, Frank G. Clement, and Buford Ellington to the hotel.

In earlier years, Democratic leader Edward Hull "Boss" Crump and his majordomos, Frank "Roxie" Rice and Willie Gerber, always stayed at the Hermitage when they were in town. Rice, with a reputation for heavy

drinking and profanity, also was known for being Crump's longtime liaison with the Shelby County Democratic delegation in the state legislature. He made sure they voted as a unit however Boss Crump dictated. Roaming the hotel's rooms, cloakrooms, corridors, and lobby, "Rice ordered, cajoled, entreated, and otherwise peddled the considerable influence of his sponsor."[6] One of Crump's many visits to the Hermitage came in 1918, when he drove to Nashville to lobby, unsuccessfully, for a charter change that would allow for a council-manager form of government in Memphis and put him in a position to name the city manager and to control Memphis politics.[7]

Governor Alfred E. Smith, unsuccessful 1928 Democratic presidential candidate, spent at least one night at the Hermitage. Throughout the decade, legislators and lobbyists stayed at there, too.

But there also were different kinds of "fighters." Jack Dempsey, world heavyweight boxing champion from 1919 until 1926—when he lost in an upset to ex-Marine Gene Tunney—stayed at the Hermitage when he came to Nashville to referee wrestling matches at the Hippodrome. On one visit, he took "Smitty," a Hermitage bellboy, with him to a match. At the teller's ticket window, Dempsey said, "I have a gentleman here with me that I want to take in." The teller complied. Joel Ralph Lamphere, a Hermitage hotel employee who knew "Smitty" and met Dempsey, remembered that the champion was a nice guy—except when he was in the ring.[8]

Dempsey would always be remembered for the "long count," referring to his controversial rematch with Tunney on September 22, 1927, when Dempsey knocked Tunney down with a left hook to the chin in the seventh round but failed to go to a neutral corner. The referee had to escort "the Manassa Mauler" to the corner before starting his count. This gave Tunney five extra seconds to get up. Tunney rose wobbly

CAPITOL BOULEVARD, LOOKING NORTH, NASHVILLE, TENN.—35

to his feet at the count of nine, but survived the round. Completely recovered by the eighth round, he won the last three rounds and retained his world championship. Dempsey retired after the fight.[9]

As the economy was flush, the Sam Davis Hotel went up on Seventh Avenue North and Commerce Street in 1927. Twelve stories tall, fireproof, and built with steel, concrete, and brick, the 250-room hotel was only thirty-seven feet wide. Frank Davis, who had been chief clerk at the Hermitage when it opened, became the manager. The Sam Davis featured all outside rooms with tub and shower baths, ceiling fans, and circulating ice water. Free parking was available at the new Seventh Avenue

Garage, advertised as the South's largest parking garage, three doors north. Rates were $2.50 per day, making the hotel price-competitive with the Hermitage. Over at the Hermitage, however, new manager Joseph L. Tall never considered the Sam Davis to be a serious threat.[10] Tall's successor, Howard E. Baughman, came in 1929.

Remembered as highly energetic and able, Baughman would become a legendary manager of the Hermitage. He ran the hotel effectively for seventeen years, a length of service that, as of 2009, had not been matched by any other general manager.

Two years after the Sam Davis opened, the James Robertson Hotel was completed at 118 Seventh Avenue North. Designed by Marr & Holman

Above: In the late 1920s and early '30s, Union Street was the home of not only the Hermitage, but also the new home office of the National Life and Accident Insurance Company (right). This company was the founder of WSM radio. Nationwide musical broadcasts from the fifth floor included a weekly program that would become known as the Grand Ole Opry. TSLA
***Opposite page, top:** Kit Kat Klub, featured in* Nashville This Week, *December 20–27, 1926. NPL-SC*
***Opposite page, bottom:** Capitol Boulevard postcard, circa 1930s. NPL-SC*

No Little Lunch

DINING IN THE '20s

Opening Saturday

MAY THE ELEVENTH

The **HERMITAGE GRILL ROOM**

With

Francis Craig's Orchestra

Featuring delicious foods, tastily served, in an atmosphere that lends itself to good cheer.

BREAKFAST   LUNCHEON   DINNER

The **HERMITAGE** HOTEL GRILL ROOM

In the 1920s, under the stewardship of Robert R. Meyer, the Hermitage Hotel dining room was the place to be for lunch. A menu from November 15, 1920, shows entrees such as beef pot roast (75 cents); Irish stew (70 cents); breaded veal chop (75 cents); fricassee of turkey wings with rice, cutlets of sweetbreads, a half dozen fried oysters (60 cents); baked Gulf red snapper (70 cents); fried fillet of sea trout (75 cents); grilled Spanish mackerel (80 cents); and native crappie fried in corn meal (40 cents).

In 1923, options included shrimp gumbo New Orleans style or celery stuffed with cottage cheese and nuts as first courses. Entrees were creamed calf sweetbreads a la king; beef pot roast with vegetables; and tuna fish salad with mayonnaise. For dessert, the diners were offered lemon custard pie or vanilla or chocolate ice cream. The meal, including coffee, tea, or milk, cost 75 cents. Dinner, including a beverage, was $1.25. The dining room was open from 11:30 AM to 8:30 PM during the week and longer on weekends.[11]

*Vegtable with Macaroni, Toureen 25　　　　*Consomme, Nature, Cup 20
Cream of Tomato with Rice in Toureen 40　　Chicken Broth with Rice, Cup 35
Chicken and Okra in Toureen 40　Clam Broth, in Cup 35　Clam Chowder, Toureen 40

FISH
Cooked Fresh to Order 10 to 15 Minutes.

Fried Oysters, Half 60—Milk Stew 40, Cream Stew 60
Baked Gulf Red Snapper, Portugaise 75　　　　Fried Filet of Sea Trout, Tartar Sauce 75
Grilled Spanish Mackerel, Maitre d'Hotel 80
Native Croppie, Fried in Corn Meal 75

ENTREES
*Beef Pot Roast, Pan Gravy, Brown Potatoes 75
*Irish Stew with Vegetables and Dumplings 70
*Breaded Veal Chop, Tomato Sauce, Spinach 75
*Fricassee of Turkey Wings with Rice 70
*Cutlets of Sweetbreads, Cream Sauce, Asparagus Tips 75
*Vegetable Plate Dinner with Beef Pot Roast or Calf Sweetbreads 75
Steak, a la Minute, Parisienne (15 min.) 1.25

ROASTS
*Turkey, Dressing, Cranberry Sauce 1.25—All White 1.40
*Loin of Corn-Fed Pork, Dressing, Apple Sauce 80
*Hot Roast Beef Sandwich, Mashed Potatoes, Brown Gravy 90
*Prime Rib of Beef, au Jus 1.00—Extra Cut 1.75

*COLD MEATS, ETC.
Small Portion Potato Salad with Cold Meats 15

Half Spring Chicken, Waldorf Salad 1.25
Home-Made Boneless Pigs' Feet, Vinaigrette Sauce, Potato Salad 75　　Sugar Cured Ham 75
Sliced Turkey 1.10—All White Meat 1.25
California Tunafish, Sauce Remoulade 65　French Sardines, Box 60　　Smoked Ox Tongue 75
Tennessee Country Ham 1.00—with Turkey 1.00　　　Roast Beef 1.00　　Corned Beef 60
Kippered Sardines, Potato Salad 60　Assorted Cold Meats with Sliced Turkey or Chicken 1.00
Fatted Chicken Liver Loaf, Potato Salad 80

VEGETABLES—Ready to Serve
Broiled Fresh Mushrooms on Toast 90

Beets in Butter 30　　New String Beans 35
Creamed Spinach 30—with Egg 40　Green Peas 35　Lima Beans 40　Asparagus, Drawn Butter 65
Baked Stuffed Tomato 40　White Midget Onions in Butter or Cream 40　Bell Pepper (1) 20, (2) 35
Whole Artichoke with Drawn Butter 50—Hollandaise 60
TO ORDER—New Cauliflower in Cream or Butter 40—au Gratin 50—Hollandaise 60
Lye Hominy Saute in Bacon Fat 25　　　　Brussels Sprouts 40　　　　Fried Egg Plant 25
POTATOES:　Mashed 25—New Boiled 25—In Cream 35—Hashed Brown 30
Baked 35—12 to 2, 6 to 8—Sweet Potatoes French Fried 25—Candied in Syrup 30

SALADS
TODAY'S FEATURE SALAD: STUFFED TOMATO WITH COTTAGE CHEESE 45
Chicken 75—White Meat 1.00　　　　Tunafish 60　　　　　　Crab Meat 75
Giant Asparagus, Vinaigrette 65—Tips 60　　Waldorf 60　　Potato 35　　Combination 50
Hermitage Fruit 60　　　　　　Florida Fruit 60　　　　　　Grape Fruit 60
Stuffed Tomato (1): Chicken 50—Crab Meat 50—Celery 40—Asparagus Tips 45—Waldorf 50
Head Lettuce 40—With Egg 50　　　　Sliced Tomatoes 45　　　Lettuce and Tomatoes 50

ICE CREAM AND ICES
CREAMS: Chocolate, Pistache or Vanilla 25　　Nesselrode Pudding 45　　Biscuit Tortoni 35
Biscuit Glace 35　　　Meringue Glace 40　　　Coffee Glace 50　　Macaroon Glace 40
PARFAITS: Hermitage 40　Nordica 40　Hazlenut 40　Vanilla C. e Chocolate or relia 25

Howard Baughman (center) was one of the hotel's longest-tenured and most revered managers. Second from the left is Pete Wills and second from the right is Bill Caldwell. The other men are unidentified. HH

Architects, the hotel had eleven floors and one hundred seventy-five rooms. It was marketed as the "apartment hotel of distinction." The James Robertson boasted of having free electricity for cooking and an electric Frigidaire in very room.[12]

Even so, the James Robertson would compete more with the Maxwell House and the Sam Davis than with the Hermitage.

A Hairsbreadth from Fame

Before the spring of 1930, W. D. Brown had opened a five-man barbershop in the basement of the Hermitage Hotel. In those days, he and his fellow barbers used scissors exclusively to cut men's hair. Some forty-seven years later, in 1977, Brown remained, but he was the only barber in the shop. He fondly recalled the days when Howard Baughman was manager. "He was one of the finest managers imaginable," Brown told a local newspaper. He continued:

> He was really a hotel man. He was always busy. I would open shop at eight o'clock. At 8:05 every morning he would walk in my door. He had already started at the top and inspected everything, hiking all the way down to the basement. There were always a lot of bellboys around in those days. If he started talking to someone in the lobby, he might motion to one of the boys. The bellboy knew what to do. He went to the desk and got the man's name and slipped it to Mr. Baughman, who always liked to call a guest by his name. He was as straight as he could be. He would do anything for a guest. If the hotel was full and a regular guest came in he would take him to his apartment. Baughman had an apartment on the sixth floor.

Baughman said his Hermitage stay had been "one long cavalcade of pleasant associations with travelers in every walk of life—princes and presidents, generals, and GIs." He left the Hermitage to go home to Florida in 1945.[13]

Highlights of Brown's forty-seven-year career at the Hermitage barbershop were visits by politicians Al Smith, Franklin Roosevelt (with his wife, Eleanor), and Richard Nixon. It was the *Nashville Banner's* Jimmy Stahlman who introduced Brown to Nixon. Brown's career at the hotel ended when Nashville Mayor Richard Fulton ordered the hotel closed because of health and codes violations.[14]

Under an Alias

The hotel boom continued. In 1930, the Noel brothers of Nashville, Oscar F. and John H., opened the 220-room Noel Hotel at the northeast corner of Church Street and Fourth Avenue North. It was a first-class property intended

Enjoying lunch in the 1936 Grill Room are second from left: Mrs. Charles (Thelma) Waterford, Mrs. Roberta Alexander, Mrs. Francis (Elizabeth) Craig and (far right) Mrs. Howard (Alice) Baughman. The other women are unidentified. DCD

Young Francis Craig would soon make his mark conducting the orchestra in the Grill Room and also as a songwriter. HH

to compete with both the Hermitage and the Andrew Jackson. No small coincidence, then, that the Meyer hotel chain—which leased the Hermitage for twenty-four years before purchasing it in 1938—renovated the Hermitage the same year the Noel Hotel appeared.[15] The Art Deco light fixtures were added to the Hermitage during this renovation and would remain for decades.

The Hermitage Hotel remained at the top of its game, evidenced in 1932 by the fact that American Airlines chose the site for a one-man ticket office.[16]

Well-heeled businessmen and affluent, upper-class couples were the norm, but they weren't the only ones to frequent the Hermitage. Gangster John Dillinger, considered by the FBI's first director, J. Edgar Hoover, as the "number one criminal at large," spent a night there, too. He came with his moll, Billie Frechette, and John "Three Fingered Jack" Hamilton. They arrived in a new Terraplane sports coupe. After checking in, Hamilton went for a walk and reportedly didn't return for hours. Having forgotten both his room number and the alias he used when he registered, Hamilton spent the day trying to remember either one. Desperate to find either Dillinger or Billie, he stood for a long time outside the hotel keeping watch. Hamilton finally described Dillinger to a bellboy, who helped him reconnect with his party at 9 PM. Needless to say, Dillinger was pretty upset with his sidekick.[17]

A Frightening Fall

TODDLER FALLS FROM A WINDOW

Raymond Garnetts, a young New York businessman, never would forget what happened to him at the Hotel Hermitage on August 1, 1927. The amazing event took place just before noon when Garnetts was walking up Capitol Boulevard a few steps away from Union Street. Suddenly, he was knocked to the pavement by a terrific and completely unexpected blow to his shoulders. His first reaction, while stunned and dazed, was bewilderment about what had hit him. Gathering his wits, he realized that a small boy, who looked to be about two years old, was lying beside him crying. The little boy's name was Roland Wolfe. He had fallen from a seventh floor window of the hotel when the screen came loose. The little boy's father, R. C. Wolfe, was in the room with his child when he heard the rustle of a curtain. He looked up and saw the toddler topple out of the window and watched horrified as his little boy hit a man on the street ninety-four feet below. By the time Wolfe reached the lobby, Roland, conscious and crying, had been brought inside. He gathered him in his arms and took him to a nearby hospital. When told what happened, the physician on duty assumed the child had massive internal injuries and would not survive.

The boy's mother had been out shopping at the time of the accident. Upon hearing the news, she hurried to the hospital, where a doctor said, "Your child is alive, but I must tell you that he cannot live. You must not cry for that will upset the baby and he should not be upset more than he already is." Mary Wolfe refused to accept the verdict. Soon, Dr. Albert Sullivan arrived, having been summoned by the hotel. He examined the child and agreed with Wolfe. Amazingly, Roland had only suffered a broken arm, a broken leg, bruises, and a cut on his chin. He fully recovered, grew to adulthood, married and had four children.

Garnetts was admitted to the same hospital. He insisted, however, that he was not hurt and was dismissed that afternoon. The story of little Roland's fall received national publicity, reaching even Mary Wolfe's aunt via a newspaper in Sioux Falls, Iowa. In the following days, the Wolfes received hundreds of get-well cards and letters, and Roland received all kinds of presents. As for Raymond Garnetts, he was reluctant to talk about the incident, usually saying something like, "Aw, let all that stuff go." In 1949, a hotel guest from Springfield, Illinois, would fall from the same floor of the hotel. Unlike the fortunate boy, however, he was killed.[18] Modern safety codes prevent windows from fully opening.

Good Reviews

Sanford "Sandy" Brandt of Chattanooga, Tennessee, would always remember staying at the Hermitage with a fellow Tennessee Valley Authority friend during the 1930s. Brandt had an almost sleepless night; his roommate kept him awake lamenting the fact that he wasted a lot of money by not staying at the YMCA next door. Brandt's son, Chancellor Robert S. Brandt would later become an outstanding Nashville attorney.[19]

Many others had near-sleepless nights that same decade, but for entirely different reasons. Governor Hill McAlister held his inaugural dance in the Hermitage Hotel ballroom on January 16, 1936. An 8:30 PM formal reception preceded the dance. A few minutes before 10 PM, couples in the receiving line lined up behind the McAlisters in the loggia. Precisely on the hour, Governor and Mrs. McAlister led them in a grand march to the ballroom. As they entered, the group passed under an arch of sabers held by officers of the Tennessee National Guard. The ballroom was decorated with large American flags, "draped effectively against the dark woodwork of the walls. Southern smilax was entwined about the wall lights and chandeliers. At the far end of the room, Francis Craig and his orchestra played for the dancing that followed."[20]

Craig was lucky to get the job; Governor McAlister was known to be tight with the state's money in addition to his own. Craig received good reviews for his work. Craig would go on to have an illustrious career at the Hermitage and became a household name during the 1940s.

Two months later, on March 25, the governor's wife was back at the Hermitage to pose with other members of the prestigious Garden Study Club

Above, top: Bellhops and supervisors, 1937. James Hasson (top row, second from the right) went on to work at Oak Ridge. He eventually retired as director of quality assurance for the Atomic Energy Commission's Iowa plant. MW
Above: Bellhop James Hasson, during a break, sent this telegram to his sweetheart from the Hermitage Hotel while working on Christmas Eve, 1935. JJH
Opposite page: 1930s street scene. Notice rival Andrew Jackson Hotel to the left. NPL-SC

Going Long

VANDY FOOTBALL WEEKENDS AND HUEY LONG'S SPEECH

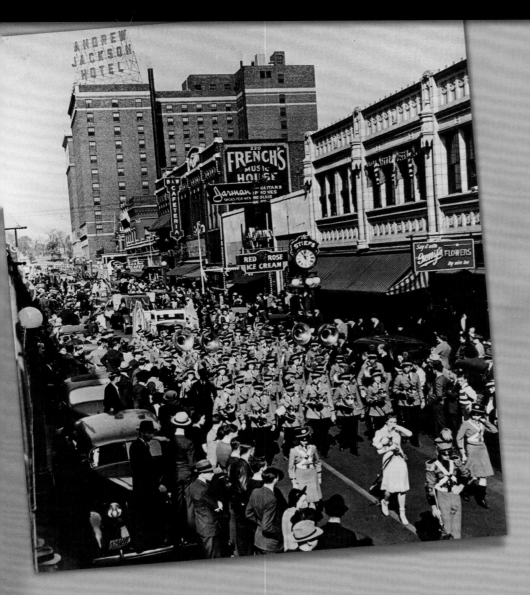

During the 1930s and continuing until World War II, Vanderbilt football weekends were highlighted both by the games and by Friday night parades through downtown Nashville. They often landed in the lobby of the Hermitage

Hotel, where students would put their cheerleaders on a desk or table to lead the cheers. The band and the school crowd would fill the lobby entrance, shouting, shoving, and cheering, and the Vanderbilt band would play its fight song, "Dynamite," which was written by the hotel's dance bandleader, Francis Craig.[21]

Vanderbilt homecoming parades could be especially spectacular. In 1938, the homecoming judges' stand was in front of the University Club on Sixth Avenue North, just down the street from the Hermitage. The homecoming theme that year was "The Gay Nineties." The students wore dresses with lace collars, high-button shoes, and peg leg trousers and rode in buggies, surries, and wagons, as well as on old-fashioned bicycles.[22]

That fall, Senator Huey Long of Louisiana was making preparations for what was called "the greatest peace-time railroad excursion in the history of America." Long distributed new gray uniforms to 1,500 Louisiana State University cadets, who would leave Baton Rouge on a Friday by railroad and head north to Nashville for the October 28 game between LSU and Vanderbilt. Railroad officials estimated that 5,000 people would make the trip, which was being offered for an unbelievably low seven dollars. That evening, railroad workers assembled the cars that made up the trains. The "Kingfish," as Long was called, paid the fare for the 1,500 cadets and band members, and lent money to a thousand or more other LSU students who lacked funds for the trip. In order for Louisiana state police to perform duties in Tennessee—including policing student behavior on the train where there was a no-drinking policy—Long had received permission from the Tennessee Game and Fish Commission for the police to enter the state as "deputy game wardens." Long's sound trucks, which would be used for speeches at the game and possibly elsewhere, left Baton Rouge on Thursday morning, October 25, and the crew stayed at the Hermitage.[23]

Just before Senator Long boarded the train, reporters asked him if he planned to use the occasion to announce his 1936 candidacy for the presidency of the United States under his "Share the Wealth" program. Long laughed it off, saying, "It will probably be for the presidency of Mexico." He also declined to reveal what he would say in his speech at Vanderbilt. The Kingfisher's six trains roared north through Louisiana and Mississippi, led by the red train that carried the uniformed cadet corps. The white train came next, carrying Senator Long, his wife, a son, and a few friends. Others followed. There were sizeable crowds at the towns along the railroad line."[24]

At 9 AM on October 27, Long, now in Nashville and arm-in-arm with Vanderbilt Coach Dan McGugin and Nashville Mayor Hillary E. Howse, led the cadets and the band on a tour of the city. Following a luncheon, during which many people asked Long questions and shook his hand, Long headed to Vanderbilt for the game. He predicted an LSU win, and he was right: LSU defeated Vanderbilt 29–0; it was Vanderbilt's worst defeat in fourteen years.[25]

Three weeks after Huey Long's spectacular visit to Nashville, President and Mrs. Franklin D. Roosevelt arrived at the Hermitage Hotel. They came to Nashville at the invitation of U.S. Speaker of the House Joseph W. Byrns. The president was in town to promote his New Deal programs, many of which Byrns had helped push through Congress. One of the largest crowds in the city's history greeted the president. The president's wife, however, would likely not have been pleased that the "Kingfish" had been a recent guest at the Hermitage, as well. Two years earlier, Senator Long had Sunday dinner with the Roosevelts at their Hyde Park home. He arrived wearing "a loud suit, an orchid shirt and a pink necktie," possibly chosen to shock the aristocratic Roosevelts. If so, he was successful. At one point during the meal, Sara Delano Roosevelt, leaned over and whispered, "Whom is that awful man sitting on my son's right?"[26]

of Nashville. The picture was taken to publicize the publication of the group's *History of Homes and Gardens in Tennessee*.

During the 1930s, Nashville ladies shopped downtown. As Catherine Henry visited her favorite stores, she would sometimes bring her young daughter, Peggy, with her. For a treat, Mrs. Henry would take Peggy to the elegant Hermitage Hotel for lunch in the Grill Room (which picked up an "e" at the end of its name along the way). Catherine's husband, Douglas Henry, would occasionally walk down from National Life to join them. Often, they would enjoy the music of Henry's first cousin once removed, Francis Craig.[27]

The Days and Nights of a Bellman

Not everyone was so fortunate. The Great Depression raged across America, and jobs in Nashville were hard to find in the mid-1930s. It was at that point, however, that two young men would get their business starts at the Hermitage Hotel: James "Jim" Hasson and Herschel "Bob" Pardue. Hasson had his photo taken with seventeen other bellboys at the Hermitage in 1937. He later recalled taking a food order to a room occupied by a state legislator. When Hasson knocked on the door, the man told him to come in. Hasson did, just in time to find the legislator in bed with a young woman. The guest never stopped what he was doing; he simply told Hasson where to put the food.[28]

As for Pardue, he began working at the Hermitage in 1938, when he as only fourteen years old. His first job was operating the back elevator, working ten hours a day, six days a week, for

$7.50 per week. The Hermitage was the first hotel Pardue had ever been in; Pardue's father had died, and Jimmy Waters, a supervisor, gave him the job because he felt sorry for him. In January 1992, Pardue recalled, "Every young man who came to work there started at the back elevator. After a while, you got promoted to the front elevator, and they gave you a uniform and you got $10 a week. You still had to work the same hours." In the evenings when business was slow, Pardue would run his elevator down to the lower level and listen to Francis Craig's orchestra. When Pardue walked out the Sixth Avenue entrance, he knew to watch his step, as the doormen sometimes allowed Western Union delivery boys to leave their bicycles under the awning while they made their deliveries.

World War II interrupted Pardue's career at the Hermitage, but the paratrooper came back after the war and worked in higher capacities at the hotel. He remained until 1949, when he left to run a hotel training program in Florida.

Above: By 1931, both the Hermitage and rival hotel Andrew Jackson advertised the new guest amenity, a radio in every room. This billboard was featured prominently along a Nashville highway. NPL-SC

Opposite page: Bellman Roy Jones makes the daily mail run. Jones worked at the hotel for three years, then entered the army after the attack on Pearl Harbor. He was killed in action in Anzio, Italy, 1944. HH

After retirement, Pardue returned to the Hermitage for a third season. This time, his role was to handle public relations, act as sales manager, and give history talks.[29]

In the 1930s and 1940s, the elevator operators, who wore snappy dark blue and light blue uniforms, were expected to learn how to be bellmen. The bellmen also dressed sharp. They made only what they received in tips. The bellmen actually had to pay the bell captain 35 cents a shift for the privilege of working. There were three shifts: 7 AM to noon, noon to 5 PM, and 5 PM to midnight. In addition to loading and unloading baggage, the bellmen were responsible for bringing ice to lodgers who requested it; delivering packages from the downtown stores; and for valet and laundry service. Pardue recalled that the first things salesmen wanted were to have their suits pressed and ice water delivered to their rooms. A driver from Model Laundry picked up the laundry and dry cleaning daily. In addition, the hotel had its own valet shop, which could handle emergency pressing, repair a ripped shirt or blouse, and replace buttons.[30]

A joint duty of the night bellman and night switchboard operator was to make sure each guest's door was locked; at that point, the hotel did not have self-locking doors. Each door had to be locked from the inside. At 2 AM each night, the bellman and switchboard operator began systematically checking locks, starting on the ninth floor and working down to the second. At each guest bedroom door, they would cautiously turn the doorknob to the right. If it was properly locked, it would not move. Conversely, if unlocked, they opened the door to see if everything was all right. Occasionally, they would surprise guests in the middle of various nighttime activities. Sometimes the guests were nude, and according to Pardue, the duty could be quite frightening. On at least two occasions, he discovered that guests had died.[31]

An Upscale Address

The hotel remained popular, as did its Grill Room restaurant; the eatery received a renovated ceiling in the summer of 1938. The Len Herndon Company, of Nashville, was the contractor.[32]

Up on the mezzanine, Walter Bauer and his wife, Fredia, ran a beauty shop, popular with fashionable Nashville women. Walter was the hairdresser while Fredia was receptionist. Among Walter's customers was Mrs. Margaret "Maggie" Craig, wife of National Life's Board Chairman C. A. Craig. The Bauers were Austrians who served hot tea and European style cookies to their largely upscale clients. During World War II, they suffered some undeserved verbal abuse because of their national backgrounds.[33]

A minor problem for the management of the Hermitage Hotel was that its tastefully decorated and restful lobby was the meeting place downtown for a lot of people who were not guests of the hotel. The YMCA was just behind the hotel on Seventh Avenue North, and several bachelors who lived in the modestly priced YMCA rooms gave the Hermitage as their mailing address. They simply pretended to live at the hotel. Pardue remembered that some of them even added titles to their names. The men would sit in the hotel lobby each morning, usually reading the newspaper and smoking cigarettes. Frequently, they would drop off to sleep with the papers still in their laps. One day Pardue noticed one such visitor sitting on the south side of the lobby near the steps to the loggia. He had not moved for several hours. Hotel rules were for the staff to awake anyone who slept in the lobby and tell him to either stay awake or leave. When Pardue touched the man, he realized that he had been dead long enough for rigor mortis to set in. Pardue was amazed that of the dozens of people who had

Herschel Robert "Bob" Pardue. HRP

A Seamstress Retires

FLOSSIE CRAFTON

new widow with a thirteen-year-old son when she took the work; her husband had been a barber. Crafton remained at the Hermitage for at least forty-two years. For the first seventeen of those years, she used a Singer sewing machine powered by a foot pedal. Decades after her original employment, in 1966, Richard "Dick" Hall threw a party for the longtime worker at the hotel. He presented her with forty-two $1 bills along with other presents. She said, "I'm going to keep my job as long as I can, although I'll be seventy-seven next Valentine's Day." As the hotel seamstress, she was responsible for darning all torn or worn sheets, tablecloths, and other linens. At that point, Crafton said she had been through twenty housekeepers, eight managers, and two owners."[34]

Hall's tender treatment of Crafton was characteristic. Many an afternoon, Hall's second wife, Grace, would get a telephone call from her husband saying that he had a funeral to attend regarding an employee or some such, and would be late getting home. He was extremely loyal to his staff and was respected and appreciated in return.

Flossie Crafton began work at the Hermitage Hotel as a seamstress in October 1924. A country girl from Red Boiling Springs, Tennessee, she did not even know how to look for a job and "had another woman come down and ask for the job for me," she later told a newspaper reporter. Crafton was a

passed by that morning, including the hotel's own staff, no one had realized the man had died.

While at the Hermitage, Pardue was introduced to gambling, women, and whiskey. He said, "There were a lot of people who came and took rooms to gamble. Auto dealers and horse trainers and a couple of big-name Grand Ole Opry stars who came to play craps, and the morticians. I walked into a room once and there were these morticians down on their knees shooting craps with one-hundred-dollar bills all over the floor. There was a horse parlor at Fourth and Deaderick, and we'd take guests' bets down there. A lot of room service calls then were for a pitcher of beer from the hotel's tap room. The only place

Edward Hull "Boss" Crump (second from right) was a pivotal figure in Tennessee politics for decades. He often held his meetings at the Hermitage. This photo taken October 11, 1947 during arrival to the hotel. Pictured from left to right, H. T. McKinney, state superintendent of buildings; Blanchard Tual, state senator from Memphis; W. T. Hale, chairman of the Shelby County Commission; Crump; and Mayor James T. Pleasants, of Memphis. NPL-SC

in town for mixed drinks was Printers Alley. They were illegal there too, but the police would just wink. Sometimes strippers would be recruited from there to come up to the hotel and entertain conventioneers in the ballroom and suites. Occasionally, even a raucous five-piece jazz band was discovered entertaining guests in an upper suite."[35]

Pardue didn't mention it, but others have noted that taxi drivers also were a problem during the Depression; the cabbies sold illegal whiskey to hotel customers. Only when the Hermitage manager threatened to take away their parking spaces on Sixth Avenue did they pull back.

Pardue saw plenty of stars. "We had Joan Fontaine and Al Jolson. Jolson would order a roll-a-way bed for his maid, who stayed in his room. He probably had a performance at the Ryman. We had Grace Moore and all the big bands: Tommy Dorsey, Jimmy Dorsey, Woody Herman, Benny Goodman and Doris Day." Pardue recalled, too, that the certain convention attendees were notoriously bad tippers. "We'd joke that they would bring along one shirt and one $10 bill and never change either."

During Pardue's years at the Hermitage, the legislature met every two years. "This was," he remembered, "when Shelby County ran the state politically. Ed Crump could ask for and get almost anything they wanted in his district. He sent two henchmen . . . to Nashville to keep an eye on the legislators. They held private meetings at the Hermitage and votes were bought and sold in some suite over a fifth of Jack Daniel's and exchange of money. Crump's men called their legislators 'trained seals.'"[36]

According to Pardue, one of those men would bring five or six suits for a two-day stay.

Pardue recalled:

When the liquor industry wanted a fair trade law, cases of liquor were set up in one of our assembly rooms and each representative took a trunkload home on Thursday. When the milk industry wanted something, they gave out all kinds of specially packaged ice cream, popsicles, and special iced containers. Money many times was exchanged.

The employees were all aware, Pardue said, of who Crump's "money man" was. "He expected and got special attention and usually had a twenty-dollar bill for the elevator operator. The elevator operators all expected and got their tips."[37]

Lots of Leaders

By 1939, the state's Democratic Party had replaced the Ladies' Hermitage Association's annual Jackson Day event at the Hermitage Hotel. The celebration was a tribute to former U.S. President Andrew Jackson, as well as a fundraising vehicle for the Democratic Party. Democratic leaders from across the state, including then Governor-elect Prentice Cooper, heard First Assistant Postmaster Gen. W. W. Howes liken the administration of

Above: Jackson Day Dinner, 1939. NPL-SC
Opposite page, top: Famed pilot and founder of Eastern Airlines Captain Eddie Rickenbacker (right) spoke at the Hermitage in March 1939 to appeal for more air routes between southern cities. From left to right: publisher James G. Stahlman, Lt. Col. Herbert Fox, Col. Harry S. Berry, and Rickenbacker. NPL-SC
Opposite page, bottom: Young Democratic Club Dinner. NPL-SC

Above: In the ballroom, Jackson Dinner, 1939. NPL-SC

U.S. President Franklin Roosevelt to that of Jackson, "the Tennessee patron saint of democracy." A photographer for *Life* magazine was there to take pictures of the event.[38]

That same year, World War I aviation hero Eddie Rickenbacker visited Nashville as head of Eastern Airlines. He spoke at the weekly Exchange Club meeting, held at the Hermitage Hotel, about the need for new air routes between Nashville and St. Louis, Missouri, as well as between Nashville and Florence, Alabama. Rickenbacker appealed to his audience for support of the routes. The Florence route would connect at the Tri-Cities airport, he said, with flights between Memphis, Tennessee, and Birmingham, Alabama. The proposed line between Nashville and St. Louis would bring Nashville a new connection with the North and Northwest and provide Nashville with two-hour mail, express, and passenger service to St. Louis. Naturally, Rickenbacker felt that Eastern was the logical choice as operator of the proposed flights, having "established a safety record second to none."[39]

The state's Democratic Convention opened in Nashville on June 19, 1940. Sitting in his hotel room at the Hermitage with the state's democratic leaders, "Boss" Crump expounded his strategy for the Democratic National Convention. He urged the leaders to have "an uninstructed delegation" so that, if U.S. President Roosevelt decided not to run for re-election, the party could throw its support to Cordell Hull. At the convention, Crump's career was praised by Sen. Tom Stewart; there was talk that the Tennessee delegation might support him for the vice presidency, should Hull refuse the position.[40]

Throughout the goings-on, Pardue continued to relish his experience working at the hotel. He once said,

> In its day, it was as fine a hotel as there was in the South. Nobody was ever given anything in that hotel, be it food, mail, or a packet of cigarettes, unless it was on a silver tray. There's an air there, that something extra you can only feel when you are there. The people that worked there made the difference. Mr. Baughman, the manager, wouldn't let guests put their own mail in the mailbox or light their own cigar. If you saw guests fumbling for a light, you were supposed to light their cigar with a brand new package of Robert Meyer matches and then hand them the pack.[41]

The Song of the South

FRANCIS CRAIG, HIS ORCHESTRA, AND THE PHENOMENAL SUCCESS THAT WAS "NEAR YOU"

Though sights and smells can instantly conjure up the memory of a specific time and place, for early visitors of the Hermitage Hotel, it was a certain sound that did the trick. Nashville society bandleader Francis Craig, backed by his able orchestra, was a staple for dances and other events. But he also had a regular gig playing lunch and dinner music at the hotel's Grill Room during the 1920s and 1930s.

Francis Craig, the next to last of ten children of the Reverend and Mrs. Robert James Craig of Dickson, Tennessee, graduated from Massey Prep School and spent two months in the Student Army Training Corps at Tennessee Technological University before entering Vanderbilt University in the winter quarter of 1919. His father had been the first Founder's Medalist for Oratory there. The young Craig soon pledged the Phi Delta Theta fraternity, but dropped out of school following the spring quarter. He returned for the 1920–21 school year.[1]

At some point during his second stint at Vanderbilt, Craig formed a band of three fellow students and five other Nashville musicians. The group's first dance was for a Sigma Nu fraternity party, for which they were paid forty-five dollars. Craig called his band the Vanderbilt Jazz Band, a name

Chancellor James H. Kirkland found inappropriate, having decided that Craig had no right to co-opt the university's name. He allegedly asked Craig to change the band's name and said that, if he didn't, he would be expelled. Disenchanted with academics and short of money anyway, Craig changed his band's name to Francis Craig and His Orchestra, and left Vanderbilt for the second and last time after the spring quarter of 1922.

Acting as his own agent, Craig began playing at the Belle Meade Country Club as well as at college fraternity dances and college and high school proms. He occasionally played in the ballroom at the Hermitage Hotel. One of the songs Belle Meade Country Club members enjoyed hearing Craig's orchestra play was George Gershwin's "Rhapsody in Blue," music that Gershwin first played on the piano backed by Paul Whiteman's orchestra. Craig's reputation spread quickly and he widened his clientele to include country club and fraternity parties across the South.[2]

In the summer of 1923, Craig landed a job playing at Cascade Plunge in Birmingham, Alabama, a combination of swimming pool and dinner and dance club. One evening at a dance at Birmingham's Tutwiler Hotel, Craig broke in on Elizabeth Lazynka Gewin. They soon fell in love and married in 1924. For the first six months of their wedded life, they lived in her hometown of Birmingham, where he worked as a salesman for a marble company. Miserable in his job, Craig persuaded his bride to move to Nashville. After returning home, Craig's orchestra had an audition with Robert E. Hyde, the manager of the Hermitage Hotel. Hyde was impressed and gave Craig a job playing during meals from an alcove in the northeast corner of the Grill Room. Craig now had a fulltime position as a musician with nine band members: three brass, three reeds, drums, piano, and a final member who could play both the tuba and banjo. Craig enjoyed the relaxed atmosphere of the Hermitage and acquired a loyalty to the

hotel. On weekends, his orchestra also played at Vanderbilt fraternity parties, as well as an increasing number of other universities in the Southeast. When he was out of town, he simply had a musician friend cover for him at the Hermitage.[3]

Over the Airwaves

The radio came to Nashville in 1922 when sixteen-year-old John "Jack" DeWitt Jr. broadcast music from a Victrola record player over a 20-watt transmitter. A year later, Dewitt started a commercial radio station, WCBQ, in his home.[4] Francis Craig and another local bandleader, Beasley Smith, broadcast their music from the DeWitt living room. On October 5, 1925, Craig's cousin, Edwin W. Craig, a vice president at the National Life and Accident Insurance Company, started a radio station with the call letters WSM. This stood for "We Shield Millions," referring to the number of National Life policyholders. The station's 1,000-watt power was exceeded in the South only by WSB in Atlanta. The WSM studios were on the top floor of National Life's new five-story office building on Seventh Avenue North at Union Street.[5]

In preparation for the dedication of WSM at 7 PM on October 5, remote broadcast hookups were set up at the nearby Hermitage and Andrew Jackson hotels, where Francis Craig and Beasley Smith, respectively, stood by with their orchestras.[6] Craig's orchestra, set up in the Hermitage's ornate ballroom, didn't get started until midnight. After finishing, they hustled up to the WSM studio, where they participated in a jamboree emceed by Jack Keefe. The on-air party lasted until after 2 AM. Craig's orchestra continued to be heard regularly over WSM through the broadcast of dinner music from the Hermitage. At that time, all of WSM's programs were local.[7]

RED ROSE

WORDS & MUSIC BY
FRANCIS CRAIG

Francis Craig

FORSTER · MUSIC
PUBLISHER · INC
CHICAGO

In 1927 WSM accepted an invitation to join the National Broadcasting Company (NBC), the country's first national network. A year later, National Life increased WSM's power to 5,000 watts. This paved the way for WSM to become, in 1928, one of forty clear channel stations in the country at 650 kilocycles.[8] Craig's association with WSM helped him attract excellent musicians and establish an even greater reputation as a first-class regional orchestra as well as Nashville's society orchestra.

In the spring of 1928, Francis and his wife vacationed in Birmingham, where he enjoyed seeing some red roses in full bloom. He quickly wrote "Red Rose" in honor of his wife. The sweet song quickly became his trademark and at the Hermitage, where he played it in the Grill Room, diners would enjoy a single red rose in a bud vase on their tables. His soft music and good food made the Grill Room one of Nashville's most popular restaurants.[9] Eighty-one years later, red roses were still being displayed in vases there.

In 1929, the *Nashville Banner* recognized Francis Craig as "one of the youngest orchestra leaders today." That same year, when his contract expired at the Hermitage, Craig left to go to work for the hotel's principal competitor, the four-year-old Andrew Jackson Hotel, a block away. He signed a two-year contract there and played at lunchtime and at dinner. The hotel advertised Francis Craig and his Andrew Jackson Hotel Orchestra as "The best all-round orchestra in the South." Most of the time, his shows were carried live on WSM.

Craig, who smoked incessantly, developed a bad cough in 1930 and was losing weight. His physician, Dr. Owsley Manier, diagnosed his ailment as tuberculosis. By mid-May, Craig was confined at home while his band continued to play in its normal Sunday evening Rhythm Symphony slot at the Andrew Jackson. In 1930, TB patients were often advised to go to Colorado, where the high altitude and dry air were thought to be beneficial. Quarantined in a sanitarium in Denver, Craig's career was clearly in jeopardy.

Meanwhile, back home, trombonist Bradford Smith held Craig's orchestra together as its interim leader. The group traveled to gigs across the South and Midwest during the summer, returning to Nashville in the fall to play for parties at Vanderbilt University and elsewhere in town. The following spring, Craig was released from the sanitarium and

BONG BONG BONG BONG BONG BONG BONG BONG BONG BONG BONG BONG

WEDNESDAY MIDNIGHTERS

Joseph MacPherson, bass-baritone, formerly of the Metropolitan Opera Company, gets a kick out of singing on the "Wednesday Midnighters" Midnighter listeners, although they are night owls, get a thrill out of his superb singing

THREE ON A MIKE—But not at the same time. Three good reasons why folks stay up Wednesday nights. Left is June Moody, lady of the blues; center, vivacious Fannye Rose Shore, singer with Francis Craig's orchestra; right, Louise Hammett, the "gal from Mississippi" returned to Nashville. His friends said the only noticeable change in Craig was that he had gained considerable weight. After regaining the allegiance of his band members, Craig took them on the circuit, playing at hotels, proms, and on radio stations through the South, Midwest, and West. In June 1932, he began a three-month stand at the exclusive Broadmoor Hotel's Nite Club in Colorado Springs. Three days a week, the band journeyed up to Denver, where they played to a national NBC audience over Denver's NBC affiliate, KOA. Friends in Nashville and Birmingham could hear his smooth music over their local NBC affiliates.

That fall, the band played at Dallas's Adolphus Hotel. There, the musicians also played to a national audience at KRLD, a 10,000-watt station whose airwaves reached Nashville. At Christmas 1932, when he was back in Denver, Craig had a twelve-piece orchestra and a female vocalist, Alpha Louise Morton. On New Year's Eve, NBC broadcast nationally a "Dancing Across the County" show that featured four outstanding orchestras, one of which was Craig's.[10]

In February 1933, Craig brought his band members back to Nashville where their families anxiously awaited. Although the nation and Nashville were in the grips of the Great Depression, Craig found steady work for his band at cotillions, at the Belle Meade Country Club, at high school and college fraternity parties, at the annual Bachelor Club dances, at wedding receptions, and elsewhere. Soon after returning to Nashville, Craig left the Andrew Jackson Hotel and returned to the Hermitage, where he played at luncheons and dinner. On Saturday nights, the cover charge for the dinner and dance was $1.50.[11]

In 1934, Francis Craig gave serious consideration to taking his band to New York City. Only at the last moment did he back out. Content to stay in Nashville, he was very proud of his orchestra's continuing contract to perform on NBC late Sunday evenings where the sweet, easy music pleased an invisible audience across America. He also was comfortable with his job at the Hermitage. The hotel's longtime manager, Howard Baughman, appreciated Craig's value to the hotel and put the orchestra's name on outdoor billboards along some of Nashville's major avenues.

The "Chocolate Drop"

To add a touch of humor to his orchestra, Craig hired Pee Wee Marquette (shown with Craig on page 91), a sixteen-year-old black midget from Montgomery, Alabama, who could sing, tap dance, play the ukulele, and do funny impersonations. Despite his youth, Marquette, who stood only three feet, nine inches tall, had already been a mascot for the University of Alabama football team for two years and a page at the Thomas Jefferson Hotel in Montgomery.[12] Craig dressed him in a bellboy uniform similar to Philip Morris's "Johnny." Marquette, often called the "chocolate drop mascot," became a great hit, singing such songs as "Shine," "Minnie the Moocher," and "Me and My Shadow."[13]

In addition to being a regular at the Hermitage, Marquette often performed at dances and at birthday parties for Craig's daughters, Celeste and Donia, and their friends. He also went on the road with Craig's orchestra. This proved to be difficult because of segregation laws. Marquette's popularity caused rival bandleaders to take notice and attempt to hire him. Finally, during World War II, Francis Craig's "diminutive darky" left Nashville for Harlem, where racial discrimination was hardly visible. There, he performed at such establishments as the Birdland and Zanzibar night-clubs.[14] Craig's musicians, most of whom had grown to respect Marquette, missed him, as did Craig and his many other friends in Nashville.

Discovering "Dynamite"

James "Jimmy" Melton had gotten his start as a saxophonist and singer in Craig's band at the Hermitage Hotel, but had gone on to New York to become one of the country's most popular radio tenors and launch careers at the Metropolitan Opera and in films. In November 1935, he came to Nashville for the southern premiere of *Stars Over Broadway* at the Knickerbocker Theatre. Melton arrived several days early to be honored at a banquet given by Gov. Hill McAlister. He stayed at the Hermitage Hotel, where he enjoyed visiting with old friends. Francis Craig and his orchestra were proud to share the billing with Melton at the Knickerbocker.[15]

On Saturdays in the mid-1930s, a small group of Peabody Demonstration School students, including Elaine Yarborough and Jane Roberts, would frequently ride the bus to town to have lunch at the Hermitage. They would each order a Swiss on rye sandwich (the least expensive item on the menu) and a coke while listening to Francis Craig's orchestra. Pee Wee Marquette would relay requests for songs from the girls to Craig, who would sometimes come by their table to socialize.[16]

PREMIER SHOWING
"STARS OVER BROADWAY"
featuring NASHVILLE'S OWN
JAMES MELTON
In Person
APPEARING WITH
FRANCIS CRAIG
and His Orchestra

2—PERFORMANCES—2
Wednesday
7:10 AND 9:40 P. M.
All seats reserved for the 7 p. m. performance
Tickets on sale Starting TODAY at Boulevard Box Office—for both premier performances.
They'll Go Fast! Better Get Yours Now!

PRICES—
ADULTS 75¢
CHILDREN 40¢

— POSITIVELY —
No Courtesies Accepted this Evening

KNICKERBOCKER
OF COURSE IT'S AT your

One night, while Craig was leading his orchestra in the Grill Room, a fire broke out in the kitchen and smoke drifted into the dining room. Craig kept his cool. His response was to change to the popular show tune, "When Smoke Gets in Your Eyes," written by American composer Jerome Kern and lyricist Otto Harbach for their 1933 operetta, *Roberta*.

In the mid-1930s, Craig hired Snooky Lanson, a young tenor from Memphis, to sing in his band. Lanson, whose original name was Landman, quickly became well known to all the teenagers who attended Alpha Chi and SAP dances at the Belle Meade Country Club or dances at the less formal Wagon Wheel on Harding Road. Lanson went on to co-star on the long running television show *Your Hit Parade*. Dinah Shore also sang with Craig's band, although she made her name as vocalist for WSM.[17]

Always loyal to Vanderbilt University, even though he didn't graduate, Craig wrote the university's fight song, "Dynamite," a few days before the annual Vanderbilt/University of Tennessee football game in 1938. On Saturday mornings before Vanderbilt games, WSM broadcast a show from the Hermitage Grill that featured the Francis Craig Orchestra playing fight songs, as well as commentary on games and predicted winners. Craig loved it.[18]

On Tuesday night, December 27, 1938, Craig's cousin, Edwin W. Craig, and his wife, Elizabeth, gave a lavish debut party at the Belle Meade Country Club for their daughter, Elizabeth, a sophomore at Smith College. The young people danced to the music of Francis Craig and his orchestra before being served an elaborate dinner at midnight.[19] The next night, Dr. and Mrs. Rufus Fort gave an equally lovely party at the club for their daughter, Cornelia. At 10 PM, Cornelia was led on the floor by her brother, Rufus Jr., for

the first dance. Naturally, Nashville's favorite band played for the dance. At midnight, Craig's orchestra took a break while the guests ate an elaborate buffet supper. After dinner, dancing continued until 2 AM. Craig and his crew must have been exhausted.[20] Three years later, Francis Craig and his orchestra played at Belle Meade Club's New Year's Eve dinner dance. This was special because the program was broadcast nationally over WSM.

Craig was over forty when America entered World War II. Because of his history of tuberculosis, Uncle Sam was not interested in him, although Craig did register for the draft. It turned out that he could do more for the morale of the servicemen by continuing as a great bandleader on the home front. With army bases ringing Nashville, from Camp Campbell to the north to Camp Forrest to the south, the Hermitage Hotel stayed full during the war with a good complement of officers and government officials. They appreciated listening to Francis Craig and his orchestra. Manager Howard Baughman also appreciated Craig. In 1945, he congratulated Craig for his record of twenty-one consecutive years at the Hermitage, "a world record for one band at one spot." Baughman conveniently forgot about Craig's six months in Birmingham, being at the Oakes Home in Denver, and working for a while at the Andrew Jackson Hotel. Craig responded with a letter, thanking Baughman for his kindness. In part, the letter said, "Wherever I go—whatever I do—I shall never forget how kind you have been to me throughout these years."[21] As for Craig's association with WSM, it grew stronger during the war. He was given the title of music director and continued a thirty-minute Sunday night national broadcast. The program was called "Francis Craig's Sunday Night Serenade."

In March 1946, Paul Whiteman, the self-proclaimed "King of Jazz," came to Nashville to buy a walking horse. While in town, he stopped by the Hermitage Hotel to renew his acquaintance with Francis Craig, whom he had first met when his orchestra gave a concert at the Ryman Auditorium in 1930. After their meeting, Craig said, "We don't believe in this knockdown type of jive music that some bands play and we are in thorough accord on the matter of keeping music soft so that the melody will be a noticeable factor."[22]

An End and a Beginning

Francis Craig's career began to slip after World War II, and for a number of reasons. Musical tastes changed with the era of the Big Band over, and there was an emphasis on vocalists at the expense of orchestras. Bands were expensive for hotels such as the Hermitage, and, perhaps Craig, who was tired of travel, and dealing with BMI, ASCAP, and musicians, had not changed with the times. New hotel management did not renew Craig's contract in 1948. A year earlier, in May 1947, NBC had cancelled his Sunday night contract. Craig considered early retirement and disbanded his orchestra.

Craig did reassemble his orchestra, however, for a recording session at WSM's Studio B. Craig and producer Jim Bulleit, of Bullet Records, wanted to record Craig's famous record, "Red Rose," on one side and another of Craig's songs on the back. "Just dash off a tune for the other side," Bulleit said. So Craig picked out a song and got Kermit Goell, a professional songwriter on his way to California, to write a set of lyrics. He reportedly did so on a Grill Room menu while at the Hermitage, and they named the new song, "Near You." Craig played the piano part himself even though he had not played the piano much since 1929.[23] The record was released March 7. DJs across the South liked "Near You" and, by November 8, the song had become number one in Atlanta, Birmingham, Chicago, Los Angeles, Louisville, New Orleans, New York, and San Antonio. "Near You" made the Billboard list in August and

remained on the Top 10 list for twenty-five weeks, seventeen consecutive weeks of which it was number one.[24] On September 27, "Near You" became the number one song on "The Honor Roll of Hits." *Your Hit Parade*, sponsored by Lucky Strike cigarettes on Saturday nights, played the song to its national audience. It was the first national hit out of Nashville, even though it wasn't a country song.

Craig, along with Beasley Smith, also wrote "Beg Your Pardon," a song that would climb as high as third on the "Honor Roll of Hits"; it was featured for eleven straight weeks on *Your Hit Parade*. The American Society of Songwriters named "Near You" the outstanding song of 1947. Craig went on a tour that lasted almost eight weeks. Exhausted, Craig then went deep-sea fishing in Florida, and visited friends, including Howard Baughman, who was living in retirement in Florida. In the 1950s, Craig did some work at WSM and enjoyed having lunch with old friends in the National Life cafeteria. Although honors continued to come, "Beg Your Pardon" would be his last hit. He and his wife, Elizabeth, vacationed in Europe in 1954, and a few years later wintered in Sarasota, Florida, in a classic silver Airstream trailer. In the early 1960s, Francis and Elizabeth moved to Sewanee, Tennessee. Craig lived there until his death on November 19, 1966.[25] Weeks before he died, he and Elizabeth had attended Belle Meade County Club's fiftieth anniversary party. The young people there insisted that he sit down at the piano and play "Near You." He was surprised but moved by the enthusiastic ovation he received. Belle Meade had been important in his life, as had Vanderbilt, the Hermitage Hotel, and WSM.

Page 93: The Francis Craig Orchestra in the Grill Room. Front row from left: Roy "Snooky" Lanson, vocals; Carter McClellan, tenor sax, and vibes; Jack Hoffman, tenor sax, and arranger; Cecil Bailey, alto sax, and vocals; Clint Garvin, alto sax, and clarinet; Pee Wee Marquette, vocals and dancer; and John Gordy, piano. Back row from left: Jerry Vroman, trombone; Audrey Royalty, trumpet; Mickey Teninity, trumpet; Walter Lenk, drums; and Ted Swinney, bass. DCD
Page 95: Band members on break from rehearsal. Pictured on Sixth Avenue looking toward the hotel. NPL-SC
Page 97: Hermitage Hotel manager Howard Baughman and Craig at his retirement in 1947. DCD

Chapter Four

TIME MARCHES ON

cross the country in the early 1940s, wartime tensions were high. After a number of hotel employees left for military service, manager Howard Baughman had the skylight over the Hermitage Hotel lobby painted black. That way it would be indistinguishable should enemy aircraft ever bomb the city.

Efforts were made, however, to keep spirits up. In March 1942, Sam Fleming, vice president of Third National Bank, presided at Nashville's Community Concerts annual meeting at the Hermitage Hotel. Fleming introduced the principal speaker, Governor Prentice Cooper. It was announced that next season the Philadelphia Orchestra and Helen Traubel, soprano, hailed as the greatest voice of modern times, would be featured attractions. Cooper endorsed the idea of community concerts during the war, because "music builds confidence and morale, inspires and uplifts the sprits."[1]

Eight months later, Fleming was appointed Lieutenant Junior Grade in the U.S. Naval Reserve. He survived the war and returned to Nashville, establishing himself as one of the city's greatest business leaders of the twentieth century.[2]

During that season, John B. Nixon of Nashville and his family lived on a farm near Murfreesboro, Tennessee. In the summers, he would occasionally accompany his mother when she came to Nashville to shop. Before they parted company at Loveman's Department Store, she would give him twenty-five cents to spend and instruct him when to meet her in the lobby of the Hermitage Hotel to return home. While she shopped, Nixon spent his time at W. T. Grant, F. W. Woolworth, and S. H. Kress on Fifth Avenue North. If Nixon reached the Hermitage before his mother did, he would admire the Gilbert Gaul paintings in the lobby. Nixon also remembered the black street musicians who played in front of the Elks Club, a block from the hotel, during the war.[3]

In the spring of 1943, Bing Crosby crisscrossed the United States on a two-month tour promoting war bond sales by giving exhibition golf matches and conducting auctions. His Nashville stop was to benefit the Nashville Rotary Club's $1.5 million "Buy a Sub Chaser" war bond campaign. Crosby and his golf partner, Ed Dudley, president of the Professional Golfers' Association, squared off at the Belle Meade Country Club against Byron Nelson, the nation's top golfer, and Nashville city champion C. A. McManus. They played before an estimated 2,500 fans, including a good number of soldiers. Following the 18-hole match, Crosby assisted in selling 600 items, including nylon stockings and automobile tires, at an auction. Before the match, he relaxed in his room at the Hermitage Hotel where he was met in the lobby by a mob of female fans. For the occasion, he wore a green sports shirt, brown slacks, and a Panama hat at a rakish angle. Whistling as he made his way up the front steps to the lobby, Crosby broke into a wide grin when confronted by his fans. Later that evening, following dinner at the Belle Meade Country Club, Crosby took a train to Chicago for another war bond sale.[4]

The year after, in July 1944, Dorothy Niederhauser, a twenty-eight-year-old Brentwood girl, had a blind date at the Hermitage Hotel that she'd never forget. She first saw Dick Wallman, a handsome pilot with Pan American World Airways, at the top of the steps leading from the Sixth Avenue entrance of the hotel to the lobby. They had dinner that evening at the hotel and then danced to the music of Francis Craig. Under the magic spell of the Hermitage, they fell in love and married August 29, 1944. For the rest of their lives, Dorothy and Dick Wallman celebrated anniversaries, birthdays, and other important events at the hotel where their lives became one.[5]

A little bit of that hotel magic left in 1945, however, when Howard Baughman retired as manager of the Hermitage. *Nashville Tennessean* political writer Joe Hatcher once called Baughman "the best in the business." Baughman and his room clerks, Bill Caldwell and Pete Wills, "knew every politician this side of the Suez."[6] Not long after Baughman left, so did Francis Craig, in 1947. They had become close friends and Craig decided not to stay around to see how he stood with the new management.

Next in Line

William H. "Bill" Caldwell, promoted to general manager to succeed Baughman, had been with the hotel's owner, The Robert Meyer Hotels of Birmingham, Alabama, since 1931. Because materials and supplies had been scarce during World War II, the hotel needed refurbishing. Roland Munford of Raleigh, North Carolina, assistant general manager of the Robert Meyer Hotels, headed the effort to launch a renovation project. On April 25, 1946,

Wartime Weekends
SOLDIERS ENJOY DANCES

During World War II, army bases and maneuvers surrounded Nashville. Sixty miles to the northwest, straddling the Tennessee-Kentucky state line, was the sprawling Camp Campbell. To the southeast was Sewart Air Force Base at Smyrna. Forty miles further, near Tullahoma, Tennessee, was the U.S. Army's Camp Forrest. In the city itself was the Army Air Classification Center on Thompson Lane. To the east, near Lebanon, the Army held extensive maneuvers in 1943 and 1944.

As a result, weekends brought both enlisted men and officers into Nashville. While the enlisted men sought cheap quarters at the YMCA or boarding houses—or free accommodations at the 250-bed Joe Werthan Service Center on Elliston Place—the officers often stayed at the Hermitage and other downtown hotels. The army also provided entertainment for officers on the bases, usually dances held at the Officers' Club. In 1944, Nashville Cotillion Club girls, including Patti Hardison and Dorothy Ann Steward, were taken by their parents to the Hermitage Hotel, where they were taken by bus to the base at Smyrna to dance with the officers. The military furnished the music. Patti fell in love with one of those officers, Second Lieutenant Ted H. "Spike" Geltz III, who was in basic bomber training. She married him three weeks later.[7]

A Horse, of Course

AUTRY'S CHAMPION GETS STAR TREATMENT

Following the Japanese attack on Pearl Harbor, Hermitage Hotel bellman Horace Bornstein resigned his job to join the navy. In September 2005, at age eighty-one, he came back to the hotel for his first visit since leaving in December 1941. While touring the Hermitage with his wife, Tina, Bornstein noticed a photograph hanging on the hotel wall of Gene Autry and his horse, Champion. Bornstein's eyes lit up as he told his host, Hermitage controller Tom Vickstrom, that he was there when the horse checked in.

In 1941, Gene Autry, a film and TV singing cowboy with a career that spanned about two decades, was in town with his horse to be the star attraction at Nashville Public Auditorium. It was natural for Autry, who had several horses with variations on the "Champion" name, to come to the area; one of his songwriters was Nashvillian Fred Rose, who would later form Acuff-Rose Publishing Company with Roy Acuff. Before Autry's arrival, his manager received permission from the Hermitage's general manager, Howard Baughman, to allow Champion to stay with him at the hotel. In preparation, Baughman had all the furnishings removed from a room where the horse could stay. The hotel staff then put a canvas down to completely cover the floor. When the horse arrived, it was brought into the lobby through the door that opened on Capitol Boulevard, stopping for a publicity shot that showed the horse pretending to check in at the front desk. Bornstein was given responsibility for Champion's care during its stay at the Hermitage. This included supplying Champion with water and walking the horse in Memorial Square. When Gene Autry and Champion checked out, Autry personally thanked Bornstein for the good care he gave the horse and tipped him with a one hundred dollar bill, even though a traditional tip at the time would have been 10–25 cents.[8]

The hotel, incidentally, remains "pet-friendly" to this day.

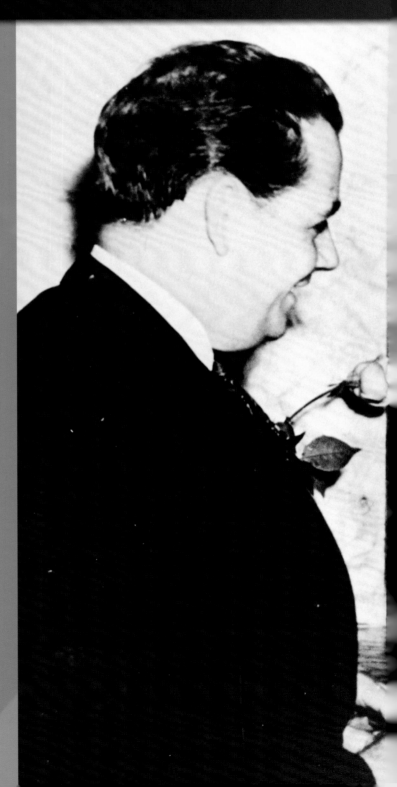

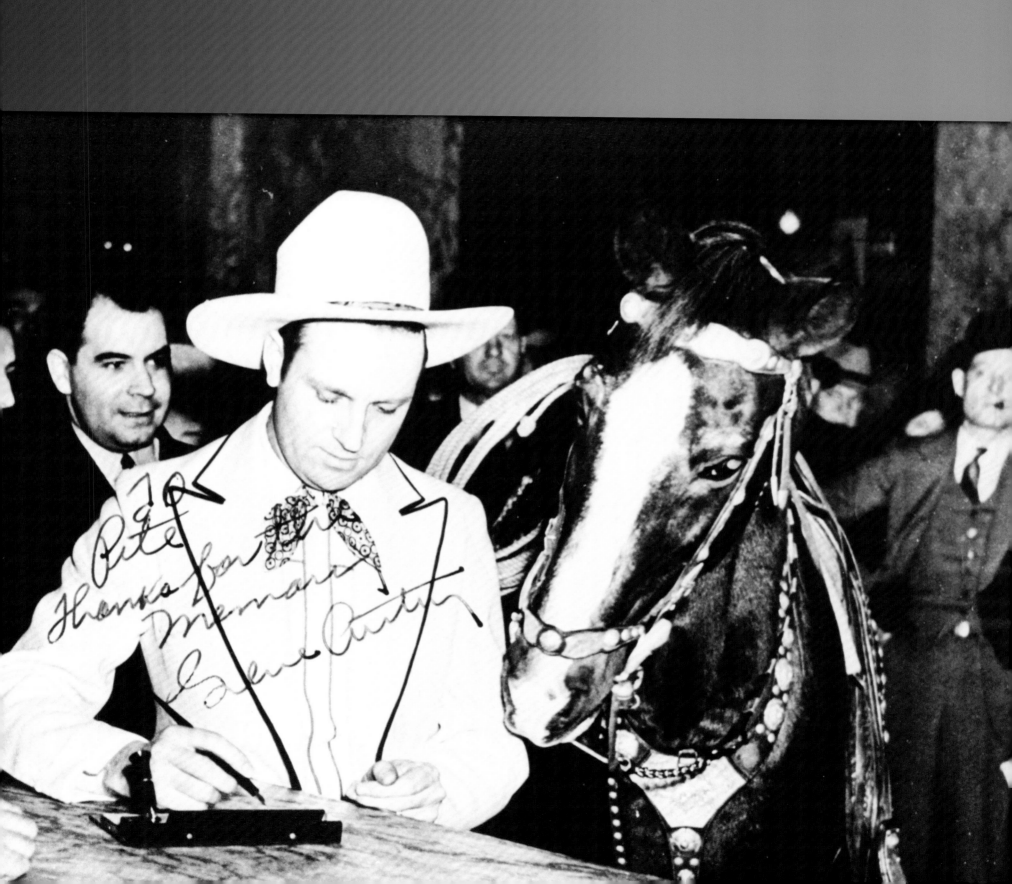

In the 1950s, Duncan Hines was a household name. His food column "Adventures in Good Eating" appeared daily in the *Nashville Banner*. In September 1953, Hines came to Nashville to be the guest of honor at a reception at the Hermitage Hotel. That evening, Mayor Ben West presented Hines with a key to the city. The next day, Mayor West proclaimed September 17 "Duncan Hines Day in Nashville." Hines, a resident of Bowling Green, Kentucky, was the author of numerous popular books in addition to his column, and they were printed at Nashville's Methodist Publishing House through Williams Printing Company. During his visit, Hines said Nashville compared favorably with other cities its size in terms of the number of good restaurants. He found fault, however, with a southern preference for fried steak. "There ought to be a law against it," he said. "Broiling is the proper treatment for any good steak." The visit was immortalized in the *Nashville Banner* with a picture of Hines sampling Hermitage Hotel chef Kirk Johnson's soup.[9]

he and Caldwell jointly announced that upward of $100,000 in improvements would be made to the hotel. Munford said, "A considerable amount will be spent for new bath and plumbing fixtures and the bedrooms are to be redecorated and modernized as rapidly as materials and supplies become available." New mechanical equipment was installed in the boiler rooms, and the kitchen and the entire hotel was repainted.[10]

In April 1946, Munford was commissioned as an honorary colonel on the staff of Governor Jim Nance McCord, who used the Hermitage for his political campaigns. Colonel Hilton Butler made the presentation in the presence of Caldwell, also a colonel on the governor's staff, and several state officials.[11]

Two years later, McCord ran for re-election in the Republican primary against country music star Roy Acuff. Shockingly, McCord lost. Acuff went on to run in the general election against former Tennessee Gov. Gordon Browning, who—despite having had the support of Ed Crump back in

1937—was by now a bitter enemy of the Memphis political boss. Browning's decisive defeat of Acuff and Democrat Estes Kefauver's easy win over Carroll Reese, the former Republican National Committee chairman, in the race for U.S. senator broke Crump's control of Democratic politics in Tennessee forever.[12] A good deal of the political infighting during these campaigns took place in the Hermitage Hotel and on Memorial Square, where Acuff held his last public rally.

A Word from the Sponsor

When WSM radio station launched its most ambitious post-war promotional effort in June 1946, the station's general manager, Harry Stone, brought

Above: This 1940s street scene features the Hermitage Hotel on the left, just beyond Memorial Square. On the right is the War Memorial Building. TSLA

Opposite page: Political meetings were often held at the Hermitage. Pictured here in the lobby are from left: Senator Herbert S. "Mr. Hub" Walters, unidentified man, Governor Jim Nance McCord, and Senator Kenneth D. McKellar. NPL-SC

Downtown Nashville played host to numerous military activities, and the Hermitage played its part. The hotel can be seen here in the background during this 1943 military parade. TSLA

a group of national newspaper and magazine writers to Nashville for a weekend junket. Naturally, he booked a suite of rooms for them at the city's finest hotel, the Hermitage. WSM's assistant manager, Jack Harris, wrote hotel manager Bill Caldwell, "You are to have a bar in operation in the main suite, which we will use as headquarters for the group." When the writers arrived, Harris told them that if they needed anything at all, they should simply pick up the phone.

He also saw to it that each room was supplied with flowers, fruit, a carton of Camel cigarettes, and a can of Prince Albert smoking tobacco. Caldwell knew, as did the writers, that Price Albert smoking tobacco, made by R. J. Reynolds, was the sponsor of a half-hour segment of the Grand Ole Opry, which had been carried live on NBC network since 1939.[13]

Eighteen months later, several hundred of Nashville's cultural elite attended a reception in the Hermitage ballroom given by the Nashville Civic Music Association. It followed the Nashville Symphony Association's fourth subscription concert of the 1947 winter season. The Civic Music Association, the umbrella organization for the Nashville Symphony Orchestra, the Nashville Choral Society, and the Nashville Youth Orchestra, had its offices on the Hermitage's mezzanine. Officers in January 1947 were Walter Sharp, president; Mrs. Charles S. Ragland, first vice-president; W. Ovid Collins, second vice-president; Reber Boult, secretary; and E. T. Proctor, treasurer. Margaret Ann Craig was general chairman for the reception.[14]

Clubs and More Clubs

In October 1947, Robert R. Meyer, president of the Robert Meyer Hotels chain, died. His son, John Edward Meyer, succeeded him as president. It took some five years to settle Robert Meyer's estate, but the Hermitage seemed not to suffer in the meantime.

It was a year later, in December 1948, that Hermitage Hotel manager Caldwell announced the appointment of Philadelphia native George E. Perry Jr. to the position of public relations manager at the hotel. For the previous three and a half years, Perry has been the executive assistant manager of the McAllister Hotel in Miami, Florida.[15]

The ballroom accommodated many large dinner meetings, as this 1948 picture of an Exchange Club meeting shows. National president Meyers Cooper was the guest speaker. Note the hardwood floor and original chandeliers. HSS

Buildings in Nashville were draped in lights for Christmas in the 1930s. From left, the Cotton States Building, the Andrew Jackson Hotel, and the Hermitage Hotel.
TSLA

Caldwell didn't last at the hotel another year. On October 24, 1949, he announced the end of his four-year tenure after meeting with Roland Munford, then general manager of the Meyer Hotels chain. At the same time, Munford announced the appointment of Edward T. Doty, thirty-five, former sales manager for hotels in New York and Washington, to succeed Caldwell, effective immediately. Doty, a native of Alexandria, Virginia, had been in the hotel business for eighteen years.[16]

That winter, the Yale Glee Club came to Nashville to perform. It was December 22, 1949, and Vanderbilt University co-ed Peggy Henry and some

A Girdle Takes Flight

STEWARDESS STORIES

American Opens New Office

Joe Torrance, representing Mayor Ben West; Stewardess Katherine Mogen of Nashville; Dr. Oren Oliver, member of the Chamber of Commerce Aviation Committee; John Gifford, vice president of General Shoe Corp., also an Aviation Committee member; P. D. Houston, Aviation Committee member and president of the First American National Bank; and Earl Bouilly, district sales manager for American Airlines, at the formal opening of American's completely remodeled and modernized ticket office at the Hermitage Hotel. The ticket office handles 590 passengers a day and has grown from a 1932 sales force of one man to the present personnel of 10. Since 1932 American has maintained ticket facilities in the Hermitage. The new office is an exact replica of the ticket office at Hollywood and Vine in Hollywood, Calif. *Staff Photo by Bill Goodman*

Once the constraints of the wartime economy disappeared, commercial airline activity dramatically increased. In the Nashville market, American Airlines shared a monopoly on commercial traffic with Eastern. American not only had a local sales office within the Hermitage Hotel, it would also house its crews there. The airline leased several rooms that were the first to be air-conditioned at the hotel. Crews arrived at any time, day or night. The rooms, each of which had twin beds, were numbered 313, 314, 315, and 327.

A crew consisted of a captain, a co-pilot, and a flight attendant, then called a stewardess. The captains and co-pilots sometimes shared rooms, but the stewardesses had their own rooms. Many times, however, stewardesses from different crews shared a room. The stewardess who arrived first would leave the door unlocked for the second stewardess. If the door was still unlocked at 2 AM, longtime employee Bob Pardue and his partner would awaken her by knocking on the door and saying, "This is the night watchman. Would you please lock your door?"

Pardue loved to recall the night when a certain "really cute" stewardess left her door unlocked. "When we knocked on her door at 2 AM," he said, "she came to the door nude and cute as a button. The night watchman got so rattled he said, 'This is the night lock man will you watch your door?'"

On another occasion, Pardue recalled, "A stewardess was staying in 327, an inside room overlooking the ceiling of the lobby. A girdle was a required part of every stewardess's uniform then. Most stewardesses were small, weighing no more than 110 pounds. Shoulder length hair was also a requirement for stewardesses. The stewardess had washed her girdle and hung it on a hanger outside her window to dry. While drying, the undergarment blew off the hanger and lodged on top of the skylight. She called the bell captain and asked if she could borrow the key to Room 227 so she could climb out the window and retrieve the girdle." Pardue answered her call and decided to go up to her room and retrieve whatever she had lost. He did and to his surprise found it was an undergarment. He put it in a laundry bag before handing it to her. "She was embarrassed," he said, "but less so than if I had not covered it."[17]

Legislators and Liquor
LIQUOR SALES AT THE HOTEL

With so much political activity and schmoozing swirling around the Hermitage Hotel, it was an ideal location for a liquor store. Harry Banniza recognized the opportunity and, in 1949, opened Hermitage Hotel Liquors on Sixth Avenue North immediately to the right of the hotel entrance. Many of his customers during the next quarter century would be legislators; lobbyists such as Tom "the Golden Goose" Hensley; and politicians, such as Frank Clement and Ned Ray McWherter. Banniza knew most of them, both as customers of the liquor store and of the hotel, where he was a bellman and, later, assistant superintendent of services.[18] When the legislature was in session, legislators and lobbyists were hardcore customers at the Hermitage bar. One legislator who enjoyed staying at the Hermitage was Jim Cummings of Woodbury, Tennessee. One night, after he had undressed to his underwear, someone knocked on his door. When he opened the door, an attractive young woman standing there said, "I must have the wrong room." Cummings replied, "No, you've got the right room. You're just twenty years too late."[19]

of her friends witnessed the event at the War Memorial Building. Following the performance, the girls attended a dance in the ballroom at the Hermitage Hotel given by the Nashville Yale Alumni Club. There, Henry met her future husband, Harry Joyce, a young trainee at National Life and Accident Insurance Company. After the dance, Henry and her friends—but not Joyce—went to Union Station to see the Glee Club off. The Yale boys, who were as excited as the girls were, threw the paper shirts on their tails out of the windows as the train slowly pulled away.[20]

In the summer of 1950, the deteriorating Chamber of Commerce building's owner announced that its dining rooms would have to be closed. The Kiwanis, Lions, Rotary, and other civic clubs that met there had to scramble to find new homes. Manager Doty, who was a Rotarian, invited the club to return to the Hermitage, where they had been until 1921. Rotary office space was identified and the move was scheduled for October. The Exchange Club, however, which had met at the Hermitage Hotel since it was founded, objected to the Rotary Club meeting there. The Rotarians decided not to fight the issue and moved to the Maxwell House Hotel in 1951, where they stayed until the hotel burned on Christmas Night, 1961.[21]

In October 1951, the City of Nashville granted the Meyer Hotels Company a building permit to refinish the Sixth Avenue front of the Hermitage Hotel. In addition, alterations and repairs were to be made in the interior on the first and second floors by contractor R. E. Dunn. Manager Edward Doty oversaw the renovations with prominent Nashville architect Edwin Keeble on the job; the work was expected to cost $67,000. A temporary walkway was constructed around the Sixth Avenue façade while the renovation was underway.[22] The work went quickly and, on January 13, 1952, Munford announced that the stores adjoining the hotel, in a building known as the Hermitage Hotel Annex, would be ready for occupancy in about a month. The development included four shops facing Sixth Avenue, seven offices facing Capitol Boulevard, and a new banquet hall and ballroom on the second floor above the offices. The office space fronted sixty-two feet on Sixth Avenue North. "The facing of contemporary design will be of yellow and green terra cotta with redwood canopy and trim," Munford said. But leases had not yet been signed. "The office space on Capitol Boulevard . . . would," Munford announced, "house the Nashville bureaus of the *Memphis Commercial Appeal* and the *Chattanooga Times*, and offices of the Tennessee Petroleum Association, Tennessee Municipal League, Tennessee Motor Transport Association, and the Reese Insurance Agency." The ballroom would accommodate four hundred people.[23]

Full House

Country music legend Hank Williams was a good customer of the Hermitage Hotel in the early 1950s when he was on the Grand Ole Opry. Bob Pardue recalled that Williams drove a nice Cadillac convertible, and that he would sometimes ask Pardue to go down to Kress & Co. on Fifth Avenue North to purchase shirts, T-shirts, and socks. Williams, who once shot up the ceiling and walls of his room with a pistol, talked a lot about his relationship with his wife Audrey, Pardue recalled, including their divorce in 1952. He also spoke about his return to drinking.[24]

Not long after being dismissed by the Opry for alcoholism, the twenty-nine-year-old star died while on his way from Knoxville, Tennessee, to a concert in Ohio. His seventeen-year-old driver stopped in Virginia when he sensed something was wrong with Williams. He found the country music star dead in the back seat, a victim of an overdose.

In those early 1950s days, sixteen-year-old Hillsboro High School sophomore Lannie Neal Jr. needed an after-school job. He wanted to save money to pay half the cost of flying to London, where his older

Local groups frequently used the hotel as a place to promote their interests. In 1957, the Nashville Exchange Club sold season tickets for the minor-league Nashville Vols. Pictured are (seated) ex-major leaguer Clydell Castleman; standing from left: Vols General Manager Bill McCarthy, Exchange Club President Tom Steele, and Drive Manager Joe Carr. Nathan Halpern is the man buying the ticket. NPL-SC

'BACK THE VOLS'
Advance Ticket Sale
(5 TICKETS $ 4.50) 30% SAVINGS
(25 TICKETS $22.50)
Youth Season Tickets
$ 6.00 (73 GAMES)
• BASEBALL IS FUN "

sister lived, to see the 1953 coronation of Queen Elizabeth II. Neal's father, a Metro policeman, knew Sue Dixon, secretary to Herbert Bingham, executive director of the Tennessee Municipal League, which had its offices in the Hermitage Hotel Annex. Through their influence, the young Neal landed a job as assistant room clerk at the hotel. The elder Neal, who directed traffic at the corner of Fifth Avenue and Church Street, also knew Allen Pomeroy, owner of the Nashville Tailoring Co. on Church Street. He asked Pomeroy to give his son a good deal on a tailored suit, and Pomeroy did so. When the young man reported to work at the front desk, he looked sharp. His face fell, however, when the clerk sent him down to the basement to see the housekeeper. She greeted him, and said that, although he looked nice, he really didn't need a suit. She gave him a green uniform, told him to change, and then go up to the sixth floor and report to the housekeeper on that floor. Word quickly got back to Sue Dixon that the boy was scrubbing toilets. She immediately complained to Edward Doty, the general manager, and that same afternoon, when Neal got back from lunch, he was assigned duties as the assistant room clerk for the 3 PM to 11 PM shift, earning him enough to make the London trip. Neal stayed at the hotel for six years.

During the six years that Neal worked at the Hermitage, hotel guests sometimes attended concerts at the War Memorial Auditorium a block away or went to the theaters on Sixth and Fifth avenues or Church Street. Other nearby attractions were the Nashville Lion's Club next door, as well as the 216 Club, Jimmy Kelly's, and Cross Keys restaurants. American Airlines and Hermitage Hotel Liquors had offices in the hotel on the street level along Sixth Avenue. There was a newsstand in the lobby run by

Ruth McCoy, a sister of *Nashville Tennessean* sports editor, Raymond Johnson. The Exchange Club office was on the veranda. The annex building next door had long-term residents, including William Anderson, the very popular Vanderbilt track coach who stayed there periodically; Mr. and Mrs. Powell Stamper, who lived at the hotel for twenty-two years; and Mr. and Mrs. Robert E. Cooper. Stamper was an assistant vice president and sales promotions manager for the National Life and Accident Insurance Co. Mr. Cooper was general manager of WSM radio.

June brought the arrival of Southern League baseball teams to play the Nashville Vols at Sulphur Dell. Invariably, they stayed in the cheapest rooms, usually paying about twenty-two dollars a night. The players often came in late in the evening even when they had a daytime game.

But the wildest time, according to Neal, was the three-month period when the legislature was in session and legislators filled the hotel. Sometimes, when legislators arrived with confirmed reservations, Neal would not have a room available, and would frantically call the Maxwell House, the Andrew Jackson, and the Noel to find space. This practice was called "walking guests." Every time this happened, Neal suspected that someone had "greased the palm" of a room clerk on the earlier shift. Neal recognized the lobbyists, including John R. Neal of East Tennessee, who also stayed in the hotel when the legislature was in session. They booked some of the best rooms. In addition to being wonderful customers of the bar, the legislators got their cigars, chewing gum, and "girlie" magazines at the cigar stand in the lobby.

Nixon, Winfrey, and Swanson

Neal was at work late in the afternoon of September 27, 1952, when then Republican vice-presidential candidate, Senator Richard Nixon of California, drove by. Nixon was on Sixth Avenue North in an open convertible, on his way

This picture from 1977 shows the hotel entrance to the Iris Room, located in the annex, where many political and social meetings were held. Note the green lobby color scheme which dates back to Bill Caldwell's tenure as hotel manager in the late 1940s. NPL-SC

Robert R. Meyer

HOTEL ICON

Few people in the early twentieth-century hotel industry have left as large a footprint as Robert R. Meyer. As founder of Meyer Hotels, he was an innovative entrepreneur with a dedication to quality. As a philanthropist, his legacy is even more lasting.

Robert Randolph Meyer was born on August 1, 1882, as one of six children of Fred and Martha Meyer of Montgomery, Alabama. He was educated in Montgomery public schools; there is no information indicating that he attended college. However, there is every indication that even at an early age, Meyer possessed a pioneering spirit that would lead him to the top of his chosen profession.

He started his working career in the laundry business, serving both Montgomery and Birmingham. By the age of twenty-two, he turned his attention to the hotel trade, which would remain his business for the next forty years.

He bought his first hotel, The Metropolitan in Birmingham, prior to 1920, and during varying times through 1947, owned, leased, or operated hotels in Jacksonville; Atlanta; Knoxville; Baltimore; Nashville; Raleigh, North Carolina; Roanoke, Virginia; Reading, Pennsylvania; and Trenton, New Jersey. Meyer was on the board of directors of the Waldorf-Astoria, as well. Although he never claimed credit for the idea, Meyer was nonetheless one of the few individuals who became proponents of the hotel chain.

Meyer's first wife, Camilla, died in 1910; he was divorced from his second wife, Cora, by 1917. He retained custody of the couple's children, Robert Jr. and John Edward, and married widow Lewis Barrett in 1922. She

Greetings from
Hotel Hermitage
Nashville, Tennessee

Other
Robert Meyer Hotels:
Hotel Winecoff
　　　Atlanta. Ga.
Hotel Farragut
　　　Knoxville. Tenn.
Hotel Sir Walter
　　　Raleigh, N. C.
Hotel Windsor
Hotel Roosevelt
　　　Jacksonville, Fla.
Hotel Emerson
　　　Baltimore, Md.
Hotel Patrick Henry
　　　Roanoke, Va.
Hotel Stacy-Trent
Hotel Hildebrecht
　　　Trenton, N. J.
These are indicated by
larger dark circles on
map.

We Drove Today

From ....

To ....

had two children from her previous marriage, Kitty and Edward Barrett. The Meyers were a commanding couple; he, a hotel magnate, and she, the first woman editor of a daily newspaper in the United States and the first female member of the Associated Press.

Meyer had clearly achieved great success by the end of the 1920s, for even though the stock market crash in 1929 ruined many businessmen, the Meyers' lifestyle remained virtually unchanged. Meyer was an avid golfer and enjoyed club memberships in several localities.

A favorite humanitarian interest was the Children's Fresh Air Farm. Founded in 1923 by Meyer, this program enabled hundreds of needy children a month-long vacation on Shades Mountain, near Birmingham.

In 1942, the Meyers established a foundation to support their charitable work, based on 1/3 of their estate. The original endowment of $2.5 million is worth about $35 million as of 2008. Support from this foundation helped to construct the Children's Hospital in Birmingham.

Tragedy struck the Meyer family in 1942, when son Robert Jr., a graduate of Princeton University and a military pilot, was reported missing over New Guinea. Following the family's tradition of philanthropy, a scholarship was established in his name by his brother John, and has since sponsored many Birmingham-area students to study at Princeton University.

In 1947, both Lewis Meyer and Robert Meyer died. The Meyer estate was so complicated and large that it took five years to sort out. Eventually, the majority of the estate was placed into the jurisdiction of the Robert R. Meyer Foundation. As of 2008, more than $51 million had been distributed to more than 340 charitable organizations over the decades. The fund continues to operate today, a testament to the man who, according to one book, will benefit generations to come "because he lived, aspired, and held steadfast to the goals he had set."[25]

from the airport to address a crowd of Republican supporters at a rally on Memorial Square. At the rally, Nixon correctly predicted that traditional Democratic states Tennessee, Oklahoma, and Texas, would vote Republican that fall.[26]

The Grill Room had a private dining room with a frosted glass front, located near the far wall where the Parthenon picture is today. Oprah Winfrey had a party for her father in the room. Lannie Neal remembered three general managers: Ed Doty, Bill Cole, and George Scharf; assistant manager Fleming Hocker; and Morris Cunningham, a colorful character who was head bellman. Overall, Neal recalled, the hotel staff was stable during his tenure there; in his opinion, the Hermitage was "the" hotel to stay at in Nashville, with the Andrew Jackson only a "poorer sister."

One of Neal favorite tales, however, involved legendary silent film diva Gloria Swanson. She stayed at the Hermitage in 1952 while promoting a women's clothing line at Castner Knott Department Store. Neal knew from the reservation ticket that someone named Gloria Swanson would be staying at the hotel, but he doubted it would be the movie star. When she checked in, he was initially speechless as it really was the diminutive Hollywood star. After catching his breath, he gushed, "Oh, Mrs. Swanson, I love you. You are the greatest actress in the whole world." She responded, "Young man, you are the only person in the world who thinks that."

A little later, Neal was summoned to the general manager's office, where he fully expected to be fired for being overly familiar with a guest. He began a plea to keep his job when the manager said, "Shut up, Lannie. I have a strange request. Mrs. Swanson wants to have dinner with you tonight." As soon as Neal got back to the front desk, he called his mother for permission, as he was only sixteen years old.

Neal did have dinner that night as Swanson's guest in the hotel dining room. He was so excited he could not remember a thing he ate. He did recall that Swanson asked a lot of questions about his parents. He, in turn, asked her about some famous Hollywood personalities. All she said was, "Anyone that was anybody in Hollywood is now dead or forgotten," including herself.

Some months later, Swanson returned to the Hermitage with a big box for Neal. In it was one of her designer hats for Neal's mother. When the young man called his mother to tell her about the present, Mrs. Neal said, "That sweet woman, we'll have to have her out for dinner." So, Gloria Swanson had dinner with the Neals at their home. Mrs. Neal served country ham, scrambled eggs, a grits casserole, Waldorf salad, and iced tea. Swanson returned to the hotel one more time while Neal was there. He recalled that each time she came, he was the only person who seemed to recognize who she was.[27]

What Kind of Calf

Edward Doty resigned as general manager of the Hermitage Hotel at the beginning of 1953. His employees thought enough of him that they presented him with a large, framed color photograph of the Hermitage, Andrew Jackson's home. On the back of the painting, every hotel employee signed his or her name. The inscription said, "To the Skipper: We wanted to do something that would somehow help to show how much we're going to miss you for we hate to see you go. And so this comes to say 'good by' and bring good wishes too. For all the very best of luck in days ahead of you."[28]

In 1953, the hotel had one hundred forty-five employees in ten departments: auditing, banquet, engineering, front office, grill, housekeeping, kitchen, laundry, office, and service. The housekeeping and service departments had the largest number of hotel employees, with twenty-nine and twenty-six respectively.

At that point, J. William Cole became the new manager of the Hermitage. Cole, who had served as vice president and general manager of the Grenoble Hotels Company, which operated twenty-six hotels and five hospitals in

Pennsylvania, Virginia, and North Carolina, assumed his new post on February 1. The twenty-five-year hotel veteran was described as a graduate of the Cornell University Hotel School, a Rotarian, and a Methodist. He and his wife had two sons, ages seven and twelve.[29]

Frank G. Clement, a young attorney from Dickson, Tennessee, and a candidate to succeed incumbent Gov. Gordon Browning in the 1952 Democratic Primary, announced that April that Buford Ellington would be his state campaign manager with headquarters in the Hermitage. Ellington was familiar with the hotel, having stayed in the hotel's least expensive rooms before he moved to Nashville from Mississippi. Recalling those days, Ellington joked, "My room was so small I could lie in bed and brush my teeth in the bathroom."[30] Clement also lived with his wife, Lucille, and their two sons, Frank Jr. and Bob, in the Hermitage Hotel for six months that year. Lucille was pregnant with their third son, Gary, who was born November 28. Little Frank and Bob loved living in the hotel and both helped their father campaign by wearing T-shirts that read "Vote for My Daddy" on the front and "Frank G. Clement" on the back.

Clement won the primary and went on to become Tennessee's second youngest governor. He served two terms, the first for two years and the second for four years. Ellington, who had served as commissioner of agriculture under Clement, succeeded him in 1959. Anna Bell Clement, Frank's sister, became Ellington's secretary, and others, including Eddie Friar and Brainard Cheney, joined the payroll.

One year during Ellington's administration, the Hotel Association had its convention at the Mountain View Hotel in Gatlinburg, Tennessee. Bob Pardue, who had known Ellington from his early days at the Hermitage, asked the governor if he would he have thought several years ago that they would be together "at a meeting of this capacity, him the governor of Tennessee and me, the manager of a nice hotel." Ellington answered, "Bob, you don't know what kind of calf will come from a sick cow."[31]

During the Clement and Ellington years, there were a number of political fixtures in the Hermitage lobby. Walter "Pete" Haynes, prominent attorney from Winchester, Tennessee, was one. Haynes who, at different times, was speaker of both the House and the Senate, would stay in a suite at the Hermitage in the odd years that the legislature was in session. What he really enjoyed was to sit in a comfortable chair in the lobby and visit with his friends while enjoying a cigar and a little Jack Daniel's whiskey. Jim Cummings, the longtime Tennessee general assembly leader from Woodbury; I. D. Beasley of Carthage, Tennessee; and George Oliver Benton of Jackson, Tennessee, were often good company. Beasley, Cummings, and Haynes were sarcastically referred to by their enemies as the "Unholy Trinity," for their efforts to benefit the state's rural communities.

Whether in the lobby or the mezzanine, Haynes also would do a little lobbying. Sometimes, he would bring his junior law partner, Tom Wiseman, with him. Although Wiseman would sleep at the less-expensive Noel Hotel, he met all the political operatives who socialized at the Hermitage. He also

Mrs. Lula C. Naff enjoyed her retirement party in the Iris Room September 1, 1955. Nostalgically, Mrs. Naff surveys autographed photos of some of the hundreds of celebrities of the world of music and theater who played the Ryman Auditorium when she was manager. NPL-SC

A Top-Dollar Stay

KEEPING UP WITH THE "JONESES"

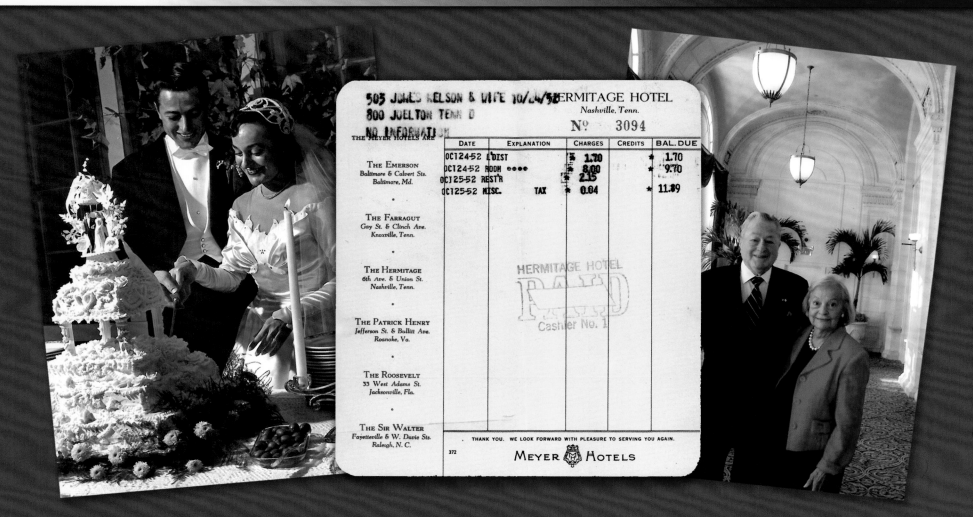

On October 24, 1952, newlyweds Nelson and Clara Rawlings Davenport checked in to the Hermitage Hotel to spend their wedding night. Nelson was apprehensive that his fraternity brothers would pull some pranks by either paying an uninvited visit or lurking in the couple's reserved room. He therefore registered under the alias "Jones," much to the chagrin of his proud new bride.

In 2008, the Davenports called again, this time spending their anniversary at the hotel. They produced their original hotel bill, complete with a room rate of $8 and a restaurant charge of $2.25. To help them celebrate—and gain a bit of publicity—the hotel offered them the same $8 rate. The Davenports own and operate a lodge named Shadowbrook in Joelton, Tennessee.[32]

learned that the liquor lobby provided Harry Banniza's Hermitage Liquors with free liquor with the understanding that Banniza would give a pint to any legislator who wanted one. Wiseman would go on to serve in the legislature from 1965 to 1969; was treasurer for the State of Tennessee from 1971 to 1974; ran as a Democratic candidate for governor in 1974; and was appointed judge on the U.S. District Court for the Middle District of Tennessee by U.S. President Jimmy Carter in 1978.[33]

In 1962, Clement made another successful gubernatorial campaign and served another four years, from 1963 until 1967. Tragically, on November 4, 1969, the forty-nine-year-old ex-governor was killed in an automobile accident near Nashville.[34]

Changing Hands

On June 29, 1954, the *Nashville Banner* announced that George A. Scharf, forty-nine, a hotel manager from Baltimore, Maryland, would succeed Bill Cole as manager of the Hermitage Hotel the following month. Cole would return to Grenoble Hotels Co. in Harrisburg, Pennsylvania, as executive vice president and general manager. It also was announced that the $450,000 modernization program begun in 1950 would be completed that September. The plan included air conditioning throughout all areas of the property; the replacement of plumbing and fixtures in sixty-four bathrooms; new room furnishings including television sets; and a beauty parlor.

Scharf's move to Nashville came only two months after the Supreme Court issued the famous *Brown v. Board of Education of Topeka* decision that declared segregated schools unconstitutional. Locally, William Adrian, bishop of the Catholic Diocese of Nashville, asked his priests to vote on desegregation. They voted for ending segregation and, as a consequence, fifteen black students entered Father Ryan High School that fall. After the city's restaurants refused to hold a desegregated prom that December, the school ended its prom and held a desegregated banquet at the Hermitage Hotel. That affirmative action spoke well not only of Father Ryan High School and the Diocese, but also management of the Hermitage Hotel.[35]

Renovations were finished at the hotel, but sales were not where management wanted them to be, so John E. Meyer, president of the Meyer Hotels Company, named Howard M. Burton director of sales for the Hermitage Hotel. Previously, Burton had been director of the Nashville Chamber of Commerce Convention and Visitors Bureau. He assumed his new duties on October 1.[36]

Burton must have been dismayed when he learned his first month on the job that stockholders of the Meyer Hotels had met in Birmingham to consider the sale of the Hermitage to an outside group. Meyer would not comment on the meeting to the press. Financial sources speculated, "The sale may be just a technical matter to settle the estate of Robert R. Meyer, who headed the Meyer chain until his death about eight years ago."[37] Sure enough, the *Nashville Banner*, on October 14, 1955, reported that the Hermitage Hotel was for sale. Meyer did say that the hotel would continue to operate as a Meyer Hotel under a long-term lease.[38]

The sale took longer than expected. It was not until May 29, 1956, that the Alsonett Hotels Company officials confirmed that a deal to purchase the Hermitage Hotel had been virtually completed at a price believed to be $2 million. The formal closing was held May 31 in Chicago, where Alsonett had its headquarters. The Nashville Hotel Company, a subsidiary of Alsonett, paid $1,710,000 for the property, $710,000 in cash and two promissory notes, one for $280,000 and the other for $720,000.[39] Plans were not announced for additions or improvements, but John McMullen, Alsonett general manager, said redecorating the guest rooms and the upstairs corridors would likely be an early priority. The Hermitage Hotel would be the Alsonett Company's 37th property.[40]

C. H. Alberding, president of Alsonett Hotels, said, "The Hermitage Hotel long has been a leading hotel of the South. Its physical location in Nashville is unique, facing as it does Memorial Square and the Capitol. To Nashville people it is an institution connected with many of their fondest memories."[41]

George Scharf, in the meantime, who had served as manager of the Hermitage for nineteen months, resigned to return to Baltimore to manage another hotel in the Robert Meyer chain.[42]

Postcard of the Hermitage Hotel when it was owned by the Alsonett Company.
RW II

Alvin York

A RELUCTANT HERO

Corporal Alvin C. York, a soldier from rural Pall Mall, Tennessee, knew he had to silence the German machine guns that killed nine of his comrades. He and sixteen other soldiers, under the command of Sgt. Bernard Early, had mistakenly ended up behind the German lines during World War I. In a brief firefight, Early was so badly wounded that he turned over command to corporals Harry Parsons and William Cutting, who ordered York to find some way to stop the Germans' assault. York led an attack that stopped thirty-two machine guns, killed twenty-eight German soldiers, and captured another one hundred thirty-two.[43]

When York returned from war, he was a sergeant; his chest was decorated with a Congressional Medal of Honor—placed there by General John Pershing—and a Croix de Guerre presented by Marshall Ferdinand Foch. "What you did," he was told, "was the greatest thing ever accomplished by any soldier of any of the armies of Europe."[44]

York received a hero's welcome after returning to the United States. He visited Washington, D.C., as a guest of Tennessee congressman Cordell Hull, as well as New York where offers to tell his story in book or on film were numerous. He refused, preferring to return to Tennessee to be with his sweetheart, Gracie Williams.[45]

The original plan had been for York and Williams to wed in a simple ceremony with her pastor/cousin presiding. Tennessee Gov. A. H. Roberts realized the wedding would generate national attention, especially after the *New York Times* covered York's homecoming with the headline, "Sergt. York Home, His Girl Says Yes."[46] Roberts made the offer to officiate and the couple accepted. With 2,500 watching, the couple married on a flat rock on the top of a slope above the Wolf River in Fentress County on June 7.[47]

Roberts persuaded the newlyweds to spend part of their wedding trip at the governor's mansion in Nashville. Nine members of the wedding party joined the newlyweds for the trip; for many of them, it marked their first time out of Fentress County. The Yorks stayed in the mansion on Seventh Avenue, while others in the party stayed at

the Hermitage Hotel. Manager Robert E. Hyde tried to make the Fentress County visitors feel at home, or, at least, not overwhelmed.

There were receptions at the Ryman Auditorium; a visit to the Hermitage, Andrew Jackson's home; some shopping for the ladies; a professional baseball game at Sulphur Dell; a Rotary Club dinner; and, on the last night, a dinner at the Hermitage Hotel given by Maj. E. B. Stahlman, a vaudeville show at the Princess Theatre, and a war movie, *The Home Town Girl*, at the Fifth Avenue Theatre.[48]

By 1920, Hollywood film producer Jesse Lasky began trying to negotiate a movie contract with York. And, as the years went by, he saw his chances improve. In 1939, despite having been given a house and a four-hundred-acre river bottom farm by the Nashville Rotary Club, York was having financial problems. The same was true of the Alvin C. York Industrial Institute, which York founded in Jamestown in 1926 as a school for mountain boys and girls. That year, Lasky appealed to York's patriotism by suggesting that his story would present a patriotic, pro-allies

message to the country. Lasky knew that York was vocal in denouncing isolationists in America and particularly their most visible spokesman, Col. Charles Lindbergh. York found something appealing in Lasky's proposition that a telling of his story might promote nationwide a patriotic stance against Hitler, as well as give him the funds he needed to start a Bible school in Fentress County.

When Lasky and York met at the Hermitage Hotel on March 14, Lasky had already tipped off the press that the movie would be made and that York would serve as a technical advisor. After much back and forth, including a stunt that had the pair signing a dummy contract for cameras while Gov. Prentice Cooper looked on, York signed the contract that gave him $25,000 plus an equal amount the day after the movie was released—or by October 1941, even if the picture was never made. He also would receive $500 per week for his services as technical consultant. If the movie made $3 million, York would receive another four percent, increasing to eight percent if the movie topped $8 million. One point that York and Lasky did not argue about was who would play Sergeant York. Both men wanted Gary Cooper, who agreed.

Sergeant York premiered in New York City at the Astor Theatre on July 2, 1941. Two images alternated above the marquee: first, a forty-five-foot-tall Gary Cooper, dressed in Tennessee homespun and holding a squirrel gun, and second, an equally-tall Cooper in his army uniform looking down the barrel of a rifle. A huge theatrical sign to the side read, "Gary Cooper in *Sergeant York*." Warner Brothers announced that the advance ticket sales were the greatest since *Gone With the Wind*. York, Cooper, and Lasky sat together for the premiere. It was the first time either Cooper or York had seen the movie, which was not shot in Tennessee.[49]

One bone of contention was the fact that Lasky had promised York that he would hold a premiere in Nashville. When it became obvious that he had no intention of doing so, York, Gov. Prentice Cooper, and Nashville Mayor Thomas L. Cummings decided to hold one on their own at the nearby Knickerbocker Theatre. York arrived in town for the September 18 premiere at midday. He and his party were welcomed at the Hermitage Hotel by Governor Cooper and others. Early that afternoon, outside the hotel, Governor Cooper read a proclamation temporarily renaming Sixth Avenue North "York Avenue." Later that day, the York party went to the Tennessee State Fair before returning to the Hermitage Hotel for an 8 PM reception. At the premiere that night, York cut a ribbon stretched across the sidewalk in front of the theater, signaling the beginning of the event.[50]

The movie made Alvin York a hero all over again and gave him a platform to speak forcefully about the importance of America intervening in the war raging in Europe. The movie, a sensation at box offices across the country, won an Oscar for Gary Cooper and a nomination as Best Picture.

Alvin York traveled extensively during the first part of World War II, promoting the sale of war bonds, visiting recruits at army bases, and speaking on behalf of the war effort. In 1941 and 1942, he wrote a syndicated newspaper column. York also was head of the Fentress County Draft Board.[51]

York was back in Nashville in 1942 for a defense bond rally at the Ryman Auditorium. While there, he met a Nashville singer named Fanny Rose, who would later achieve stardom under the name Dinah Shore. It may have been one of the last times he stayed at the Hermitage Hotel, as arthritis and other physical ailments—aggravated by his 275-pound size—made travel difficult.[52]

Chapter Five

THE DICK HALL ERA

The Hermitage

Richard "Dick" Hall had known since he was only seven years old that he would be a hotel general manager someday, and on June 30, 1956, that dream came true. Hall was about to begin a twelve-year, memorable run at the helm of the Hermitage Hotel.

At age seventeen, Hall joined the U.S. Navy, and later served for two years in the Korean War. He graduated first in his class at Cornell University Hotel School before entering the hotel management business. Before moving to Nashville, the Illinois native had been sales manager of the Robert E. Lee Hotel in Winston-Salem, North Carolina, where he married Drusilla "Dru" Darr, daughter of R. J. Reynolds Tobacco Company president E. A. Darr. At the time Hall was recruited for the Hermitage position, he was resident manager of the Maxwell House Hotel, president of the Tennessee Hotel Association, and chairman of the Chamber of Commerce's convention and visitors committee.[1]

Above: Richard R. "Dick" Hall was the manager of the Hermitage Hotel from 1956–1968. GH

Right: An article in the June 18, 1957, Nashville Banner *featured Betty and Benny Fox, aerial artists for the Tom Pack Shrine Circus. The couple perched on an eighteen-inch platform atop the Hermitage Hotel to publicize the circus. The platform protruded into open air ten stories above street level.* NPL-SC

One of the most frequent guests at the Hermitage during Dick Hall's years as general manager was Mae Boren Axton, a schoolteacher from Jacksonville, Florida, who worked out of her room at the Hermitage as a publicist for Hank Snow. Snow was a songwriter, manager, and board member of the Academy of Country Music. One day, Axton showed singer Elvis Presley a song, "Heartbreak Hotel," that she and Tommy Durden, another Jacksonville songwriter, wrote. She asked Presley to see if he might be interested in recording it. He liked the song and recorded it at RCA Victor in Nashville, his first recording at that studio. When it was released in January 1956, "Heartbreak Hotel" became the first number one pop record Presley had recorded. It remained number one for seventeen weeks on the Billboard Country Chart, reached number three on the Billboard Rhythm & Blues Chart, and was the best-selling single of 1956.[2]

That same year, the new management of the Hermitage was quickly becoming acquainted with the hotel's permanent tenants: American and Braniff Airways, the first on the corner to the right of the Sixth Avenue North entrance and the second immediately to the left; Citizens for TVA; the Exchange Club; the Hermitage Beauty Salon; Hermitage Hotel Liquor Store; the office of Hazel Mathias, public stenographer; the Nashville Symphony Association; and the Tennessee Road Builders Association.

In April 1958, American Airlines, which had occupied a one-man office in the Hermitage for

Above, left: 1950s street scene, facing south. MA

Above, right: Nighttime street scene featuring Sixth Avenue North, early 1950s. Fourth, Fifth, and Sixth avenues were shopping meccas, as well as Church Street, one block south. MA

thirty-two years, formally opened its completely remodeled and modernized ticket counter. The office, manned by ten people, handled 590 passengers a day, and was an exact replica of the ticket office at Hollywood and Vine in Hollywood, California. Mayor Ben West and several members of the Aviation Committee of the Chamber of Commerce attended the ceremony.[3]

The 1950s were the heyday of shopping downtown as suburban shopping malls had not yet—but would soon—materialize. In 1959, the stores facing the Hermitage on Sixth Avenue North offered men's wear, furs, and shoes. There also was a cafeteria. On the west side of Sixth Avenue North, it was but a short walk south to Eastern Airlines, Cross Keys Restaurant, Grace's Shop for Ladies, Broadway Bank, and the Knickerbocker Theatre.[4]

Blazes and Music

Dick and Dru Hall got quite a scare the previous November when a fire broke out in their 6th floor hotel apartment. It happened about 8 AM in a closet

The Dick Hall Era

131

Vice President Richard Nixon and his wife, Pat, dined at the Grill Room during a campaign stop in Nashville on September 27, 1956. Escorting them is hotel manager Dick Hall (far left). Nixon spoke to a large crowd at the War Memorial Auditorium. NPL-SC

in their daughter Drusilla's room.[5] The baby was not injured and neither was her three-year-old brother, Darr, who slept through the commotion in another room. However, almost all of Darr's clothes were destroyed before firemen extinguished the blaze.[6]

Each April, Dick and Dru Hall would host Derby Day parties at their Hermitage suite. Among those friends who frequently attended were Sally and Eddy Arnold; Joanne and Paul Callis; Betty and Ed Graham; Peggy and Harry Joyce; Emmie and Hunter McDonald; and Mary Elizabeth and Richard "Red" Norvell. Arnold was godfather for the Halls' daughter. In 1959, while with the Halls, Arnold sang his newest song, "Tennessee Stud." It rose to No. 5 on the country music charts that year.[7]

Kennedy, Nixon, and a Gubernatorial Song

May 1, 1958, was a big day; between 3,000 and 4,000 people passed through the doors of the Hermitage Hotel to shake hands with Buford Ellington, who had officially opened his gubernatorial campaign headquarters in the hotel. Veteran political observers said it was the largest crowd ever seen at a political event there. Visitors came from every county in Tennessee, providing evidence of Ellington's tremendous political strength.[8]

That same year, Dick Hall got some welcome sales help when he persuaded Jennie Mizell, wife of Nashville Federal Court Clerk Andrew H. Mizell—as well as a sister of Third National Bank president Sam Fleming—to assume the role of sales manager for the Hermitage. Hall termed it "something of a reunion" as he and Jennie Mizell had worked together when he was assistant manager and she was sales manager of the Maxwell House Hotel. Mizell would

Southern Governors Gather

LEADERS VIEW HISTORIC SPEECH

Governor Buford Ellington welcomed governors from fifteen states to the twenty-seventh Annual Conference of Southern Governors in September 1961. The visiting governors and their guests were housed in the Hermitage and Andrew Jackson hotels with all business sessions held at the Hermitage Hotel. Shortly after Governor Ellington's welcoming address on Sunday, the initial business session was interrupted; television sets were wheeled into the Hermitage conference room so the governors could hear and see U.S. President John F. Kennedy challenge the Soviet Union to a "peace race" to save mankind from extinction. Following the address, the southern governors passed a resolution "congratulating the president on his magnificent speech" and "expressing support from this body on his suggestions for peace." Vice President Lyndon B. Johnson flew into Nashville on Monday to attend the annual state dinner that evening.[9]

make contacts with state and regional groups planning future Nashville meetings, as well as with local sales organizations, businesses, and professional firms looking for bookings.

At the time Mizell came on board, renovations had just been completed in two of the hotel's six "function" rooms. Work was then in progress on a new front desk and registration desk in the lobby. It included "a new 'cut-down' front," the newspaper reported, "and lavish use of cherry paneling featured the modernization of the registration area." Additional work was scheduled for that summer.[10]

In November 1958, WSM's seventh annual National Disc Jockey Celebration was held in Nashville. On the night before the convention, "two-hundred straw-hatted disk jockeys, google-eyed tourists, and run-of-the-mill lobby sitters" heard Gov. Frank Clement sing "No Help Wanted" in the lobby of the hotel as his wife, Lucille, accompanied him on the piano. Minnie Pearl, the mistress of ceremonies, talked the governor, who claimed he could not sing, into doing so. Next, Pearl and the Clement sang "You Are My Sunshine," accompanied by Mitch Miller on the oboe. It was a great start for the celebration.[11]

Desk clerks Gladys Burton and Mabel Louthan always cherished having seen a pre-presidential John F. Kennedy at the Hermitage in September 1960. Burton recalled in 1977, "Our night auditor wasn't allowed to move around and a doorman, who had a pistol registered in his name, wasn't allowed to work that day." Longtime Hermitage employee Lannie Neal actually met Senator Kennedy on the hotel steps on September 21, when the Hermitage was state headquarters for Kennedy's presidential campaign. A photograph taken that day showed a large crowd on Memorial Square extending down Capitol Boulevard, all listening to Senator Kennedy's speech. On the north side of the

Above, top: The WSM-sponsored National Disc Jockey Convention was held at the Hermitage in 1956. MA
Above: A highlight of the convention was Gov. Frank Clement singing with Minnie Pearl. Clement is pictured here with his wife, Lucille, and Minnie Pearl. MA
Opposite page: The Hermitage served as a backdrop to Gov. Buford Ellington's inaugural parade in 1959. TSLA

The Dick Hall Era

Senator John F. Kennedy visited Nashville on September 21, 1960, while campaigning for United States president. He spoke to a crowd of 15,000 in Memorial Square. The Hermitage Hotel, with political banner displayed on the exterior and facing the Capitol, typifies this era. NPL-SC

Hermitage Hotel was a photograph of Kennedy, along with a banner that extended all the way across the façade. It read "TENNESSEE—VOTE DEMOCRATIC—KEFAUVER-FOWLER." Above the fourth floor level, there was a smaller sign for "NIXON-LODGE." There also was a "KENNEDY-JOHNSON" sign.[12]

Mickey McGuire, an inspector with the Tennessee Highway Patrol, drove Kennedy during his visit to Nashville. He recalled being in Kennedy's room at the Hermitage while the crowds waited to hear Kennedy speak. Former governor Frank Clement knocked on the door. Later, McGuire heard Kennedy say that his father liked Clement and that, if Joe Kennedy had his way, Clement might have been vice president.[13]

That same evening, shortly after 11 PM, Harry Banniza Jr. left his father's liquor store on the hotel's ground floor and started walking up the steps to the cashier's office; he intended to put the store's receipts for the day in the hotel safe. Suddenly, two men pinned his arms behind his back and pushed him against the wall. They wanted to know how he got in the hotel and where he was going. After explaining what he was doing, the two Secret Service agents escorted him to the safe and then out of the building.[14]

On October 6, U.S. Vice President Richard Nixon made a brief stop in Nashville, also speaking at Memorial Square. With Nixon were his wife, Pat; two cabinet members; and both of Tennessee's congressmen, Carroll Reese and Howard Baker. The day before, on October 5, Rose Kennedy had charmed a cheering Democratic women's rally in the ballroom of the Hermitage Hotel.

She told her audience, "I am here to get the grandmother vote." Fashionably dressed, Mrs. Kennedy was relaxed and firm-voiced; she reiterated her Catholic family's position that religion was not a legitimate issue in the presidential campaign.[15]

Even after the presidential campaign was over, manager Hall continued to look for opportunities to keep the Hermitage Hotel in the public eye. In December 1960, he purchased the 820-pound champion steer of the Junior Fat Cattle Show and Sale at the Tennessee State Fairgrounds. Hall and Donald Wood, executive chef at the hotel, and Glenda Fox, exhibitor of Davidson County's champion steer, had their photograph taken for the *Nashville Banner*.[16]

Sitting In

Earlier that year, after months of workshops in the techniques of nonviolent protest had been held in the basement of Rev. Kelly Miller Smith's First Baptist Church, Capitol Hill, one hundred thirty-four students from American Baptist Theological Seminary, Fisk, and Tennessee A&I had converged on downtown Nashville. They broke up into small groups of twos and threes, and entered a number of five-and-dimes on Fifth Avenue North. There they bought inexpensive items and then sat down at the lunch counters. The store owners closed the counters and, after two hours of quiet protest, the students left. The sit-ins spread to other stores, and

Vice President Richard M. Nixon visited Nashville on October 6, 1960, during his campaign for the United States presidency. The former ladies' entrance to the hotel on Union Street is seen at the right of the photograph. NPL-SC

A Tasty Wintertime Treat
THE CHRISTMAS VILLAGE CHEF

In December 1956, the hotel's head chef, Robert E. Steiner, displayed his creative culinary skills by fashioning a miniature snow-covered Christmas village out of sugar. The houses were fruit covered and—except for the mirror pond and figures—everything was edible. Steiner, who had previously worked at the Robert E. Lee Hotel, was a native of New York City. He graduated from the Culinary Institute of America in 1952, and his first job was as head chef of the Ali Gahn Shrine Club in Cumberland, Maryland. He also was head chef at the Irvin Cobb Hotel in Paducah, Kentucky.

Steiner's efforts were center stage in the hotel lobby. Manager Dick Hall said of Steiner, "He's absolutely tops. He loves his work and so do those who sit down to it."[17]

blacks boycotted those who would not serve them. This went on until April 19 when the protesters met Mayor Ben West on the courthouse steps. There, protest leaders pressed him hard. In response to a direct question about his feelings on desegregating the lunch counters, Mayor West agreed they should be desegregated. This was a turning point. By summer, the movement broadened to include H. G. Hill grocery stores, accused of not employing blacks as clerks.

At one point, when the protesters of segregation were marching downtown, there was uncertainty as to whether or not the march would be peaceful. The Capitol was barricaded and members of the Tennessee National Guard, armed with machine guns and protected by sandbags, were posted in front. Suddenly, a police scanner reported gunfire from the top of the Hermitage Hotel. Upon being notified, Dick Hall grabbed a 30-caliber carbine and headed for the roof. On the way up, he met a highway patrol sergeant, armed with a machine gun. They ran up the stairs from the top floor, hitting the roof together. There they confronted three schoolteachers from Toronto who had come to Nashville to attend the Grand Ole Opry. The women had gone up on the roof to take pictures of the Capitol with their "flash cameras." Hall later said, "We didn't know what we would find. We were lucky. It could have gone the other way."[18]

On the bad luck side, Nashvillians, including Dick Hall, who loved the historic Maxwell House Hotel, were horrified to read in *The Nashville Tennessean* on December 26, 1961, that the once-grand hotel had burned to the ground Christmas night. A fire roared out of control due to freezing temperatures and frozen water hydrants. Four hook and ladder companies and sixty-eight firemen had fought the blaze to no avail. Seventeen businesses, including the Rotary Club, were destroyed. Gone were the

John Lewis, chairman of the Student Nonviolent Coordinating Committee (SNCC) and future U.S. Congressman, confronted Nashville policemen near the front of the hotel on May 13, 1963, during civil rights protests in downtown Nashville. NPL-SC

Rotary Club's ledgers, attendance records, photographs, scrapbooks, and minutes. The Rotarians found a new home at the Hermitage, where they had originally met from 1914 until 1921. Two weeks before the fire, the Rotary Club had shelled out $4,600 for the Big Brothers annual auction of territories. The Exchange Club paid $4,502.45 for the wealthy Belle Meade territory. The auction, attended by more than two hundred Big Brothers, took place in the ballroom of the Hermitage, preceded by a steak dinner and Christmas music.[19]

More racial demonstrations came about in January 1962 when students staged sleep-ins in the lobbies of the Hermitage and Andrew Jackson hotels. Eight black girls and two white girls attempted to register at the Hermitage at 6 PM on January 31. When they were refused, they sat down in the lobby prepared to spend the night.

Concurrently, twenty-four black boys unsuccessfully tried to register at the Andrew Jackson. Several white men at the Andrew Jackson shouted insults at the students. One man threw a beer bottle that hit a student in the shoulder, though the student was not injured. There was no violence at the Hermitage. Nashville policemen came to the Andrew Jackson about 7:40 PM and stayed until all the men left.[20] Two weeks later, John Lewis, the future Georgia congressman who was then a student at Fisk University, attempted to register at the Hermitage with two white exchange students. At that time, blacks were not allowed as guests at the hotel, and they were asked to leave. Apparently, one did manage to spend the night in the hotel during that turbulent period—by slipping up the stairs after he had been registered by a white friend.[21]

After the downtown sit-ins, which took place from 1960 through 1963, segregation all but disappeared from Nashville hotels, including the Hermitage and the Andrew Jackson. Thanks to responsible negotiations between protest leaders and Nashville's white business community, the city earned respect from the nation and was applauded for its handling of desegregation.

Let's Meet at the Hermitage

In 1962 and 1963, former Vanderbilt University basketball star Bob Dudley Smith was a lobbyist for the Tennessee Savings and Loan League. His office was on the fifth floor of the 226 Capitol Boulevard Building, next door to the Hermitage Hotel Annex. "Almost every day," Dudley later recalled, "I would walk through the hotel security entrance on the Capitol Boulevard side, since they knew me, have a meal, visit with business associates and friends and, on Fridays, attend the weekly luncheon of the Kiwanis Club in the ballroom."

He would have coffee and

Opposite page, top: The Maxwell House Hotel was completed in 1861, prior to the Civil War. It was used during the Union occupation as barracks and housing for Confederate prisoners. The Maxwell House was destroyed by fire on December 25, 1961. NPL-SC

Opposite page, bottom: Police and demonstrators scuffle during a civil rights demonstration across from the Cross Keys Restaurant and hotel in Nashville in 1963. NPL-SC

Below: High school sororities often held their dances at the Hermitage. ETC Preparatory School Sorority held its winter dance at the hotel on December 14, 1962. NPL-SC

beverages with the state senators and representatives, government officials, and congressional people throughout the year at the hotel. Occasionally, a state senator from West Tennessee would charge drinks for his friends to Dudley's account.

Bob Dudley Smith and his wife, Jeanne, loved the hotel. His sister, Reita Smith Petsch, had been a singer for WSM radio with Dinah Shore and sang with Francis Craig and Beasley Smith when they played at the Hermitage and the Andrew Jackson. Jeanne Smith's fondest memories were of the sorority balls that were held at the Hermitage. "I met my husband there and had my first dance with him," she later recalled. "Oh, I remember it well as that was the time when stag lines were long and I was thrilled to dance with the handsome Bob Dudley Smith at my sorority Cinderella Ball. I still dream of high teas and ball gowns when I hear 'Let's meet at the Hermitage.'"[22]

Those preparatory school sorority dances continued to be held in the Hermitage ballroom each winter through the 1960s. The ETC Winter Dance, held on Friday evening, December 14, 1962, was an example. With Francis Craig retired, Tommy Knowles and his orchestra provided the music. Among the members and their escorts who enjoyed the music was Yvonne White, sorority president.[23]

A Bear but No Snowman

In the summer of 1962, Davidson County Tax Assessor Clifford Allen established his Campaign for Metropolitan Mayor headquarters at the Hermitage Hotel. Real estate agent Glenn Bainbridge leased rooms 505 and 506 for the duration of the campaign. Charlie Burke, night auditor at the Hermitage, told a reporter for *The Nashville Tennessean* that a 128-foot sign boosting Allen's candidacy would be erected on the hotel's exterior on Monday, August 27.[24]

Countless times in Nashville's business history, developers have announced construction projects that never materialized. That happened in 1962 when Dick Hall held negotiations with the Southern State Building Corporation of Knoxville, for a plush $65,000 private membership club to be constructed on the Hermitage Hotel's roof. The city's Board of Zoning Appeals approved plans for the unusual air-supported, translucent nylon sky dome atop the Hermitage to house an International Sky Dome Club. Sonny Morris, spokesman for the project, said, "Construction is expected to get underway in the very near future," and that the club would open December 10 with Dave Gardner, well-known comedian, performing for the first week.[25] The sky dome never materialized.

Although Nashville missed out on Dave Gardner, someone equally famous did visit the hotel that October. Sir Edmund Hillary, the New Zealander who conquered Mount Everest, was in Nashville to talk about his latest expedition to the Himalayas and his search for the Abominable Snowman. Hillary spoke at a banquet at the Hermitage hosted by World Book Encyclopedia, which sponsored the 1961 expedition. Hillary said that, after examining all the evidence on his last expedition, he was convinced the Abominable Snowman never existed.[26]

Another famous guest during the 1960s and 1970s was legendary Alabama football coach Paul "Bear" Bryant. He came every other fall with his Crimson Tide football team to play Vanderbilt. Harry Banniza knew that Bryant would want a bottle of Bell's Scotch Whisky as well as some buttermilk for his ulcer, and Banniza made sure Bryant had both.[27]

Dorothy Baumgartner, who had a decade of experience in Nashville hotel sales jobs, was appointed sales manager of the Hermitage Hotel on October 10, 1962. Previously, the bright and outgoing Baumgartner worked at the Noel Hotel.[28]

Dick Hall's wife, Dru, died of cancer in 1963. This left Hall with full responsibility for rearing the couple's two children, Darr, eight, and Drusilla or "Drusie," six. The kids lived in the hotel's Suite 601 with their father. In

The Nashville City Club built a new lounge in the hotel in an unusual place—the upper half of the veranda. MA

August 1965, Dick married Gracie Ward, who took over as the children's stepmother.[29] Young Drusie had an extensive collection of stuffed animals. The Hall children also had pets, including turtles, a snake, and a dog named Chug-a-lug that they walked in Memorial Square. On weekends, Darr and Drusie often went with their father on his forty-foot cabin cruiser. One of Darr's favorite hotel haunts was the carpentry shop, where manager Albert Hicks generously allowed the youngster to use his nails, hammer, and boards.

Both children enjoyed helping in the kitchen and were special friends of Chef William Weaver. Howard Slagle, elevator operator, would sometimes let Darr run the elevator. The roof was normally off limits, but when Darr was a little older, he kept a miniature greenhouse from FAO Schwarz there. The elder Hall and his close friend, Harry Joyce, would occasionally go up to the roof to shoot pigeons.

The Hall children attended Ensworth School, driven there and back by the same taxicab driver. Their Ensworth friends often had the novelty of spending weekend nights at the hotel.[30] A little later in the decade, Darr and Alex Joyce, an Ensworth friend and son of Harry and Peggy Joyce, gathered golf balls from Richland Creek at the Belle Meade Country Club. One night, they brought them to the hotel and dropped them out of a sixth floor window facing Sixth Avenue North. The balls bounced wildly. One hit the edge of the sidewalk and flew across the street, shattering the plate glass window of Sam Wilson Shoes at 230 Sixth Avenue North. In a few minutes, the police arrived and detained a homeless man who had been sleeping nearby, but the boys escaped detection.[31]

During the 1960s, the Hermitage remained an Alsonett Hotel, completely air-conditioned, with two hundred fifty attractive rooms and suites. It could handle convention and sales meetings for groups of five to five hundred. The AAA was located at the hotel, as well as airline offices off the lobby, and the City Club on the second floor. On January 2, 1964, Rogers C. Buntin, president of the City Club, announced that work would begin within a week on a new one-thousand-square-foot lounge for the club. Guy McComas was the architect.[32]

In the Middle of Things

Whenever there was excitement at the Hermitage Hotel, manager Dick Hall was part of the action. On one occasion, after getting the word that someone was robbing the front desk clerk, he alerted the police and then ran to the lobby where he kept a stranglehold around the robber's neck until the police arrived. On another occasion, he got a call in the middle of the night that a hotel robbery was in progress. He threw a coat over his pajamas, grabbed his slippers, and flew out the bedroom door. His wife, Gracie, warned him he might get hurt, but his response was, "They better be fast."[33]

There was always something going on. The third week in September 1964, Democratic nominees from across the state assembled in Nashville for the official opening of the party's state headquarters at the hotel. Joe L. Evins was campaign chairman.[34] This set the stage for the biggest story in Nashville in 1964: the short visit of U.S. President Lyndon Johnson. The presidential plane arrived at Berry Field at 10:30 AM October 9. He was met by Representative Evins; a reception committee; thirty-seven bands; and the "Johnson girls" a group of beautiful young ladies including Martha Ellen Truett of Tiptonville, who was 1963 Miss Tennessee, and Jayne Ann Owens of Paris, the 1964 Miss Tennessee runner-up.[35]

A motorcade took the president to the War Memorial Building where, shortly after noon, after being introduced by Gov. Frank Clement, he spoke to a crowd of an estimated 85,000 people. It was one of the largest crowds in the city's history. At 1 PM, the president was the guest of honor at a President's Club reception in the Hermitage Hotel's Iris Room; it was attended by those who

Hoffa at the Hotel
TEAMSTER DINES WITH ENTOURAGE

International Brotherhood of Teamsters union leader Jimmy Hoffa was in Nashville in 1964 being tried by the United States Department of Justice for jury tampering. Young Nashville attorney, James F. Neal, earned a national reputation for his skill as prosecutor of Hoffa. Neal had some help. While Hoffa and his entourage stayed at the Andrew Jackson Hotel, they often ate lunch and dinner at the Hermitage. They had no idea that the FBI had rented a room above the Iris Room in the hotel's annex, opened the window and listened to the conversations at the Hoffa table. One day, when the Hoffa group was eating at the Hermitage, several female schoolteachers sat at an adjoining table. A waiter overheard Hoffa say to his friends, "All right men, watch your language, and keep a clean mouth."[36]

had contributed one thousand dollars or more to the Democratic Party in the 1964 campaign. Johnson slipped away from the reception to do some hand-shaking at a reception Amon Carter Evans, the chairman of *The Nashville Tennessean*, was having for the visiting press in the ballroom. "I don't want to miss Amon's party," Johnson explained.[37]

When President Johnson and Governor Clement stepped out of the elevator on the lobby floor on their way to the limousine that would lead the motorcade back to the airport, Johnson noticed two young boys standing expectantly in the lobby. Despite his tight schedule, Johnson sat down with Bucky Katzman, a Peabody Demonstration School seventh grader, who was there representing the Young Citizens for Johnson Committee, and Irwin

Kuhn, a politically active fifth grader at Ensworth School. President Johnson gave both boys a card that read, "Admit to The President's Gallery, United States Senate." The president scratched his initials on the back. "You can get in anytime," Johnson told the boys. Katzman still had his card years later; Kuhn lost his before he got home.[38]

In February 1965, Metro introduced a new traffic plan that annoyed not only Dick Hall, but also area legislators. Metro changed Seventh Avenue North into a one-way street going north. This meant that those legislators who stayed at the Hermitage and drove their cars the "hop, skip, and a jump" from the hotel to the Tennessee State Capitol every day would have a difficult time getting back to the hotel in the evenings. They had to wind their way behind the Supreme Court Building to Charlotte Avenue, then proceed west on Charlotte to Eighth Avenue North. From there, it was a left turn on Eighth to Union Street, and another left on Union to Capitol Boulevard. This, at least, would get them to the back of the hotel. An equally depressing alternative was to go the other way through the state parking lot to James Robertson Parkway, then proceed to Charlotte or Union and drive the remaining few blocks to the hotel. Some lawmakers and Hall complained. Other legislators simply walked.[39]

Just before Christmas 1964, WSM television and radio personality Barbara "Babs" Moore got the attention of manager Hall by commenting on a morning radio show that the flag atop the Hermitage Hotel "looked like a tribe of hungry little goats had been nibbling on it." Hall decided to make the best of the disparaging remark. He managed to obtain a twelve-year-old billy goat named Rudolph, brought him to the hotel, and locked him up in the basement for the night. The next morning, he drove the goat to Moore's farm in Brentwood, where he left it with a note. It said that the goat was a birthday present for her and that it had indeed been tethered atop the Hermitage, where it had enjoyed nibbling on the American flag. As expected, his prank received publicity in *The Nashville Tennessean*.[40]

Opposite page: President Lyndon B. Johnson at the Hermitage Hotel, October 9, 1964. President Johnson is on the lower left, speaking with Beverly Briley, Nashville's first Metropolitan mayor. Future Tennessee gubernatorial candidate, John Jay Hooker Jr. is in the center. To the left of Mr. Hooker is Elmer Dissypane, Cookeville businessman. Behind Mr. Hooker, in the upper right-hand corner, is Jayne Ann Owens, Vanderbilt student and Young Citizens for Johnson volunteer. To the left of her is Jayne Ann's future husband, Frank A. Woods. He served as chairman of Young Citizens for Johnson. Standing just behind them is Bob Brandt, a Vanderbilt law student and Young Citizens for Johnson volunteer. WOODS

Although no goats really were nibbling on the flag, its frayed edges did symbolize a slow decline in the vitality of downtown business district. The reduction in the number of people downtown also impacted the health of the Hermitage and other downtown hotels. The Madison Square and Green Hills shopping centers, both some miles from downtown, were becoming increasingly popular. Other shopping centers would soon pop up in the suburbs, draining business from Cain-Sloan, Harvey's, and other downtown retail stores.

Hall had another problem. The Metropolitan Government charged that the Hermitage Hotel and the Nashville City Club were engaged in the sale of alcoholic beverages in violation of state statutes. The City Club sued Metro, Mayor Beverly Briley, and the police chief, H. O. Kemp. The club's argument was that the enforcement guidelines imposed by the police department were inappropriate, and that the law prohibiting the sale and storage of liquor was nullified by the 1939 local option law allowing package liquor stores in wet counties.[41] The suit was never heard; nine months later, Nashvillians voted for liquor-by-the-drink. In 1969, after the Third National Bank opened its new twenty-story building on the corner of Church Street and Fourth Avenue North, the City Club moved to Third's top floor.

From Bad to Worse

Conditions continued to deteriorate at the Hermitage. By the late 1960s, the hotel was in a poor condition. One evening in March 1968, flames that ultimately shot more than fifty feet in the air broke out on the roof. Twelve engines and six companies quickly answered the three-alarm blaze that started in the hotel's air-conditioning system. Shooting ladders to the roof, the firemen put out the blaze within minutes. Although the hotel was full, only one guest on the ninth floor had to be relocated. The other guests rushed out when shouts of "Fire!" caused them to head for the street. Quickly they came back in, laughing and talking about how lucky they were. Thinking the fire was worse than it actually was, Mayor Briley came on the scene.[42]

He learned that a welder had been working in the cooling tower all day and that a spark from his torch ignited the fire. Fortunately, the fire was confined to the tower, which was a total loss. John J. Hooker Jr., one of the owners of the Andrew Jackson Hotel, offered rooms in his hotel free of charge to any guests at the Hermitage in case they needed to move.[43]

That year, after twelve years as manager of the Hermitage Hotel, Dick Hall resigned to try a new venture: president of Eddy Arnold's Tennessee Fried Chicken.

On June 5, Charles H. Alberding of Chicago, president of Alsonett Hotels, announced that Richard McGoldrick, manager of a hotel in Huntington, West Virginia, would succeed Hall as manager that same month. McGoldrick was then president of the West Virginia Hotel and Motel Association as well as the Huntington Hotel Association. A native of Moberly, Missouri, he also was vice president of the Southern Hotel Association.[44]

Eleven months later, Dorothy Baumgartner, director of sales for the Hermitage Hotel since 1962, resigned to take a position as sales manager for Holiday Inns of America, the Memphis company that had a number of motels in the Nashville area, including the 158-room Holiday Inn Capitol Hill on James Robertson Parkway, only a half dozen blocks from the Hermitage. Losing two key employees with a combined nineteen years of service was not a good sign.[45]

It was not that the hotel had quit trying; it was simply a challenging time. The Hermitage Hotel had modernized in 1967, adding the Telemax Reservation System, with instant

communication to 2,000 hotels across the country. It was the first hotel in Nashville to offer the service, which reported current reservation data and could signal when incorrect information was put into the system.[46]

In January 1970, Jimmy and Joan Gallivan were introduced to the Hermitage when they moved to Nashville from Greenville, South Carolina. For their first month in town, the Gallivans lived in a three-room suite at the hotel with their three children, Clark, Jim Jr., and Joe. The first day, Gallivan warned his children not to run around the hotel, particularly since it was filled with boisterous legislators. The children, the oldest of whom was fourteen, took him seriously. That night they pushed a chest of drawers against the outside door. Before the month was over, the children had learned every nook and cranny of the hotel and were completely comfortable socializing with the legislators and the hotel staff. Joan Gallivan was probably more relieved than her husband when they gained possession of their new home. While at the hotel, he walked the three blocks to his office at J. C. Bradford while Joan had to drive her children to Harpeth Hall and Montgomery Bell Academy.[47]

Within a few months, a disquieting sign came. In June of that year, the Andrew Jackson Hotel closed. One month later, Fred Gregg Jr. sold the building to the Nashville Housing Authority. The downtown urban renewal plans for the building were undecided, and the hotel, ultimately, was imploded.[48] The site is now the location of the Tennessee Performing Arts Center (TPAC).

In time, darker days would come for the Hermitage, too.

Above: The demolition of the Andrew Jackson Hotel, once the Hermitage's biggest rival, June 12, 1971. NPL-SC
Opposite Page: Aerial view of downtown Nashville from above the cupola of the Capitol, 1969. Memorial Square would be converted into Legislative Plaza in 1973–74. TSLA

DOWNWARD SPIRAL

A mid the opulence and grace that is the Hermitage Hotel today, it's hard to imagine the depths to which it fell. The landmark came precariously close to being "history" long before its time.

Richard McGoldrick's tenure as manager of the hotel was brief; he was replaced by John Dewey, who also stayed only a short while. Next, Richard Barney, an Alsonett Hotels Company official, served as interim manager until a more permanent replacement could be found. In October 1970, veteran hotel man Leon Womble, former manager of the soon-to-be-razed Andrew Jackson Hotel, accepted the challenge.[1] Womble did not stay long enough to have much impact. Neither did his successors, Jack Grigsby, Bill Boswell, James E. Arnold, Sam Bass, Russell Nichol, Steve Andrews, and Leroy Arnold, none of whom lasted more than two years.

This art deco chandelier was taken from the hotel lobby and used at the 1974 Swan Ball. While it hung in the hotel lobby for many years, it was not original to the hotel's décor. These massive chandeliers were installed in the 1930s. NPL–SC

In an effort to stay competitive with newer hotels and motels in Nashville, the Hermitage installed an interconnect telephone system designed by Ericsson Centrum, Inc., of New York City, the North American division of a company in Stockholm, Sweden.[2]

Another boost came when State Party Chairman Jim Sasser announced on September 22, 1973 that the Democratic Party would open a state headquarters at the Hermitage within a couple of weeks. He added that the State Democratic Executive Committee formerly staffed an office in the Hermitage, but they had closed down several months earlier. The office was on the first floor and faced Capitol Boulevard.[3]

Sasser's announcement was good news as tenants were leaving. For example, radio station WNAH, owned and operated by Van T. Irwin Jr., left the hotel in about 1974 to move to a new location at 1701 West End Avenue, where they would have more room. WNAH had been on the Hermitage's veranda facing Sixth Avenue North since 1962.[4]

In 1974, the theme of Cheekwood's twelfth annual Swan Ball was "The Great Gatsby." For the June 8 gala, Clara Bass's art committee planned a major summer exhibition of Art Deco architecture, artifacts, fashions, and furniture. Corinne Franklin and Tom Connor hustled to assemble the exhibit. One of the people they called on was then-manager Bill Boswell, since the hotel was "a virtual Art Deco museum." They asked him if they could borrow a sample of the wonderful art objects in the hotel for the Cheekwood exhibit. Boswell graciously lent Cheekwood a monumentally proportioned chandelier from the lobby; poplar chairs painted black in imitation of lacquer from the Iris Room; a poplar table made to fit between two chairs; a wooden dressing table with a scroll shape showing neo-classical influence; the chrome shoeshine chair with a stylized falling water motif from the men's room; a small dressing table and light fixture from the women's room; a curved brass and glass newsstand that had not been used for many years; a copper and brass samovar with a brass

The modern lobby features several of these classic chandeliers, installed during the 2002 renovation. JA

spout; and several frosted and ribbed architectural tiles found in the boiler room. Clara Hieronymus, who wrote a story on the Swan Ball for *The Nashville Tennessean*, was in the hotel lobby when workers climbed scaffolding and removed one of the four handsome chandeliers. While excited about the wonderful art objects and how much they would add to the Cheekwood exhibit, Hieronymus also stated that the hotel "is now somewhat seedy and run-down."[5]

Hieronymus was not the only person who thought so. Dr. Joseph Bistowish, Metro Health director, stated on September 27, 1974, that, "The Hermitage Hotel kitchen facilities, target of four or five pages of deficiencies," had been closed down. Bistowish continued, "We have been having problems with them for months." The facility was cited for improper cleaning; an inoperative dishwasher; peeling paint; plumbing leaks; and a nearby sidewalk crack that could admit rainwater or rats. Russell Nichol, who had the misfortune of being hotel manager at the time, wistfully described the infractions as minor.[6]

The Exchange and Kiwanis clubs, which still met regularly at the Hermitage, had their meals catered after Bistowish closed the kitchen. A month before, the Lions Club had fled the Hermitage for Gay Street. The Sertoma Club also had left. The Rotary Club moved to the Silver Wings dining room at Statler Hilton Airport Inn, managed by Dick Hall, the former manager at the Hermitage. The Capitol Club, also in the Hermitage, simply closed.[7] The Exchange Club, which had been at the Hermitage since 1920, held out for two more years before moving its headquarters and weekly meetings. As for the Kiwanis Club, it eventually moved to the Cumberland Club on the twenty-sixth floor of the Nashville City Center, where it stayed for about fifteen years.

When the kitchen reopened in early November 1974, new manager Sam Bass reported that the kitchen deficiencies had been corrected and that the Capitol Club and one or two civic clubs that held weekly luncheons at the hotel had remained. The extended closing happened, Bass said, because, "We were a little short of cash at the time and it took time to do cleaning and wait for parts for major appliances." He added that the health department had issued a new kitchen permit.[8]

Down the Drain

During the 1970s, AMTRAK leased rooms in the Hermitage Hotel for its railroad crews. If anyone in management had been there in the 1940s and 1950s, when American Airlines did the same thing, they would have realized that the latter group was considerably different than that of airline pilots and stewardesses. Ann Reuss, a member of the Metropolitan Historical Commission (MHC) in the 1970s, recalled how distressed MHC members were about the hotel's decline. Many of the hotel's 238 rooms were occupied by permanent residents, including derelicts, while most of the others were often vacant. The "glory days" were unquestionably over.

Protesters against the Shah of Iran gathered outside the closed hotel during a visit from President Jimmy Carter on October 26, 1978. NPL-SC

Even so, Robert "Rob" Stallings of Bolivar, elected to the Tennessee State Legislature in 1976, stayed at the Hermitage when the legislative body was in session. The general manager gave him and all other legislators a state rate and put their names on their room doors if they were regular customers. One day in 1976, Jim Free, chief clerk of the House of Representatives, saw Stallings and some other legislators at the hotel. He asked them if they wanted to meet the future president of the United States, Jimmy Carter. Stallings and his friends, some of whom didn't know who Jimmy Carter was, said, "Sure." Free then introduced them to Carter, who had, the year before, completed four years as governor of Georgia. Later, Free worked for Carter in

In 1974, the construction of the new Hyatt Regency Hotel amplified the worsening condition of the Hermitage. NPL-SC

Washington, D.C. During that time, he took Stallings and Judy Barnes, Stallings's future wife, on a tour of the White House, including the oval office.[9]

But that was a long way away. At the Hermitage, the situation may actually have been worse than historical commission member Reuss recalled. In June 1976, Paul Carlisle, a twenty-seven-year-old Nashvillian just out of the navy, was hired by Russell Nichol as the night auditor, working from 11 PM until 7 AM six days a week. Although Carlisle's job at the Hermitage only lasted until late February 1977, he saw enough of the seamy side of life there to last a lifetime. Once, a resident accosted him for turning off the Muzak system at 11 PM. When Carlisle paid him little attention, the man threw a lit cigarette in his face. On another occasion, another resident, a country musician on hard times, confronted Carlisle in the middle of the night and pushed him to the floor. Carlisle called 911 and soon the police arrived to arrest the man. They entered the hotel through the Sixth Avenue entrance without a key, as the doors were so warped that they were able to simply be pushed open. Shortly before Carlisle left the hotel, a dentist committed suicide by jumping from his inside room to the courtyard over the lobby.[10]

With the Hermitage short of cash and customers, the mid-1970s opening of the Hyatt Regency Hotel on the site of the old YMCA across Capitol Boulevard from the Hermitage was not good news. The new hotel was spectacular, with twenty-eight floors and an atrium that extended from the lobby to the very top. Four glass elevators on the inside of the hotel provided an exciting ride to upper floors and three slowly revolving restaurants and lounges high above.

Finally, Alsonett officials made a decision. On March 3, 1976, Steve Andrews, manager of the Capitol Park Inn, another Alsonett-owned hotel in downtown Nashville, announced that the Hermitage would be refurbished to the tune of $3 million; another $1 million would be spent on the Capitol Park Inn. In his statement, Andrews said, "There is a renewed interest in the downtown area and the Hermitage offers a unique type of accommodations. It is the last of Nashville's grand old hotels." The renovation was expected to start on the Hermitage "in the very near future," he continued.[11] The fact that the manager of the Capitol Park Inn made the announcement suggests that there may not have been a manager at the Hermitage at that time.

The ballroom as it looked after the 1977 closing. NPL-SC

A year later, in June 1977, it was apparent that the $3 million restoration plan for the Hermitage had gone down the drain. Only recently, Fire Marshall Howard Boyd had hauled Hermitage officials into court for "failure to carry out orders to install emergency lights, a lobby sprinkler system, an alarm system, and another exit from the Capitol Club." Charles Alberding, president of Alsonett Hotels Company, who had come to town to meet with Boyd, admitted that the hotel was a problem and was for sale. Alberding also told Boyd that he had tried unsuccessfully to sell the hotel to Hyatt. Contacted by Larry Brinton, *Nashville Banner* staff writer, about the March 3, 1976 story that the hotel would be renovated, Alberding said that he knew nothing about any plans to renovate the hotel and that Andrews, who made the announcement, had no authority to do so. Andrews, by then, had left the Alsonett Company. Alberding told Brinton that he had $250,000 invested in the hotel and that "it had lost money for several years."[12]

Concerned over the fate of the Hermitage, the Metroolitan Historical Commission's executive director, May Dean Eberling, identified three reasons why the hotel should be saved. First, the hotel "offers an alternative hotel to those who prefer marble and wood to chrome and plastic." Second, "The architectural style, although not old, is the only commercial example of Beaux Arts in Nashville." And third, "If the Hermitage Hotel is proven unfeasible [*sic*] as a hotel, other alternative uses should be explored." Earlier, in 1975, the commission had successfully nominated the hotel for inclusion in the National Register of Historic Places. Staff member and architect Leonard Marsh, who wrote the nomination, ended his petition by saying: "Today, urban renewal plans of the late sixties has Nashville undergoing a formidable change to wide avenues and to concrete, glass, and steel of contemporary

Opposite Page and above: The dilapidated condition of the hotel in 1977 left few who believed it would ever be restored. NPL-SC

Above: Pieces of the ceiling litter the stairway to the restaurant area. NPL-SC
Opposite Page: *The exterior of the hotel as it looked in 1977.* NPL-SC

architecture. The Hermitage Hotel is the last of the prestigious hotels and is one of the few early twentieth century commercial structures remaining near the state capitol." Only as a last resort should the demolition of the building be considered, Marsh said. He also spoke of new tax incentive programs, specifically the 1976 Federal Income Tax Act and the Tennessee Historic Property Tax legislation, which were enacted to encourage preservation efforts.[13]

Eberling alerted Mayor Richard "Dick" Fulton to the distinct possibility that the Hermitage could be demolished. She sat on a stool beside his office desk, described the terrible conditions at the hotel, and told him, "We at the Metropolitan Historical Commission felt we had to do something." Fulton listened and the two discussed the possibilities. "While I sat there," Eberling recalled, "he picked up the phone and called codes and the fire department and told them to go to the hotel and enforce all the codes violations immediately." Very soon thereafter, Mayor Fulton issued the notification to close the hotel. She felt he deserved a great deal of the credit for saving the hotel by getting the process underway.[14]

Fulton also received other warnings about the critical situation at the Hermitage, including an angry letter from Renea Franz of Pittsburgh, Pennsylvania. She wrote that, while she loved her stay in Nashville, she didn't like the Hermitage. She had chosen the hotel because it was the only place in town that had a vacancy during the Country Music Association's Fan Fair week. To buttress her complaints about the hotel's run-down condition, she enclosed photographs with her letter. Joe Williams, the mayor's development aid, said the mayor's office had received numerous other complaints, as well.

In all, four departments inspected the hotel: codes, the fire and health departments, and water and sewerage services. All found problems of a serious nature. Metro Health Director Bistowish suspected that water from the hotel's

Lobby view from the southwest corner, showing conditions of disrepair. The former doorway to the manager's office can be seen on the loggia level in the background. NPL-SC

laundry was getting into the same pipes that brought water to bathrooms. He also cited evidence of "water bugs, roaches, gnats, mosquitoes, and spiders."

Leroy Arnold, the hotel's newest manager, was furious with the crackdown. Arnold felt that the city was either trying to run the hotel out of business, or, at least, to force them to sell it. "It seems very unfair," he said, "that we are being singled out. If they do this to us what about all the other hotels I know are worse?"[15] Fire Marshall Howard Boyd did say that his most recent inspection found only minor problems and that most of the problems found earlier were being corrected. Conversely, Walter England, codes administrator, said his men found ten pages of violations.[16]

Wanting Fair Play

On July 1, 1977, Mayor Dick Fulton ordered the Hermitage Hotel closed in thirty days because of health and building code violations. That morning, barber W. D. Brown was sitting in his shop in the Hermitage, as he had done for forty-seven years. One of the first customers that morning grinned and quipped, "I thought I'd get a haircut before they kicked you out." Brown replied, "That is a bunch of junk." He claimed not to have noticed any of the problems mentioned by the Metro departments. The hotel's eighty permanent residents, nearly all of whom were elderly, were worried about what they would do. Ruben Edmondson, a twelve-year resident, said, "I don't like the idea of moving at all. I think the mayor wants to drive the owner out of town because he won't sell the Capitol Park Inn." Harry Notgrass, who moved to the hotel a year earlier because of its proximity to the B&W Cafeteria on Sixth Avenue North, said, "Well, the cafeteria closed a few months ago and now I'll have to move again."[17] Mrs. Belle Lambert, who had lived in the hotel since 1965, said, "I'm shocked, I don't see how I can ever get ready in a month. I need more time to look for a place to live." Monsignor Charles Williams, a retired priest who ran the St. Mary religious bookstore in the hotel, said that the bookstore had moved several times and his hotel location was the best he had ever had. He recommended that the bookstore close if it had to move. "I've moved before and I don't think I could go through this again," he said.[18] "We're heartbroken," added Harry Banniza, who had operated the hotel liquor store since 1949.[19]

James Brookland, Hermitage Hotel newsstand vendor, was so angry, he wrote U.S. President Jimmy Carter. In his letter, mailed to the White House, Brookland said, "All I want is fair play about the whole thing since you are trying to get a lot of people back to work and our mayor is trying to put a lot of people out of work." Brookland also stated that, in the five months he had run the newsstand, "I have not even seen a mouse."[20]

Charlie Howell was another preservationist alarmed over the possible destruction of the Hermitage. In a speech to the Rotary Club at its new Statler Hilton Airport Inn location, Howell deplored the deterioration of the sixty-seven-year-old property. He went on to remind his fellow members of the loss of other historic structures, including the Andrew Jackson Hotel, Commerce Union Bank, and First American National Bank, and said that only public pressure was "holding up" Union Station, which had been condemned with no program underway to save it.[21]

An article in the Nashville Banner *on July 1, 1977 tells the stories of the Hermitage residents forced to move after the hotel was suddenly closed by the mayor.* NB

RUBEN EDMONDSON
'I don't like the idea'

HARRY NOTGRASS
Came for the convenience

MRS. BELLE LAMBERT
'Can't get ready in a month'

Hermitage Tenants In State Of Shock

JUL 1 1977

By RICH RIEBELING
Banner Staff Writer

Barber W.D. Brown was sitting at his shop in the Hermitage Hotel basement this morning as he has done for the past 47 years.

One of the first customers walked in, grinned and quipped, "I thought I'd get a haircut before they kicked you out."

Brown, the hotel's other businesses and about 80 permanent residents were in a state of "shock" after learning today Mayor Richard Fulton ordered the hotel closed in 30 days because of health and building code violations.

The barber, who has operated the shop since 1930, was more optimistic than other tenants that the hotel will not close.

"That's a bunch of junk," Brown said.

He said he hasn't seen any of the problems listed by the Metro departments.

Others were not optimistic.

Mrs. Belle Lambert, who has lived at the hotel since 1965, said, "I'm shocked. I don't see how I can ever get ready in a month. I need more time to look for a new place to live."

Her friend, Mrs. Kathryn Redmond, said "You can look at Mrs. Lambert's room or mine. They're both pretty and all of this has been exaggerated. We don't have any rats here like they say."

Ruben Edmondson also has lived at the hotel for 12 years. And like Mrs. Lambert, "I don't like the idea at all (of moving)."

He said he thinks the mayor wants to drive the owner (who also owns the Capital Park Inn) out of town because he won't sell the Capital Park Inn.

"I've never had a problem while living here and I've lived on five different floors," he said.

Msgr. Charles Williams, a retired priest, runs the St. Mary religious bookstore in the hotel.

He said the store has moved several times, but the space in the hotel, at the corner of Sixth Avenue North and Union Street, is the best location he has had.

The priest said he wouldn't recommend to the Nashville diocese that it remain open if the store has to move.

"I've moved before and I don't think I could go through it again."

The city will lose this if the hotel closes, he said.

Harry Notgrass said he moved to the hotel a year ago because it was convenient to a nearby cafeteria.

"Well, the cafeteria closed a few months ago and now I'll have to move from here."

— Banner Photos by Vic Cooley
Brown sits in one of his barber chairs at the Hermitage Hotel.

The Never-Never World

Clara Hieronymus, art critic for *The Tennessean*, went to New York in 1977 to see a major exhibit at the Museum of Modern Art. It was called "The Architecture of the École des Beaux-Arts," and it harkened back to nineteenth century Paris for its drawings in watercolor and ink, depicting what *New York Times* critic Ada Louise Huxtable called:

a never-never world of palaces of kings, palaces of justice, and palaces for the arts, of cathedrals, conservatories, stock exchanges, state banks, and thermal baths, emperor's pavilions, ambassadors' compounds, and mansions for rich bankers, public granaries, and markets, barracks for the military, and, later in the century, railroad stations . . . nothing small or humble.

Hieronymus was spellbound by the exhibit. When she returned home, it dawned on her that Nashville had a fine example of commercial Beaux Arts design and that it was in danger of being razed. She agreed with local preservationists that every avenue must be explored before a decision was made on the hotel's future as few, if any, structures in Nashville had the "profusion of decorative detailing" as found at the Hermitage. Many features, including the remarkable cornice at the top of the ninth floor with its lion heads and leaf and tongue enrichment, could never be duplicated, she wrote.[22]

In response to requests from commercial tenants, and with the understanding that a plan to upgrade the Hermitage was underway, Mayor Fulton wrote Alberding that the city would give the fifteen commercial tenants another thirty days before they had to vacate their spaces. They could, said Joe Foster, the mayor's press aide, remain open until August 31. Earlier, the city had given the hotel six months to repair the deficiencies.[23] Some of these commercial tenants were the Capitol Club, Hurst Construction News, Delta Airlines, and the Nautilus sandwich shop.

An Ultimatum

Meanwhile, the hotel's permanent residents all moved out during July, meeting the August 1 deadline. On August 26, the hotel was given an ultimatum to either submit acceptable plans to bring the hotel up to standards, or completely close its doors. Mayor Fulton wrote this in a letter to Alberding. Before sending it, the mayor met with two Metro department heads and with Metro Fire Marshal Howard Boyd. They told Fulton that improvement plans submitted by Alsonett did not meet codes standards or water, sewer, and fire regulations. Alsonett was given until the first of September to submit the plans. This was in accordance with the previous order extending the date for compliance sixty days from July 1.[24] Outside the hotel's Sixth Avenue entrance a sign had been posted since July. It read, "This building is unsafe and its use or occupancy has been prohibited."[25]

Late in August, reports of a completed lease agreement surfaced. In response, Alberding, who was in town to appear before the Metro Board of Tax Equalization to request a reduction in his property tax assessment and to meet with contractors, said he didn't know anything about the rumors.

The September 1 deadline for businesses to vacate their premises came and went. Mayor Fulton gave the merchants another extension until December 31. He told a reporter that he wanted to give them time to sell inventories they had ordered for the Christmas season.

Above: On August 1, 1977, health inspectors determined too many deficiencies in the hotel's operation, and after the mayor's order to close, tenants scrambled to find other living arrangements. NPL-SC
Opposite page: The August 1977 Sixth Avenue entrance advertised weekly rates. NPL-SC

The fate of the Hermitage hung in the balance as government and business officials scrambled to create a plan to save it. NPL-SC

Despite Alberding's natural reluctance to speak to reporters about current negotiations—for fear they would fizzle—he did have a deal in hand. That very week, he signed a lease-option agreement with Highland Inns Corporation. The lease was contingent on Troy A. Waugh, president of the Nashville firm, securing sufficient financing. Announcement of the development was made in Mayor Fulton's office. Waugh said the work should coincide with the opening of the James K. Polk State Office Building and the Tennessee Performing Arts Center in 1979, and that his intention was to make the Hermitage "the grandest hotel in the central South." A source close to the situation said, "A minimum of $2 million is expected to be invested." A danger signal was the fact that Highland, which operated eight hotels in four states, had a net loss of $70,000 during the quarter ended June 30, 1977.[26]

When Pete Bird, business news writer for the *Nashville Banner*, interviewed Troy Waugh in early October, Waugh conceded that persuading a major lender to advance more than $3 million for the project was his biggest hurdle. Bird learned that Highland Inns Corp. had until January 31, 1978, to exercise the option to buy the Hermitage. That option cost $5,000 per month. Despite the uncertainty, Nashville architect Doug Roberts had already been hired and was developing a master blueprint for the restoration project. Robert C. H. Mathews, Nashville contractor, also was waiting in the wings.

Waugh said that with room rents about $40, the two-hundred-room hotel could be "very profitable." Skeptics questioned whether an organization whose major experience had been running a few medium and low-priced motels, had the expertise to turn around the Hermitage.[27]

The skeptics were right. The financial hurdles proved to be too great for Troy Waugh and his dreams for restoring the deteriorating, but once grand hotel went by the boards. The Hermitage remained closed during 1978 as Alsonett's Alberding continued to look for prospective buyers. Doubtful that the building would ever be a hotel again, he had given away all the hotel's china and flat silver.

No organization was more dismayed with the Hermitage Hotel being vacant than Historic Nashville, Inc., whose executive director was Cherrie Hall. Historic Nashville volunteers began intensive research on the hotel and developed a slide presentation called "The Hermitage: Nashville's Grand, Old Hotel" that Historic Nashville made available to interested people and organizations. Their hope was that someone would notice and step up to prevent an architectural calamity. And soon.

In 1981, the newly refurbished hotel boasted new window treatments and contemporary furniture in the lobby.
NPL-SC

Chapter Seven

A CHANCE AT REDEMPTION

As the 1970s drew to a close, the future of the Hermitage Hotel hung in the balance. Finally, there was a real break—though not in the direction some had anticipated. On February 1, 1979, Alsonett Hotels Company President Charles Alberding confirmed that he was negotiating with out-of-state parties about purchasing the once-grand hotel. Alberding said that his asking price was about $5 million, but cautiously added, "There is no deal yet." A few months later, on May 15, B. B. Andersen, head of B. B. Andersen Companies, Inc., a Topeka, Kansas, contracting firm, signed a thirty-five-year lease with an option for an additional fifteen-year lease. It was done on behalf of a group of Kansas investors who planned to renovate the Hermitage into an office building. They envisioned turning the lobby, the ballroom, and part

Historic Nashville, Inc., took on the task of helping to save the Hermitage in the late '70s. Pictured, left to right: Dennis Morgan, general manager, Dorothy Baumgartner, director of sales and catering, Cherrie Hall, executive director of Historic Nashville, Inc., and May Dean Eberling, executive director of the Metropolitan Historical Commission. This photo was taken January 1981 prior to the grand opening. TN

of the floor beneath into a 10,000-square-foot restaurant and lounge; sprucing up the mezzanine into space suitable for a private club; and remodeling some 3,000 square feet of retail space then fronting the street. The eight floors above the mezzanine would be gutted and refurbished for offices.[1]

Later that month, Jerry Carroll, a Nashville entrepreneur and chairman of Leasing Management Development Co., confirmed that his company would handle the marketing, leasing, and management of the renovated building. Carroll said that he had already begun talking with potential clients about the 64,000 square feet of office space available. Financing was not thought to be a problem.[2] Andersen also planned to tear down the annex on the back of the building and build a three- or four-story parking garage in its place facing Sixth Avenue North.

Sonny West, attorney for Metro Codes Administration, said the only way for the developers to acquire codes permits for renovation of the hotel would be to completely replace the building's plumbing and electrical wiring. This, too, did not seem to be an obstacle.[3]

In late February, the Kansas investment group asked for a bond issue of roughly $5 million through the Metro Industrial Development Board to help finance the project. Andersen was grateful that Mayor Dick Fulton had pledged his support of the request. In mid-March, the Metro Industrial Development Board gave preliminary approval for a $5 million bond issue. Metro Legal Director Peter Curry told Andersen that document preparation for final board approval would take several months.[4]

On February 28, the state legislature stepped up to the plate when the House of Representatives passed and sent to the Senate a bill permitting cities to use revenue bonds to construct or renovate central city business establishments, including hotels. The bill, pushed by Memphis and Nashville legislators, was designed to finance renovation of the Peabody Hotel in Memphis, but could also apply to the Hermitage Hotel and other structures in downtown Nashville.[5] Meanwhile, Knoxville legislators seemed indifferent. Their premier hotel, the Andrew Johnson, built in 1930, had a history of not making money. It had been sold at public auction in 1974 for $405,000 after its owner, Andrew Johnson Properties, Inc., entered bankruptcy.[6]

While nervously waiting for the final financing, Carroll was working hard to line up subleases. In early April, John Gilmore, senior vice president and general counsel of Hospital Affiliates International (HAI), said moving HAI's corporate offices to the building was one option the company was considering. At the time, HAI, which was operating more than one hundred hospitals nationwide, was leasing space at 4525 Harding Road. Their lease would expire in March 1980. The Hermitage was attractive because it would give the company a "high profile" in a prime downtown location.[7] Wayne Oldham, president of Wendy's of Nashville, also had his eyes on the building. He hoped to put a lounge and eating establishment on the lobby floor.[8]

Good News

By May 18, the final approval of the industrial revenue bond issue had been received. The other good news was that the Metro Board of Zoning Appeals granted Andersen a variance in off-street parking that he needed to make the project viable. These accomplishments brought a bustling commercial center two blocks from the Capitol closer to reality.

Nine days later, B. B. Andersen confirmed that his group had subleased the Hermitage to HAI. George Vann, HAI president, said his company planned to

make the building its world headquarters. A six-story parking garage would, Vann continued, be built on Sixth Avenue North adjacent to the hotel, and construction of the parking garage and restoration of the hotel were already underway. Not surprisingly, The B. B. Andersen Construction Co. was awarded the contracting job.

As one of the world's largest hospital companies, with 18,381 beds, Vann said his company had run out of space. "We think a company of our size should do something for the community, and we are happy to fit into Mayor Fulton's program of downtown redevelopment."[9] Carroll, who handled the leasing negotiations with HAI, said the hotel would be gutted from bottom to top, leaving only outside walls, supporting posts, and concrete floors. New plumbing, heating and air conditioning, fixtures, equipment, floor and wall treatments, drapes, etc., would be installed at a cost of about $5 million. Because the building was on the National Register of Historic Places, careful attention would be given to preserving the integrity of the building to make sure that the marble, brass, and other important features would be maintained in their original condition. They would not, for example, sand-blast the building's exterior.

HAI would use the lower level as an employee health club, a barbershop, and a 9,000-square-foot gourmet restaurant with a sidewalk café on Capitol Boulevard. Carroll said that, although HAI would occupy about 80 percent of the building, there would be about 35,000 square feet left for five retail shops fronting Sixth Avenue North and Union Street.

The parking garage would be used by HAI during the day and be open to the public after 6 PM with a valet. Gresham and Smith, Inc. were the architects. The Sixth Avenue North entrance was being remodeled, and the entire renovation was being financed by the $5 million bond issue still being considered by the Metro Industrial Development Board. HAI had a fifteen-year lease for the eight upper floors, the lobby, and part of the lower level, a total of more than 90,000 square feet.

Specialists estimated that the lease to HAI would call for payment of approximately $10.5 million over the fifteen-year period. The one-hundred-twenty-car parking garage was expected to open in January 1980, while HAI hoped to move the next month. When the company moved to the Hermitage, HAI's name would be displayed on the outside of the building.[10]

But HAI's hopes and dreams to be in the center of a revitalized downtown Nashville faded as over the summer, Andersen and Carroll could not convince the lenders to go along with a five-year cancellation clause in HAI's lease with Andersen. Having already gutted the building, Andersen and Carroll, who was very much involved in the negotiations, put together an alternative plan quickly. On September 8, Andersen announced that the Hermitage Hotel would be reborn as a luxury hotel. Topeka Inn Management, Inc., (TIMI) promised to build an all-suite hotel, which was relatively rare at the time. The

Opposite page: February 18, 1979, Mayor Richard Fulton (right) discusses the multi-million dollar renovation plans for the once grand Hermitage Hotel with project coordinator Lloyd Buzzi (center) and leasing agent Jerry Carroll (left). TN

Holidays at The Hermitage

'Tis the time before Christmas and all
through the hotel, employees are hustling,
making sure all is well. The rooms are
resplendent with trimmings and greens,
just waiting...
all of th...
your ro...
beau...
table t...
can they...
ners, pl...
the ve...

231 6th A...

The...

Celebrate this Christmas with the charm and splendor
that is The Hermitage Hotel. Steeped in tradition, The
Hermitage is the perfect place to carry out the traditional holiday parties that make the season complete.
And after the party, there's no need to drive. Stay at
The Hermitage for the special rate of $50 plus tax,
double occupancy. Be sure and book your party in advance
as available dates are going fast.

Christmas Holiday Buffet

Fresh Spinach Salad
Salade Au Caesar
Marinated Vegetable Salad
Fresh Fruit Salad
Fresh Relish Mirror
Imported Cheese Salad
Fancy Baked Breads
Acorn Squash
Zucchini Provencale
Candied Sweet Yams
Winter Mix / Broccoli & Cauliflower
Roast Tom Turkey & Dressing w/ Giblet Gravy
Baked Schrod w/saffron rice
Hand Carved Roast Round of Beef
Roast Pork Loin w/natural gravy
14.50
An Array of Holiday Desserts

Prices are not inclusive of sales tax and appropriate gratuities.

*Minimum of 35 persons for a buffet please.

*Opposite page, top: The new veranda
included comfortable seating for
cocktails. NPL-SC*
*Opposite page, bottom: The redecorated
guest rooms reflected the contemporary
style of the early 1980s. NPL-SC*

new hotel would be called The Hermitage, a Park Suite Hotel. Construction would begin as financing was arranged and was expected to last fifteen to eighteen months.[11] A few days later, the senior vice president of Topeka Inn Management, Inc., was in Nashville to select an architectural firm for the soon-to-be remodeled property.

Once again, however, there was a snag. Around the first of December, Metro Council's budget and finance committee refused to recommend an ordinance that would allow developers to obtain tax-exempt financing for their projects. The council deferred action on creating a special "business improvement district" exclusively for the Hermitage project that "would turn the dilapidated structure into a 112-room luxury hotel."[12] The council had already approved on two readings a bill declaring the Hermitage property as being within a historical area.

The Metro Industrial Development Board met in early January to consider the Andersen group's request for $10 million in tax-free, low interest industrial revenue bonds. Of this amount, $7.5 million was for Hermitage Hotel, Inc. while $2.5 million was for Topeka Inn Management. The board asked the developers to submit a list of their financial backers. One member of the Industrial Development Board, Richard Lewis, president of Citizen's Savings Bank, said his concern was because, "I don't know whether the developers are from Nashville or are a lot of outsiders." Lewis had a problem with "outsiders coming in and profits eventually going outside Nashville."[13]

Jeff Rippy, an official with J. C. Bradford & Co., the bond underwriters for the project, stated that to his knowledge, there were no local people in either The Hermitage Hotel company or Topeka Inn Management Co. The board's deferral meant that construction would be delayed past a scheduled January 15 public hearing.[14]

That hearing aimed to assess public reaction to the creation of a Hermitage Hotel Central Business Improvement District. It bothered some people that the creation of such a district would benefit only the hotel and an adjacent parking facility, and that it could lead to the formation of dozens of redevelopment districts in downtown Nashville. Earlier, Robert Horton, Metro Finance director, had predicted that there would be strong support for the project and little opposition.[15] That turned out to be the case.

Finally, on June 1, the Metro Industrial Development Board approved a $6.46 million bond issue to Hermitage Hotel, Ltd., for the restoration and rehabilitation of the hotel and completion of the parking garage already well under construction.[16]

112 Luxury Suites

The on-again, off-again Hermitage Hotel project was on-again with Topeka's Brock Hotel Corp. The nation's largest independent franchise operator of Holiday Inns was ready to make a deal with J. C. Bradford to manage the sale of $7.84 million in industrial revenue bonds.[17] This happened and, on June 22, J. C. Bradford Jr., managing partner of J. C. Bradford & Co., said, "Investor interest has been so strong that most of the bonds are already sold. Once approval is granted Monday morning, we will give Brock Hotel Corp. the money to start the project and we will begin distributing the bonds to investors." David Pringle, senior vice president of Brock Corp., said the architect, Gresham and Smith, Inc., "has done everything to make this a sensitive restoration and has worked hard to preserve the original downstairs and lobby areas in the renovation that will preserve much of the hotel's ornate façade."[18]

Final documents were signed on June 24 to restore The Hermitage Hotel and reopen it with 112 luxury suites. Just as J. C. Bradford Jr. suspected, all

$7,840,000 worth of industrial revenue bonds of the Metro Industrial Development Board were bought by approximately five hundred people. There were two issues, one for $6,460,000 to be used to restructure the gutted building, and the other of $1,380,000 to pay for furnishings and equipment. R. Murray Hatcher, a Bradford partner, said the big issue would bring buyers an average return of 10.3 percent and the small one would yield approximately 9.5 percent.[19] Hermitage Hotel, Ltd., a partnership consisting primarily of stockholders, employees, officers, and directors of Brock Hotel Corporation, borrowed the larger issue. They subleased the hotel to Brock Hotels on a forty-year lease with Charles Alberding of Chicago as owner. Brock borrowed the small issue.[20]

New Life

In June 1980, Clara Hieronymus toured the soon-to-be-restored Hermitage and wrote lovingly of what she saw and hoped to see. In her article "Hermitage Hotel Returns to its Youthful Beauty," Hieronymus informed *The Tennessean*'s readers that the old hotel would soon be given "a new lease on life." She challenged Nashvillians to recall the old hotel with its elaborate plaster ceiling, marble floors, ornate cornices, and gilded moldings in the lobby. "Its ballroom, even run-down as it was in recent years," she said, "had a genuine elegance in its walnut paneling, fluted pilasters, coffered ceiling, and fine plaster work."

Hieronymus talked with Ms. Jerry Law, ASID, IBD, president of Jerry Law Interiors, Inc., and of Interior Exports, Inc., who had been retained for the renovation and restoration of the hotel's public spaces. Law convinced Hieronymus that the company would recreate the elegance and sophistication of the original and that the restoration "will not disregard these fine architectural elements of the past." Law, who also was impressed with the beauty of the building, said, "The formality and grandeur created by the Hermitage's existing architectural elements are unsurpassed in quality and could not be reconstructed in today's market." The large skylight, she said, "will be restored to give natural light during the day. At night, backlighting will make it a focal point and prevent it from looking like a blank surface." She commented that the ceiling fixtures, Art Deco in style, were not original to the building but were added during a renovation decades before. "Plans are to restore them, in keeping with historic preservation principles holding that such changes reflect the evolution of the building," she said. Her design concept for the lobby called for letting its architectural splendor be the main attraction. "Upholstered furniture will be plain for contrast, with velvet (as in the original furnishings) specified as harmonious with the area's plaster ornamentation and pronounced marble veining," Ms. Law said. She added that she planned to relocate the large gilt mirror, then in the Palm Room, and place it on the central arched wall where the cigar stand had been. Hieronymus wrote that Law's plans called for one large Oriental rug with mellow, rich colors, too.

Law pointed out that the 99-foot-long, 14-foot-wide loggia, "a story and one half tall," extended the width of the Sixth Avenue side of the hotel. Law continued:

When the hotel was built, this area was open. But soon after the hotel was in operation, it was enclosed with French doors. It has natural, glazed, terra cotta in a stone pattern on the walls, with cross-vaulted ceilings between the pilasters. The arched treatment in the ceiling is repeated with the arched

Restoration work in progress,
January 1981. NPL-SC

windows on each side and the end. Our design makes this area into a bar, with an adjacent room as the actual bar and the loggia as a lounge with comfortable seating. The ballroom will become a meeting or banquet room and will retain its Circassian walnut paneling and wood floors, its fluted pilasters with their Ionic capitals, and the Greek key and egg and dart cornices and friezes. Plans call for portraits of Tennessee's three presidents, with that of Andrew Jackson centered since the hotel bears the name of his home.

Law stated, "The natural wood of the raised paneling (in the Grill Room) will be refinished and the existing acoustical tiles will be removed." To create a private feeling, Hieronymus wrote, Law intended to use some angular, built-in seating units, along with more conventional tables and chairs in the open areas. "The renovation calls for uplighting around columns and palms to create a garden look with light filtering through leaves to make shadows on the ceiling."[21]

The Brock Hotel Corp. began work on restoring the hotel shortly after Hieronymus visited. By fall, management could see the end of the tunnel, and

Today's overnight guest is pampered with a comfortable bed, fine linen sheets, adjustable lighting, music, bottled water, a luxurious bathrobe, and complete house-keeping turndown service. JA

was anxious to begin marketing efforts. Accordingly, in October, they employed Dorothy Baumgartner, who had served as the old hotel's sales director and catering manager during the 1960s. She returned in the same position. Several weeks later, Baumgartner opened the Hermitage sales office.[22] In November, Dennis Morgan was appointed general manager of The Hermitage Park Suite Hotel. Morgan came with more than twelve years of experience in hotel management, seven of those years with Brock. Until the restoration was complete in January or February, his offices would be with Baumgartner in the Capitol Boulevard Building.[23] A few days later, as the

A Chance at Redemption

Tennessee's Three Presidents

NEW PORTRAITS HONOR FAVORITE SONS

During the 1980–81 renovation, plans called for the hotel's ballroom to be totally refurbished to serve as a meeting and banquet room. Part of the plan included the commissioning of large portraits to hang in the ballroom honoring Tennessee's three presidents: James K. Polk, Andrew Jackson, and Andrew Johnson. In its early days, the ballroom had featured a portrait of Jackson, but these would be all-new works of art.

Janet Swanson, an artist from Franklin, Tennessee, was responsible for creating the acrylic portraits of the presidents to be displayed in the thirty-six-foot by eighty-six-foot room.

Swanson developed an interesting technique for correctly capturing the men's faces and body positioning. She used Jackson's likeness on a twenty-dollar bill to paint his face, and asked friends to pose in period costume to complete his torso, as well as those of Polk and Johnson. These beautiful works now proudly greet visitors to the hotel, with Jackson positioned in the middle as a tribute to the man whose home shares the name of the hotel.

Swanson also used her innovative talents to paint substitutions for irreplaceable marble and tile elements that had long since been destroyed.[24]

hotel neared the final days of its restoration, John Loukmas was appointed master chef. He promised to prepare such specialties as Chateaubriand and Fettuccine Carolina in the hotel dining room.[25]

Baumgartner kept one eye on the construction and the other on her competition—particularly the nearby Hyatt Regency and the Radisson. Between the two downtown hotels, they had a total of 828 rooms and charged from $49 to $72 for double rooms. Only one local hotel, the Spence Manor on Music Row, had suites. Their rates ranged from $60 to $190 nightly. Suites in the Hermitage would rent for an average of $80 to $85 per night, a little more than they had hoped.[26]

Little Touches

Sam Polack, senior vice president and director of operations for Brock Hotel Corp., reported on January 4, 1981, that after six months of construction, the Hermitage should open around February 1. He made the point that, "when it reopens, the hotel will depend on traveling executives, tourists, and small groups for its trade. We do not have the meeting rooms for large groups."[27] In other words, the Hermitage would not be competing with Opryland Hotel, the enormous hotel-convention center outside of downtown.

The same day, the Hermitage manager, Dennis Morgan, said, "We'll have a six-person concierge staff and there will be little touches like mints placed at bedsides in the evening and complimentary newspapers. Bellmen will wear gray military jackets. Desk clerks will wear dark blue coats and vests with gray pants." Pete Bird, writer for *The Tennessean*, toured the building. He considered both the restoration and the prices to be first-class; the suites were complete with wet bars and two television sets. Three independently run shops would open simultaneously with the hotel, and hiring of the 150-person staff was well underway.[28]

Dennis Morgan told Bird that they would hold a soft opening sometime in February, and that the grand opening would be held February 27 through March 1. He then proudly described some of the public areas to Bird:

The lobby, with its ornate plaster ceiling and marble floors, has been fully preserved and restored. The stained glass skylight, rich with color and detail, now has a fresh glow. When we started working on the skylight, it looked just like plain glass that had turned black. We couldn't believe the beautiful color that was underneath. A few steps up from the lobby along the Sixth Avenue side of the Hermitage is the lovely veranda, a comfortably furnished space lined with sets of French doors. Can't you picture this on a warm summer night when we open the doors?

People can sit here like sitting in their own living rooms. Waiters will circulate and serve drinks. The old ballroom will be used as a meeting and banquet room. Its ornate ceiling has been carefully restored and decorated in gold. It took two painters six weeks just to do this ceiling. On the lower level, the old Grill Room will serve as the hotel's restaurant. The vaulted ceilings, once blistered by peeling paint,

Opposite page, top and bottom: "Before" and "After" views of the restaurant from 1977–80 era, fashionably restored as the Hermitage Room. MA

have been renewed and hung with new brass chandeliers. The adjacent Oak Bar retains its paneled walls.[29]

Two weeks later, Morgan rescheduled the grand opening by a week, to March 6 through 8. Hosting the weekend with Brock Hotel would be the Metropolitan Historical Commission and Historic Nashville, Inc. Cherrie Hall, of Historic Nashville, was training approximately thirty volunteers to act as docents for the weekend.[30] At the dinner, there was one empty chair at the Historic Nashville table. It was soon occupied by a woman whom everyone assumed was someone else's guest. She turned out to be a prostitute.[31]

A Masterpiece

Caroline McNeilly, the *Nashville Banner*'s art editor, called the new Hermitage "an artist's masterpiece." She said most of the artists and craftsmen who helped re-establish the hotel's original grandeur were local. She learned that the hotel's skylight had been painted with tar pitch to keep out all light. Dennis Harmon and Chettie Mastroianni, of Nashville's Emmanuel Studio, cleaned, photographed, and numbered every square of glass in the twenty-five panels. Then, Harmon fashioned a new design for the center of the skylight, since the original was missing. It included the letters "HH." He then reconstructed the enamel-painted designs on the skylight, many of which were faded or broken, and replaced three hundred of the eight hundred pieces of glass. The work had been completed the previous November. As for the seven-foot by eleven-foot gold gilt mirror in the lobby, it was restored by representatives of Temptation Gallery and Draper Jewelry Co. Several sections—some one hundred fifty pieces—of natural, glazed terra cotta on the walls of the loggia had to be replaced. That work was done by Lewis Snyder, a Murfreesboro potter.[32]

The next day, Clara Hieronymus wrote in *The Tennessean* of her elation that the hotel had regained its former status as "an elegant resident of downtown Nashville." She was particularly pleased that the new owners had been able to keep the unique exterior intact. In the public areas, she found that the restoration was a matter of removing the ugly accumulation of the years and redesigning the decorative components. A project coordinator for architect Gresham and Smith spoke of how small the rooms were and explained that, in 1910, the lobby was the main gathering point as there was no television to watch when the Hermitage was built. Consequently, his company had removed many interior walls to create the new, larger suites. He was particularly proud of the craftsmen, especially the painters and plasterers, who worked on the project and who took such a personal interest in doing the job correctly.[33] Hieronymus noted in the article that the restaurant on the lower level had been renamed the Hermitage Room and that it featured oak paneling, maroon carpeting, and velvet upholstery. An antique sideboard became a serving station in the room that once excluded women. What many Nashvillians remembered as the "writing room," Hieronymus said, featured a grand piano where Myrna Rose would play each day from 4 PM to 7 PM.

Let the Parties Begin

General manager Dennis Morgan had assembled his staff, and the challenge was on. One early task was the attempt to find a place setting of china and flatware used in the hotel

Polychrome terra cotta tile arch intrados located on the veranda balcony. JA

before it closed in 1977, as it had all been given away. The quest of the maitre d' made *The Tennessean*, and the hotel offered a dinner for two to anyone who brought back a place setting for framing in a dining room window box.[34]

On Friday evening, March 6, 1981, Brock Hotel officials welcomed 1,200 guests to a preview cocktail party in the ballroom. Cocktails were served with heavy hors d'oeuvres. The guest list came from friends of Historic Nashville and the Metropolitan Historical Commission, provided by Cherrie Hall and May Dean Eberling, executive directors of those organizations. During the party, the guests enjoyed seeing slides of scenes of the Hermitage from past years. The following night, there was a formal seated dinner for ninety business and government leaders, as well as people who had worked on the bond issue. While a local orchestra played, Brock Company executives and their spouses mingled with the guests.[35]

The refurbished Hermitage hotel reopened for normal business on March 16, 1981, about a month behind its original schedule. Customers who had visited the hotel a decade or two earlier were pleased to see that the gaudy bright green and black tile in the men's restroom was the same as they remembered. This time around, however, there was a modern sprinkler system throughout the hotel. Sam Polack, senior vice president and director of operations for Brock Hotel Corp., explained that the opening was delayed due to a combination of mechanical problems and special supplies required to restore the hotel according to Metro Historical Commission guidelines.

Grand opening parties were held at the Hermitage on Wednesday, April 8, as well as the two following days. There also was a seated dinner on Saturday, April 11, marking the official opening of the hotel. Three hundred pounds of beef tenderloin, lobsters from Maine, and fresh fish from the Gulf were among the many items flown in especially for the invited guests. Terry Hagan, executive chef, was assisted by chefs from across the country and by students from the Nashville Area Vocational School and CETA.[36]

On Saturday, Mayor Dick Fulton released a bouquet of balloons into the noon sky at the ribbon-cutting ceremony. Attached to each balloon was a key to one of the hotel's suites. Whoever brought in a key would get a night's free lodging in one of the suites.[37] Late that month, fourteen-year-old Tommy King and his father, Ken, of Aaron, Kentucky, noticed a balloon coming while they were fishing on Lake Cumberland, about one hundred fifty miles northeast of Nashville. Tommy retrieved the balloon, found the key and, with his dad's help, arranged to have a free $110 suite in the Hermitage. While in Nashville, the Aaron family enjoyed the races at the Tennessee State Fairgrounds.[38]

B. B. Andersen was so proud of having pulled off the restoration of the Hermitage and so grateful for his subcontractors, he put a long advertisement in *The Tennessean* on April 10. In the ad, he said his company and the Brock Hotel Corp. had been able to restore the Hermitage to its former grandeur despite almost everyone telling them, "It can't be done. You can't bring back the past." Andersen's answer was, "Well, today it has been done. The past glory of a prestigious address will live anew for thousands of guests, now and for years to come. We did not do it alone." He went on to list all the sub-contractors who had performed so well. Andersen thanked Mayor Fulton and the entire Metro Council for their unanimous support:

Without their approval and continued support, this project would have been doomed. Cities all over the South are wrestling with the dilemma of too little money,

Myrna Rose, the pianist at The Hermitage Hotel, shown here in 1987, played music in the lobby for many years. MA

not enough space, and growing needs. The Hermitage Hotel is one very graceful contribution to that problem's solution in one city, Nashville, Tennessee. As important in the actual completion of this renovation were the skilled craftsmen and dedicated professionals to whom a job well done means as much as a paycheck. To those hundreds of men and women we say, "Thanks."[39]

More accolades were on the way. In June, the Hermitage won first place in the ASID/Scalamandre Restoration and Preservation Award competition. Their first prize, in this national competition, was in the historic preservation category. Jerry Law, president of Jerry Law Interiors, accepted the award at the national ASID convention in St. Louis in July.[40]

Among the Nashvillians with a special interest in the reopening of the Hermitage was Donia Craig Dickerson. Because her father's orchestra played for so many years at the hotel, Donia, her mother, Elizabeth Craig Lancaster of Sewanee, and Donia's sister, Celeste Craig Abernathy of Bell Buckle, wanted to give the hotel a 1943 photograph of Francis Craig and his orchestra at the Hermitage. Confident that the hotel was on solid footing, they made the presentation that same summer.[41] The photograph can be seen on page 93.

Minnesota Fats

THE MAN WITH A GOOD GAME

The rich history of The Hermitage Hotel includes a near-endless stream of memorable guests. But none quite compares to the most illustrious of all: Minnesota Fats, considered the world's greatest billiard player. So strong was his presence at the hotel, where he lived for eight years beginning in 1985, that the Hermitage gave him a $3,200 Steepleton table. It was placed outside hotel manager Bruce Bommarito's office and formally presented at a reception, during which the famed player performed many of his trick shots for a number of guests, including local business and governmental leaders.[1]

Minnesota Fats, whose real name was Rudolf Walter Wanderone Jr., had spent most of his life as a pool hustler, having played the game since he was four years old; he was playing for stakes just two years later. He even claimed that his baby bed was under a pool table in his parents' home in New York City. Wanderone, who was born January 19, 1913, quit school after finishing the eighth grade to ply his trade. As he wrote in his 1966 autobiography, *The Bank Shot and Other Great Robberies*, "I've been haunting pool rooms from here to Zanzibar for almost 45 years. I've played every game in the book and some fantastic propositions you wouldn't imagine."[2] Some of the colorful characters he played against were better known by their nicknames: Cornbread Red, Tuscaloosa Squirrelly, the Knoxville Bear, Daddy Warbucks, and Weanie Beanie. Fats became a public figure after a series of pool matches with Willie Mosconi, one of the best tournament players who ever lived, was televised. An even better player, in Fats's mind, was Ralph Greenleaf. Not modest about his own abilities, the "Fat Man," as Wanderone also was called, once bragged, "I'm the greatest money player of all time."[3] With a 52-inch waist and one hundred pounds overweight, Fats had few peers as a poolroom hustler. He also was a raconteur, an entertainer, animal lover, "and the last of the high-rolling gamblers to wear $100 bills in his handkerchief pocket and play pool for outrageous stakes."[4]

By Any Other Name

Wanderone, who had several other nicknames in his prime including "Fats" and "New York Fats," appropriated the name Minnesota Fats after the release of the movie *The Hustler* starring Paul Newman and Jackie Gleason in 1961. Gleason played a character called Minnesota Fats, and the Fat Man boldly claimed the movie was based on his life. Walter Tevis, the author of the novel on which the movie was based, denied it. Besides,

Minnesota Fats

Wanderone had never even been to Minnesota. Nevertheless, he gained the nation's attention by his skill, his showmanship, and by being written up in *Sports Illustrated* and appearing on the television shows like *What's My Line?* in 1965 and *Celebrity Billiards* in 1967. These national shows were followed by his guest appearances on *The Joey Bishop Show* in 1968, *The Tonight Show Starring Johnny Carson,* and *The David Frost Show*, both in 1971. In 1979, Minnesota Fats played himself on *Vega$*.[5]

Following his years as an active player, Fats and his wife, Evelyn Inez, lived in Dowell, Illinois, sometimes with as many as twenty-seven cats and fourteen dogs. Soon after their divorce, he moved to Nashville, a city he had visited many times in the 1920s, 1930s, and 1940s when he would shoot pool at the old Maxwell House Hotel. But when he found the Hermitage, he found a new sense of home. While there, he mesmerized guests not only with his phenomenal skills at the table, but also with his recollection of the good ole days, of pool sharks he had "whacked," and of his escapades. He considered himself to be the Hermitage's ambassador to Nashville. John Cougar Mellencamp and Bruce Springsteen were said to have invited Fats to be their guest at a concert at Middle Tennessee State University. They even gave him a backstage pass.

"Billions of Dollars"

In 1986, new hotel manager Paul Kraft would normally take an early morning run. When he did so, he would wave to Minnesota Fats who invariably was outside, often in the Legislative Plaza, feeding the birds bread that the kitchen staff had left for him in plastic bags. Usually his dog, Side Pocket, was with him. Later in the day, Fats would sit in the lobby facing the Sixth Avenue North entrance. From there he would greet every attractive young woman who entered the hotel with, "Hi, Babe. Come sit down." During happy hour, from 5 PM to 7 PM, Monday through Friday, Minnesota Fats would head to the bar to partake of the free hors d'oeuvres that bartender Semra Triplett, provided. His nickname for her was "my tomato." Fats would tell her and others that he had gone through "billions of dollars." When she would say, "Don't you mean millions of dollars, Fats?" he would insist that billions was correct."[6] Fats loved sweets, particularly Lorna Doone shortbread cookies. Patrick Franzone, assistant food and beverage director, would bring Fats a pack of shortbread on his birthdays. Late in the evenings, about the time the dining room closed, Fats would wander down to see if any of pastry chef Judy Beard's delicious cakes were left over. Usually, the staff would bring him a piece of Chocolate Indulgence or Black Forest cake.[7]

Other times, Fats would challenge anyone who happened by the hotel mezzanine to a game for ten dollars. Fats would give his opponent the break shot. Once it was Fats's turn, he would quickly

run the table. Fats would then give his opponent a printed card that read, "I played pool with Minnesota Fats." The other side of the card said, "And lost!"[8] On weekends, he usually had a country music celebrity playing with him, often someone who was performing at the Grand Ole Opry on Saturday night or in town for a recording session. Sales and marketing director Alton Kelley remembered Johnny Cash and Bono playing with

Fats, who was not bashful about giving them tips for success in the music business.

On Friday evenings, after playing pool or eating hors d'oeuvres, Fats and his party would pile into the hotel's Rolls Royce and head to the Stockyard Restaurant, where he had a standing reservation for his own booth. Every young lady there seemed to have her picture made with Fats. After dancing and signing autographs—or stamping them with his silver stamp, as he usually did—Fats and his entourage would head back to the hotel and his suite or the Oak Bar. Fats never drank intoxicating liquor but thoroughly enjoyed the company of those who did.[9]

The Great "Shine-Off"

Alton Kelley and his assistant, John R. Davis, came up with a series of relatively inexpensive, but innovative promotional ideas in the late 1980s to keep the hotel in the limelight. Their best may have been in May 1987 when they gathered in the ballroom all of the city's mayoral candidates, including Eddie Jones, Bill Boner, Betty Nixon, Gale Robinson, Charlie Daniels, and WKDF-FM disc jockey Carl P. Mayfield, alias Bubba Skynyrd; Minnesota Fats and his pool table; a parrot named Wacah; a nine-foot Burmese python; festive showgirls; William Russell, the self-proclaimed shoe shine expert of the world; five of Russell's shoeshine stands; James Pruitt, Russell's manager; and country music stars including Chet Atkins, Brenda Lee, Stella Parton, and Dan Seals. The contest was between Fats and Russell. In a grand "shine-off," the Fat Man would attempt to clear the table of balls before Russell could shine the five pairs of shoes of the mayoral candidates. Supremely confident, Minnesota Fats said, "I don't prepare for nothing because I don't have to." Russell, on the other hand, practiced by having a friend sit on some milk cartons in a field and "keep time with his watch while I shined his shoes." At the showdown, Russell won the best-dressed award as he appeared in a tuxedo, draped with the nine-foot Burmese python, and with a showgirl on either arm. That's all he won as the shine-off was a slaughter. Minnesota Fats cleared the table before Russell was halfway through shining shoes. The Hermitage received a great deal of publicity, and the then-proposed Nashville Zoo was the beneficiary of the one-hundred-dollar-per-ticket event.[10]

The End of a Good Run

During the eight months in 1987 that Stan Ockwig was general manager of the Hermitage, he became fond of Minnesota Fats, so much so that he invited the Fat Man to Christmas dinner. Thirty members of Ockwig's family in Minnesota flew down, knowing that Minnesota Fats would be there. In front of a fireplace in Ockwig's home, Minnesota Fats mesmerized them with outlandish stories. Ockwig recalled in 2008 that, while he was general manager at the hotel, Minnesota Fats received a check, delivered by UPS, once a month. It was enough to pay his hotel bills and meet his other expenses. Fats, who once let Ockwig beat him in pool, never divulged where the money came from, or who paid for the new limousine that suddenly appeared one day.[11]

In 1991, Minnesota Fats had knee surgery. While in the hospital, he suffered a heart attack. He recovered with the aid of his health care giver, Theresa Ward Bell, whom he married in 1992. They had four years together before he died of congestive heart failure in January 1996, four days short of his eighty-third birthday. That he lived to that ripe old age seemed pretty impressive for an overweight pool legend who bragged about leaving "the working dodge to other people" and who once said, "I wouldn't know a calorie from a chrysanthemum."[12]

Page 192: Rudolf Wanderone Jr., better known as Minnesota Fats, in 1935 looking dapper and slim at the age of twenty-two. TBW
Page 196: Fats and bellman Buddy Potts shoot a few in the mezzanine location. A poster for "The Hustler," proudly framed, hangs on the wall. HH
*Page 197, **top**: Fats and second wife Theresa Bell.* TBW

Chapter Eight

MAKING IT WORK

W hile things came together for the refurbished Hermitage Hotel, much attention was placed on the bright and enthusiastic staff. Manager Dennis Morgan, who found most of the workers locally, encouraged creative input. Morgan was particularly proud of chef Terry Hagan and maitre d' John Heffner, both still in their twenties. Morgan turned over to them full responsibility for food preparation, menu planning, and entertainment. One of the first things they did was to change the menu, eliminating dishes that had proven unpopular before the hotel closed, and adding others that were well received.

In July 1981, however, before Hagan and Heffner had time to settle down with their new menus, a food critic for *Nashville Magazine* came in for dinner. He "regretfully reported that the food,

The intricately beautiful Hermitage Ballroom offers the graceful surroundings of another era to enhance any corporate function or social event. Groups up to 350 can enjoy the charming ambience of this magnificent room.

In the fine tradition of the Hermitage Dining Room, you'll find gourmet dining at its best with exceptional service and an array of items specially prepared by our master chef. Overlooking Sixth Street, The Vernanda Bar offers cocktails, imported teas, and a selection of sumptuous desserts.

The ultimate in luxury awaits guests in our elegantly appointed suites. Designed with the discriminating traveler in mind, each suite features spacious bedroom, separate bath with dressing area and a living room with wet bar.

In the tradition of the world's famous hotels, evening turndown service, luxury soaps, toiletry items and complimentary morning newspaper is provided.

although above reproach on some counts, did not live up to its magnificent setting, a room which is by far the most romantic and elegant place to dine in Nashville."[1]

Five months later, the staff had another chance when the critic returned. This time, the Pheasant chartreuse and quail (Cailles à la Normande) sent him "into orbit." The pheasant dish was the French version of what later became pheasant under glass. The quail was baked with apples and grapes to "juicy tenderness."[2]

Another food critic, Homer Blitch, said in his restaurant review of December 10, 1981, that the Hermitage dining room was the most popular formal place in town. He was particularly impressed that the maitre d', captains, waiters, and busboys knew their business and went about it with ease. The flatware and crystal were gleaming the night Blitch was there, and the napkins folded in the shape of a fleur-de-lis. Chef Terry Hagan had prepared:

an excellent silky potato and spinach soup. Veal was tender, white and succulent; beef dishes included prime ribs with Yorkshire pudding, tournedos forestiere, a filet mignon, a chateaubriand for two, fillet Wellington, and a strip. One party had a fillet of salmon carefully skinned and boned, and baked until golden brown. Desserts were chocolate mousse, crème caramel, a daily soufflé, and ice cream.

Blitch rated the quality, quantity, atmosphere, and service an A, and the price B+.[3]

When The Hermitage Park Suite Hotel reopened in 1981, it was one of only two hotels in Nashville to have doormen.

Morgan explained why he decided to have them, and what sort of person he wanted for the job. "The first impression is the most important one, and if the first impression is a bad one, that's the impression that remains," he said. "We want someone who's self-motivating, who represents the image of what we want to portray in the hotel: well-groomed, outgoing. We also look for someone with stamina." One doorman said he didn't get many tips, but he felt rewarded because so many people would tell stories of the old days at the hotel, and what things were like then.[4]

Hagan and Heffner came up with an idea of having a New Year's Eve party at the Hermitage. Guests would be served a gourmet dinner, and then dance to the music of a full orchestra in the grand ballroom. At 1:30 AM, they would be served breakfast before retiring upstairs to sleep in one of the hotel's luxury suites. The number of party guests would be limited and it would cost $175 per couple.[5]

The Christmas spirit permeated the hotel throughout that December. In the lobby stood a twenty-foot Christmas tree, decorated with handmade ornaments, bows, popcorn balls, and gingerbread men, most made by hotel employees. The lobby, veranda, and dining room were adorned with pink and red poinsettias. Those guests for Christmas who did not want to attend the ballroom party could enjoy haute cuisine fare in the dining room and either dance there beginning at 11 PM, or listen to a jazz trio on the veranda.[6]

Turnover and More Turnover

Despite having a good staff, however, manager Dennis Morgan had to continually deal with turnover. Keeping bellmen was a problem, primarily because it was a low-paying job. On the other end of the pay scale, outstanding executive chefs were hard to keep, as larger hotels and restaurants were always on the lookout for the stars. In addition, many aspire to own their own restaurants. Terry Hagan, one of the brightest young chefs ever to be in Nashville,

The hotel's six-hundred-fifty-pound gilded mirror was painstakingly restored to its former glory, shown here in the Nashville Banner *on February 3, 1981. The mirror, with its original glass, still reflects a bygone era from its prominent display above the lobby fireplace.* NB

A magnificent Christmas tree in the lobby was a tradition for many years. It is seen here at a wedding reception in December 1986. MWS

left in 1982 to run his own restaurant in Michigan. John W. Goddard replaced him. Dorothy Baumgartner changed jobs, assuming the role of concierge for the hotel. Her sales position was filled by Bill Corey, who was given a new title, director of sales and marketing. He had been director of national sales for Ramada Inn's western regions.[7] Corey would not stay long.

The turnover eventually extended to top management; Brock Hotel Corp. took a hit when Hermitage general manager Dennis Morgan resigned after having brought back the hotel to its former excellence. His replacement, Bruce Bommarito, arrived in 1983 to try to keep the momentum going. One of his employees at the Hermitage, Patrick Franzone, assistant food and beverage director, remembered Bommarito as a hands-on manager who cared about his employees, as well as a great trainer. Franzone was an example of Bommarito's training skills. After leaving the Hermitage in 1985 to accept a position as assistant manager of The Residence Inn in Huntsville, Alabama, Franzone went on to become general manager of Nashville's Millennium Maxwell House Hotel in 2000. He was still at the Maxwell House in 2009.[8]

Bommarito was forward-thinking. Anticipating that Nashville Christmas shoppers might come in numbers to the Hermitage for lunch, he scheduled a series of noontime musical events. These public events included, for example, a free concert by the Belmont Brass Quintet. There also was another twenty-foot Christmas tree in the lobby to encourage the Christmas spirit,[9] and a few days after Christmas, the hotel served a turkey dinner to thirty Salvation Army guests in the ballroom.[10]

Chocolate Intemperance

On March 15, 1984, the Hermitage celebrated the third anniversary of its restoration and reopening. To mark the occasion, Bruce Bommarito featured a special anniversary dining room menu in addition to its regular dining room fare.[11] During his time at the hotel, Bommarito utilized the advertising skills of Louise Mandrell to publicize events at the hotel. She designed brochures as well as billboard advertisements. Louise was a sister of country music star Barbara Mandrell.[12]

James H. Jesse, retired president of Nashville's Newspaper Printing Corporation, wrote a food review for *The Tennessean* in 1984 after eating at the Hermitage. He found the food was not as exceptional as it had been when chef Hagan had been there, but it was still very good. He thought the service was excellent and that the hotel's pastry chef was the best in town. His party found her cakes, soufflés, and a concoction she called "Chocolate Intemperance," superb. The Hermitage was the only restaurant in town Jesse knew of that had a separate *cuisine minceur* menu. It provided fewer calories

Hermitage Hotel waiter Hashem Salem chats with three-year-old Kathleen Mohre just prior to a turkey dinner served to thirty Salvation Army guests in December 1983. At center is father Louis and second daughter Michele. TN

and exciting tastes. Entrees the evening Jesse dined there included a boneless chicken poached in stock with fresh vegetables and langoustines; red snapper sautéed with onions and tomatoes, filet of lamb sautéed in butter with vegetables; scallops of veal with artichoke bottoms; and tournedos of beef, one topped with Boursin cheese.[13] It is unusual that in 1984 and 1985, the Hermitage's food and beverage department, which oversaw banquets, restaurants, and the bar, had more revenue than the hotel received from room rentals.[14]

The accolades kept coming. In March 1985, the American Automobile Association selected five Nashville hotels for its Four Diamond Award. The hotels, all repeat winners, were: the Hermitage, Opryland Hotel, the Hyatt-Regency, the Radisson Plaza, and the Marriott. Hotels were rated on such criteria as service, cuisine, cleanliness, and the overall hotel operation. Eight other hotels in Chattanooga, Gatlinburg, Knoxville, and Memphis earned the rating; the only Mobil Five Star hotel in Tennessee that year was the Spence Manor in Nashville.[15]

Executive Chef Terry Hagan (center) assembled extra culinary support for three consecutive nights of grand opening parties and dinners in April of 1981. At left are Suzie Edmondson and Jon Polkow, and at right, Michael Rasys and Charlotte Perkins. TN

Bruce Bommarito's tenure as general manager was brief. When he left the company in the fall of 1985, Brock Hotel Corporation announced that Allen Lonstron, then director of marketing and sales at the Hermitage, had been promoted to general manager. A former pilot who spent eighteen years with Pan American World Airways before going in the hotel business, Lonstron said, while looking at the lobby, "It's warm. It kind of hugs you when you come in. To me, this is the ultimate." One of Lonstron's employees described him as outgoing, as well as sales oriented.[16] To remedy the weak weekend traffic, Lonstron inaugurated a weekend package, and it worked. Overall, occupancy rates were consistently in the high 70s.

Despite Lonstron's positive attitude, he took over the reins at a precarious time. Within six months, the financially strapped Brock Hotel Corp. was trying to sell The Hermitage Hotel for approximately $8 million so the company could pay off its debts. Brock had been unable to make monthly bond payments to Third National Bank since January. The outstanding principal in industrial revenue bonds bought by Brock and Hermitage Hotel Ltd. Partnership in 1980 was still $6.1 million with only $360,000 having been paid. If Brock could not find a buyer by December 1, the ownership of the Hermitage would default to the bank, as trustee for the bonds. Tom Corcoran, vice chairman of the Brock board, told a newspaper reporter that Brock officials had met with several potential buyers, including Belz Enterprises of Memphis, which owned Memphis's Peabody Hotel and Nashville's 100 Oaks Shopping Center. Corcoran said he intended to revive negotiations with Belz officials. Another source said that the Hermitage was not making money because its average suite rate of $81.52 per night was insufficient. The same unidentified source added that the reason for the uncertainty had more to do with Brock's financial problems elsewhere than it did with the Hermitage. The company had gone into the pizza/entertainment parlor business, a move that proved to be disastrous. A recent edition of *Forbes* magazine stated that Brock ended fiscal year 1985 with an estimated loss of $70 million and a negative net worth of around $60 million. According to the article, "Corcoran stressed that since Brock Hotel Corp. was only an operator, not the owner of the hotel, it could not be construed to be selling it."[17]

Third National confirmed what Corcoran said. Keith Keisling, an assistant vice president of Third National, had already mailed letters to

THE TENNESSEAN MAR 21 1981

The Elegance of Another Era

Now Open in Nashville

The Hermitage

A Park Suite Hotel

231 6th Avenue North
Nashville, TENN. 37219
RESERVATIONS
IN NASHVILLE CALL 244-3121
TOLL FREE (800) 342-

bondholders advising them that bond payments were not being met and that a buyer was being sought. Keisling went on to assure the bondholders that "although no purchaser has been located as of this time, we anticipate that any purchase of the hotel would be contingent on assumption or payment of all outstanding obligations." He did not know if Brock Hotel would be able to make bond interest payments on June 1. Should they not be able to do so, Keisling said that bondholders would be protected at least through their December interest payments because of an $800,000 reserve fund.[18]

The impending sale of the Hermitage was further clouded by the development of two quality lodging facilities in downtown Nashville: The Union Station Hotel and the Stouffer Nashville Hotel being built at the new convention center.

Haunting Tales

Within a year of Lonstron's battlefield promotion to general manager, he was replaced by Paul Kraft. Despite the hotel's problems, Kraft presented an optimistic face to the public. In November 1986, he told Max York, staff writer for *The Tennessean*, that the hotel was top-notch but it his goal was to make it even better.[19] "We try to greet everybody with a smile. We cater to the needs of the individual," Kraft added. He planned to start some new traditions, such as giving every female guest a rose as she left the dining room, and taking guests to and from the airport in a hotel limousine.[20] He never achieved his dreams for the hotel, however, as soon after his conversation with Max York, he too left the hotel. His replacement, Stan Ockwig, was brought in because of his expertise in renovations, something the hotel management wanted to do. Although he was general manager for only eight months, Ockwig was there long enough to hear at least one ghost story. As he understood it, an enraged husband had killed a man whom he caught in bed with his wife on the fifth floor. When asked if he believed the story,

Ockwig told the author in 2008 that twice he noticed wall sconces on the fifth floor askew. Both times, he asked the hotel engineer to straighten them. Twice, the engineer found them perfectly aligned.[21]

In addition, a bartender reported seeing a ghost walk through the dining room late one evening after everyone in the kitchen had gone home. The ghost supposedly resided on the ninth floor where he had died the night of his wedding. One night a security guard claimed that, when he checked an outside door on the ninth floor, the ghost pushed him out and locked the door behind him, stranding him on the landing. Of course, the hotel's many celebrity guests during the 1980s seemed like ghosts, too—especially since they often came in the service entrance on Capitol Boulevard and went up the freight elevator. There were, for example, Michael Jackson and Tina Turner.[22] Other celebrities that Patrick Franzone remembered staying in the hotel in the early 1980s were Clint Eastwood, Boy George, George Lucas, Louise Mandrell, Lionel Richie, Linda Ronstadt, Red Skelton, Sissy Spacek, Bruce Springsteen, B. J. Thomas, and the Thompson Twins.[23]

Regardless of the goings-on, however, when Brock Hotels put the renovations on hold the following winter, Ockwig accepted another position with Country Clubs of America in Florida, where he opened the Inverrary Country Club and Resort.

Mathew Thomas, a forty-two-year-old man born in India, was next in line. Described as a sharp dresser who looked the part of a hotel manager, he was well-liked, and a true professional. His hotel experience included stints as food and beverage manager for the Radisson Plaza Hotel in Nashville, and, later, as general manager for Holiday Inns in Topeka, Kansas, and Fort Meyers, Florida.

Dramatic Improvements

General manager Mathew Thomas seemed to have a better chance at success than his three most recent predecessors. In the summer of 1986, before he was employed, the default crisis was averted when the Hallwood Group of Cleveland, Ohio, a company that specialized in financial rescues, poured $40 million into Brock Hotel Corp. This enabled Brock to resume payments on a $1.38 million bond issue and remove the hotel from technical default on the $6.46 million issue. In return, Hallwood became owner of a majority of Brock's stock.[24] The hotel also gained momentum in 1986 when it was given the prestigious Mobil Travel Guide Four Star Award.

By August and September, there was a dramatic improvement in the Hermitage's bottom line, and there was more good press, too. On August 29, Robert and Mary Craighead of Nashville were caught off guard when their six children held a surprise fiftieth anniversary party for them in the Hermitage's banquet hall. Lured to the hotel on the ruse that they had won an all-expenses-paid senior citizens weekend, the Craigheads still thought that to be the case until the doors of the banquet hall opened and they saw the smiling faces of their six children, their spouses, and sixteen grandchildren. Family members came from Ohio, Tennessee, Colorado, and California for the special event.[25]

In addition, Gov. Ned Ray McWherter had a governor's suite on the ninth floor, where he often stayed.

Thomas predicted that the hotel would be at a "break-even situation" either in 1987 or 1988. The Hermitage's occupancy rate was about 62 percent when Thomas arrived. This was considerably lower than the occupancy rates for some of the larger, newer hotels on Briley Parkway near

Custom carpet today in the Governor's Salon on the mezzanine level. JA

Opryland. Thomas hoped to build it to 76 percent. His strategy to give the Hermitage a "grand hotel image" was as follows. First, he had rebuilt the sales staff into a four-person group that focused on the corporate market, which provided the Hermitage with 70 percent of its business. Toward that end, in December, he employed Alton Kelley and Dorothy Cummings as director of sales and marketing and group sales manager, respectively. Kelley and his bride, Sheree, would later stay in the hotel on their honeymoon, as had his parents, Everett and Eleanor Clark Kelley, and his grandparents, Louis and Mary Palmer Kelley.

Thomas planned to renovate one or two floors designed to meet the needs of businesswomen. He knew, from his experience running a Holiday Inn in Fort Meyers, Florida, how important security was for women traveling alone. He also brought back a complimentary shoeshine service. Gentlemen could either leave their shoes outside their rooms before retiring or have their shoes shined by William Russell, a twenty-nine-year shoeshine veteran in the historic men's room, a facility that, in its earlier years, had shower stalls for hotel guests whose rooms did not have them. Finally, Thomas would convert the veranda overlooking Sixth Avenue North into a moderately priced deli. He wanted this to be in place by the following spring to attract the downtown lunch crowd. At that point, one bedroom suites at the Hermitage ranged from $98 to $128 a night. Two-bedroom suites went for $148 a night. Thomas felt comfortable with the Hermitage's ability to compete effectively with his downtown competition, and he planned to

Lobby with central seating evokes a classic design of a bygone era. KRS

The veranda as it looked in 1988. MOP

increase those rates following a proposed renovation and redecoration tentatively planned for the late summer, pending completion of a feasibility study.[26] Others took note. A national bed and breakfast convention came the Hermitage's way in March, and more than eighty B&B operators in town for the event stayed at the Hermitage. In past national conventions, those members had stayed at local B&Bs.[27]

June 1987 brought another promotional idea for Nashville's All Suite Hotel. Thomas arranged for the hotel's kitchen staff to provide one hundred fifty free box lunches for cab drivers who normally brought customers to the hotel. The box lunches were distributed outside the hotel's Capitol Boulevard entrance by a bevy of pretty girls.[28] This idea worked, but probably not as well as the "shine-off" publicity stunt that pitted the pool skills of legendary cue man/Hermitage staple Minnesota Fats in a timed match against the shoeshine talents of expert William Russell.

The Hermitage began to make a little money during Thomas's tenure as general manager. Still, there were inevitable problems. On Halloween night, at 4:30 AM, an underground city water main at the corner of Fourth Avenue North and Union Street ruptured, damaging electrical cables and causing a blackout of the Hermitage. It was the first time this had happened in the hotel's seventy-seven-year history. In the lobby, the only light came from some jack-o-lanterns on a table. Although the hotel was filled to capacity that night, guests did not start complaining until they woke up to no electricity. By afternoon, the use of some of the elevators had been restored, but the 112 suites would still be without electricity for a few more hours. The outage was particularly frustrating for participants of a two-day fur show at the hotel.[29]

Things Could Be Better

Vanderbilt's Institute for Public Policy Studies (VIPPS) held its second annual public policy lecture dinner at the Hermitage on January 19, 1988. Arkansas Gov. Bill Clinton was the principal speaker. The title of his talk was "The Changing Role of Governorship." One attendee, Peggy Henry Joyce of Nashville, recalled that he spoke primarily about himself and for too long.[30]

By spring 1988, Robert Adams III was the Hermitage's general manager. Unfortunately, his introduction was marred by the revelation that an administrative assistant had embezzled at least $17,000 by falsifying payroll records. Integra, Inc., the successor name of Brock Hotel Corp., pressed charges.[31] Vende Morris quickly followed suit as general manager. She lived in the hotel and survived for about a year before moving to Anderson, South Carolina, to operate a bed and breakfast, a much less stressful position. Her successor, Ron Seddon, lasted only one month. The hotel operator, Westbrook Hospitality, turned to the Hermitage comptroller, James Braden, and asked him to assume the additional role of interim general manager while the company searched for a more permanent replacement. Braden accepted and held both jobs for about five months.[32]

In the meantime, new staff in the food and beverage department tried another avenue: the focus would be on American cuisine, rather than the heavy sauces previously used. A review in the *Nashville Scene* that December was noncommittal about the food but found the dining room still to be a place of elegance and romance. On Christmas Day, brunch was offered from 11 AM until 3 PM.[33]

Integra, the hotel and restaurant company based in Irving, Texas, that owned the Hermitage, realized things could be better. Former manager Mathew

Thomas had said renovations and redecorations were needed years earlier. Without the funding available, Integra considered franchising the hotel. On June 7, 1989, Embassy Suites, a wholly owned subsidiary of the Holiday Corp., announced that it had bought the franchise rights for the Hermitage. The hotel would become an Embassy Suites Hotel as early as the end of the year, following approximately $3 million in renovations. Ownership and management of the hotel would remain the same.[34]

The franchise with Embassy Suites never materialized. Integra was left, once again, to cope with an unprofitable situation on its own. In October, Westbrook Hospitality recruited Doug Vandenberg as the Hermitage's general manager. Vandenberg replaced James Braden, who was reassigned by Integra to a Days Inn in Houston. Vandenberg did not know that he was the hotel's eleventh general manager since it had reopened a decade earlier. He was familiar, however, with the Nashville market, having been general manager for the Holiday Inn Vanderbilt from 1984 until 1989. He also realized the challenges he faced. Among other deficiencies, the Hermitage's parent company, Integra, was financially strapped, and the Hermitage did not have a national reservation system to draw on for guests as did competing hotels, such as Holiday Inns, that were part of a national chain.[35] Quickly, Vandenberg hired Steve Nagy as food and beverage director, and Jim Napolitano as executive chef. That was a start.

An Unwelcome Suit

The next summer, on July 17, 1991, it was announced that Third National Bank was suing Integra for more than $5.4 million. The flap was over the defaulted bonds that had been issued by the Metro Industrial Development Board back in 1980 to Hermitage Hotel Ltd. for the restoration of the hotel and the construction of the parking garage. As security of the bonds, the partnership assigned its right, title, and interest in a lease agreement to the industrial board. The industrial board, in turn, assigned its right, title, and interest to Third as collateral for its own bond obligation. This partnership subsequently leased the hotel's land and buildings to Integra. The total sum included the $5.4 million principal owed on the bonds, plus interest, and expenses including attorneys' fees. Integra had unconditionally guaranteed to Third the payment of principal and interest on the bonds.[36]

Interest of $281,323 was due on the bonds December 1, 1990, but the bond fund didn't have enough money to pay it, according to Third National's complaint. The industrial board had also defaulted on its obligation by failing to pay interest. Third National accelerated the industrial board's obligations on July 10 by declaring due all outstanding bonds.[37] Hermitage Hotel Ltd. sought bankruptcy protection in October 1991.

No Parking Lot

Despite the lawsuit, life went on pretty much as usual at The Hermitage Hotel. In mid-January, the Tennessee State Museum held a fundraiser in the hotel ballroom to offset the expense of the museum's special World War II exhibit. Guests were encouraged to wear costumes from the 1930s and 1940s. The slogan for the event was "History Will Kick Up Its Heels at the Hermitage."[38]

The next fall, Doug Vandenberg experienced a highlight of his term as general manager. Governor Bill Clinton spent the night at the Hermitage during his presidential campaign swing through Tennessee. Vandenberg recalled in 2007 that Clinton shared the podium at the dinner that night with Tennessee's Democratic governor, Ned Ray McWherter.[39]

The Case of the Crumbling Cornice

FAÇADE CAUSES HEALTH HAZARD

In the early 1990s, the scaffolding was up along Sixth Avenue North. The Hermitage Hotel was undergoing renovation of its terra cotta cornice as part of a long-term project.[40]

Concerned residents were worried that the architectural integrity of the hotel was being compromised. *Nashville Scene* reporter Christine Kreyling chronicled the issue in an article called, "Architecture Crimes: The Case of the Crumbling Cornice."[41] "They're taking the cornice off and replacing it with something awful," she reported one caller as saying. Under the scaffolding, part of the cornice, with its familiar lion heads, had been taken down. Carl Morse was the project manager with Western Waterproofing, which had been hired to stabilize the building and make it safe. Morse explained that, with all the dynamiting for nearby downtown construction, including the City Center, the hotel's brick had slipped, allowing water to corrode the original steel supports. Consequently, the sidewalks were unsafe to walk on. Morse said, the terra cotta cornice was being removed

because the steel anchoring system behind it is dust. The same is true of the water table ornament at the second level. It's hanging by a thread and has to come off before it falls and kills somebody. There's been years of neglect, zero maintenance. Things like caulking haven't been done and lots of water has penetrated the façade.

The hotel felt it was imperative that they restore the façade in some way. One option was to restore the anchoring and put the original ornament back up. The other option was to replace the terra cotta with GFRC (glass fiber reinforced concrete). It would take half the labor to install and could "reproduce exact replicas, color and everything." After Historic Nashville Inc. (HNI) obtained a façade easement on The Hermitage Hotel in June 1988, the non-profit organization owned any material removed from the hotel's exterior. HNI made the original pieces removed available for sale. Morse estimated that the lion heads could sell for up to $10,000 each. Individuals bought some pieces while the hotel bought many of the original lion heads that had not been sold to the public. These were left on the hotel roof for a number of years before being stored more securely. In 2009, there were two terra cotta lion heads still on display, one in the lobby and the other in the Oak Bar.

But the hammer was about to fall. On December 16, 1992, Third National Bank filed a Chancery Court lawsuit requesting the appointment of a receiver to straighten out conflicting claims by creditors of the financially troubled Hermitage Hotel. People close to the situation suspected that the bank felt that the building would be imploded and turned into a parking lot. They were naturally anxious for that to happen on someone else's watch. The wording of the lawsuit suggested that the hotel's demise was near. It stated, "The property is not generating sufficient income to cover its costs of operation and service the debt. . . . Currently, the hotel is worth less than the debt on it and is suffering from physical deterioration." Additionally, creditors were asserting conflicting claims for payment. For example, the company that installed the hotel's telephone system had taken steps to repossess the telephones, which could "cripple the operations of The Hermitage Hotel."[42]

The partnership still owed $6.8 million in principal and interest to bondholders who financed the renovation in 1981. Third National remained the trustee for those bondholders.[43]

Soon after, The Hermitage Hotel had been placed in the hands of Robert Waldschmidt, a Nashville attorney with Howell & Fisher, as receiver. His charge was to do whatever needed to be done with the property. He knew that, if he was going to find a buyer, he needed to improve the cash flow of the hotel and that was impossible as long as netting covered the Sixth Avenue North face of the building. The netting was there to prevent the deteriorating terra cotta

Above: Lobby social function, 1990s. Note the classic statuary in the background. MOP
***Opposite page:** This lobby bar was popular with legislators and the downtown crowd. Yet another fascinating adaptation of architectural interiors. Note the inset stairway below, which then turned left to the restaurant level.* KRS

ornamentation from falling off and hitting pedestrians. Because of the netting, however, many people assumed the hotel was closed. Waldschmidt, who ate lunch at the hotel nearly every day, argued that the hotel was still operating just as it always has been.[44] During this time, Waldschmidt made temporary repairs to the terra cotta ornamentation and spent an average of three hours a day at the hotel, working with the general manager, Doug Vandenberg, on the cash flow. With the improved outside appearance, they were able to convince the public that the hotel was still open, which resulted in increased occupancy and a positive cash flow. This gave them the money to replace the obsolete computer and telephone system, as well as upgrade the elevators. These changes also improved the chances of saving the hotel.[45]

Another milestone came when Davidson County Chancery Court Judge Robert Brandt authorized Waldschmidt to sell the hotel for $2.5 million to Cooper Companies of Memphis. According to court documents, there were no other bids. Terms of the pending sale called for $2 million of the purchase price to go to Third National. This amount fell well short of the money owed on the

This carpet was recently donated to the hotel archives collection by Pace Cooper. Cooper Companies had new carpets designed for the hotel in the 1990s. TCV

bonds, and it was not clear who would absorb the loss.[46] What was clear was that the price would be a bargain for whoever acquired the hotel, primarily because of the $6.46 million renovation in the early 1980s.[47] It was also clear that, in fifteen months, Waldschmidt had done his job. The Hermitage would not become a parking lot.

How "Suite" it was

In April 1994, when Cooper Companies took ownership of The Hermitage Hotel, the stated intention was to make the historic hotel Cooper's flagship property. In addition to the $2.5 million sale price, president Pace Cooper announced plans to invest another $3.5 million in restoration and improvements. Cooper gave two reasons why his company bought the Hermitage. "For one thing, we intend to maintain the hotel's appearance and to re-invest in it as needed, not just do a one-time upgrade. And the timing is much better now than it was then what with so much happening in downtown Nashville." The average cost of a one-bedroom suite is now ninety-five dollars a night.[48]

With the Hermitage under new ownership, it was time for general manager Doug Vandenberg to leave. In 2007, Vandenberg, then the general manager of Nashville's Holiday Inn Express Broadway, recalled that he had never worked harder nor enjoyed a job more than during the nearly four years he was general manager of the Hermitage. It was, he said, "a great hotel."[49]

Vandenberg's replacement, Richard Markham, was announced April 26, 1994, in the *Nashville Banner*. Originally from Hawaii, Markham got his Nashville start at the Hyatt Regency. He then managed Loews Vanderbilt Plaza and the Maxwell House.[50] Later, Cooper reflected on the state of the Hermitage at the time his company acquired it. "It was in a state of financial disarray," he said, "harboring a dismal 50 percent occupancy rate and charging about $50 per night." After three years and the promised $3.5 million in renovations, however, 1997 occupancy was up to 73 percent and rooms cost $115 per night.

Occupancy improved because Cooper Companies made extensive improvements to the lobby, grand ballroom, the Capitol Grille (formerly the famous Grill Room), Oak Bar, and veranda, the latter of which reopened as a piano bar. Each of the hotel's luxurious guest suites was completely renovated. The hotel's name was changed to "The Hermitage Suite Hotel." Atlanta designer Stan Topol, who was recognized by *Town & Country* as one of the top twenty-five designers in the United States, spearheaded the renovation efforts. Topol spoke of his goals for the hotel.

One of several suites formerly located on the mezzanine level for private dinners and meetings. KRS

We wanted to preserve 99 percent of the hotel. The parts that we changed we really only enhanced. We tried to create an oasis in Nashville—a place for business and a place to relax. The Hermitage Suite Hotel is a place for everyone. It's kind of nice to come home to a place that's not just a room, but a place where you feel like you belong. I want everyone to belong.

According to Topol, the rooms had an English interpretation with rich fabrics, unique prints, distinctive accessories, and a lot of color.[51]

Speaking of the renovation in April 1995, Manager Richard Markham said, "This should take us comfortably into the new century, noting that everything inside and outside except the famous green marble men's room has been completely renovated. The [public] response has been overwhelmingly favorable." All 120 guest rooms were remodeled, the grill was redesigned, there was

The 1990s Oak Bar, sporting a club atmos-phere, remained popular. An open doorway to the dining room shows a built-in buffet. Behind frosted glass windows in the back-ground, the restaurant also had two private dining rooms. KRS

a new menu, and the seven-month renovation covered all the common areas, such as "the lobby, ballroom and arched veranda, which is being reopened as a piano bar. . . . With the renovation comes a room rate increase from the current average of $60 to $70 a night to over $100."[52]

Around the same time, Rudolph Gomez, who had come up through the ranks in the Hermitage kitchen, was executive chef. Gomez remembered in 2008 the elegant Sunday brunches that his staff prepared, usually for good crowds. Gomez, who enjoyed handling the omelet station personally, also enjoyed meeting a number of celebrities, including recording star Victoria Shaw.[53]

Also at that time, the *Nashville Banner* lauded the recent renovations, calling the hotel "all the more elegant." The eighty-five-year-old property had been redone from top to bottom in the previous seven months, the article said, and the veranda had been reopened for piano music, afternoon cocktails, and light snacks.[54]

Changes in Ownership

Historic Nashville, Inc., however, was still concerned that the owners had not brought the exterior of The Hermitage Hotel back to its original appearance. Looking to the future, the non-profit organization received a preservation easement for the hotel in 1995. That meant that HNI could legally enforce the preservation of the exterior of the Hermitage in return for a tax break for the owners. Susan Richardson, HNI director, explained that the owners had a complete run of the missing design elements, including lions, rosettes, and cove moldings, and could make fiberglass casts. When the ornamental pieces were taken down, some were damaged while others were sold by HNI as a fundraiser, making a complete restoration impossible. "But they have to put the fiber casts back up, in a timely manner," she stressed.[55]

Pace Cooper, president of Cooper Companies, expressed justifiable pride in what his company had accomplished. He predicted, "Nashvillians will love it because it represents a very colorful part of the city's past and provides a unique atmosphere for all kinds of social events." The Capitol Grille featured an "eclectic, creative menu with southern influences." The grille also offered "a prix fixe wine maker's dinner, a delectable four-course dinner chosen for uniqueness and flavor. Each course is paired with a glass of perfectly complimentary California wine. Chef Guillermo Thomas changes the wine maker's menu every two weeks to ensure only the freshest seasonal ingredients." Thomas, who replaced Gomez, would prove to be another excellent chef.[56]

Kay West, food critic for the *Nashville Scene*, let Nashvillians know who Guillermo was. In her article, "Glory days again at Capitol Grille," she stated, "Young chef Guillermo Thomas, fondly referred to as Willie by the staff, comes to us from Cape Cod, although he has also spent some time in Vail, Colorado. His menu, which he worked on

Quiet and sophisticated dining elegance in the 1990s Capitol Grille. KRS

The Grand Ballroom, 1990s. Note the darkened condition of the walnut paneling.

KRS

for seven months, suggests a multi-cultural frame of reference and a particular affinity for unusual combinations."[57]

It was time, however, for Cooper Companies to move on. Nashvillians learned that The Hermitage Hotel had been sold, once again, when they read an article by Will Pinkston in *The Tennessean* on March 12, 1997. Pinkston reported that Starwood Lodging Trust, a Phoenix-based real estate investment trust, had paid close to $15.9 million for the Hermitage, more than double what Cooper Companies had invested in it. Having paid $2.5 million for the property in April 1994—and having spent another $3.5 million in renovations—the Coopers made $9.85 million in cash and stock profits on their investment. They also had the satisfaction of knowing that they had turned around the 120-room all-suite hotel, a landmark believed to be the only example of a commercial Beaux Arts structure in Tennessee.[58] Irby Cooper, founder of Cooper Companies, told newspaper reporter Cree Lawson that, "We just loved the place. We think we've done very well in fixing the place up and in pleasing Nashville. It's a great city."[59]

Starwood Lodging Trust was, according to Lawson's article, the largest hotel real estate investment trust (REIT) in the nation with $2.2 billion in equity capitalization. It was a subsidiary of SLT Realty Limited Partnership, and partnered with fellow subsidiary Starwood Lodging Corp.[60]

The change in ownership meant the departure of Richard Markham, who had managed the hotel since the Coopers acquired it. Jeff Wagner replaced him, but not for long. Following him was Eric Smith, who stayed until early 1999.

Although Starwood promised to spend millions of dollars in renovations, they did not do enough to elevate the hotel to the ranks of the country's elite hotels. Beginning on December 4, 1997, the Hermitage became part of the

Westin Hotels and Resorts chain, a Starwood subsidiary. The hotel's name was changed to The Westin Hermitage. Westin had, at the time, 109 luxury hotels around the world.[61]

Less than two years later, however, Barry Sternlicht, chairman and chief executive officer for Starwood Hotels and Resorts International, announced that the company was planning $6.8 million in renovations to two Nashville properties: the Sheraton Music City and the historic Westin Hermitage. Starwood, the largest lodging firm in the world with more than seven hundred hotels in more than seventy countries, took over ownership of the local Sheraton and Westin hotels in February 1999, but had just recently combined its management and operations. Already, $1 million in renovations were underway at the Hermitage, including redoing the exterior brick, and replacing carpets and sofas.[62] For the rest of that year and half of the next one, the Westin Hermitage was managed by Hugh Harper, who oversaw the Sheraton Music City, as well.

The hotel's road to recovery was now on solid ground, its return to full glory just around the bend.

Chapter Nine

GLORY RESTORED

T he dawning of a new century brought a new owner for The Hermitage Hotel, along with aspirations that, decades earlier, no one could have imagined. Historic Hotels of Nashville, LLC bought the property in June 2000 with a plan to gain the American Automobile Association's coveted Five Diamond rating. The $14 million sale included the building and .54 acres of land.[1]

In order to make the lofty goal a reality, the hotel underwent an extensive, $17 million interior and exterior renovation. The program would include:

- total demolition of all guest rooms, rebuilding with completely new and spacious designs and new furnishings;

- new marble bathrooms with five fixture appointments in all rooms;

*Artist's rendering of the
redesigned veranda area.* FP

- complete replacement of mechanical, electrical, and plumbing systems;
- restoration of all lobby, restaurant, and public spaces; and
- exterior repairs and renovations.[2]

The Hermitage stopped accepting guests in late March 2002 to begin its quick but difficult renovation. At eleven o'clock in the morning on April 1, the Sixth Avenue entrance of the hotel opened to hundreds of people who had lined up as early as 6 AM to buy a bargain in the Hermitage's furniture sale. By 1:30 PM, an estimated 85 percent of the hotel's sofas, chairs, nightstands, and tables had been claimed. Some latecomers never even made it inside. The sale resumed the next day to dispose of what remained, primarily mattresses, TV stands, coffee tables, and draperies.[3]

The owners fully realized the task at hand; the group had already turned Richmond's 105-year-old Jefferson Hotel into a Mobil Five Star and AAA Five Diamond property and also owns Kiawah Island Resort with its crown jewel, The Sanctuary, near Charleston, South Carolina. This new hotel earned its first AAA Five-Diamond Award as of 2007, and its first Mobil Five Star designation in 2008. Sea Pines Resort, on Hilton Head Island, which includes The Inn at Harbour Town as well as the famous Harbour Town Golf Links have also become part of this fine collection.

By the time the Hermitage renovations were complete, the famous green-and-black Art Deco men's room and the hotel's Capitol Grille would remain essentially the same. The rest of the hotel was transformed into a premier

Workers creating the blue sky ceiling. TGP

property, giving honor to its past, but with a vision for the future. Modern additions included a new fitness center and spa on the mezzanine level; a 2,000-square-foot presidential suite; four executive suites; seven junior suites; and 111 guest suites. The presidential suite would include a butler's pantry, a combination dining and sitting room with a plasma screen TV, a king-size bed, a garden bath, separate shower, and enclosed rest room with phone.

Teresa Silo, the first general manager of The Hermitage Hotel under its new ownership, assisted employees in finding alternative employment when the hotel closed in March 2002. Silo recalled that the employees knew that the hotel needed a significant upgrade and understood why they had to seek jobs elsewhere. Many said they wanted to return to the Hermitage after the renovation was complete.

Timeless Elegance

LOBBY MARBLE

The Hermitage Hotel possesses an air of quality, strength, and substance that is evident the moment one walks through the bronze door entrance. The impression is reinforced upon ascending the steps into the lobby. Marble serves as the visual foundation and subtle backdrop of the grandeur of the main lobby.

The central floor is composed primarily of three native Tennessee marbles: Continental Rose, Tennessee Continental Gray, and Tennessee Chocolate. The chocolate marble is also called Tennessee Cedar. The three are found in Knox, Blount, and Sevier counties in east Tennessee and have been quarried since the 1820s. They have been used all over the world. Examples of this unique marble can be found in the National Gallery of Art, The Smithsonian, the Jefferson and Lincoln memorials, the National Cathedral, and most recently the U.S. Capitol Visitors Center.

Adorning the grand lobby stair is a variety of Italian Sienna in rich, yellow-gold-ochre hues known as Giallo Sienna. This particular material is very difficult to quarry, cut, fabricate, and install. Due to its brittle nature and complex striations, the rock is prone to shear and crumble. This high degree of failure, along with the desirability of the stone's rich color dating back to the Etruscan and Roman periods, has made the stone all but extinct. The stone at the Hermitage was varnished at some point, possibly to protect it or to create a desired effect. The oxidized finish was removed in 2002, restoring the stone to its original look.

The beautiful white-and-gray marble comes from the famous Carrera Marble Quarry in Tuscany, Italy, in the Apennine Mountains. Carrera has been in used since the time of ancient Rome; the Pantheon and Trajan's Column are constructed of it. Many sculptures of the Renaissance, such as Michelangelo's David, also used Carrera marble.

The time-tested marble that graces The Hermitage Hotel stands much as it was when first installed in 1910. An esti- mated ten million people have walked upon this marble since the hotel first opened.

—*Stephen Brown and*
Tom Vickstrom

Above, left: Director of Engineering John Powers participated in the renovation. He stands in the former circular staircase, near street level at Sixth Avenue. HH
Above, right: As in 1980, a bobcat was used to remove all interior walls on guest room floors 2–9. HH
Opposite page, top: Experimentation with decorative treatments led to outstanding success. JA
Opposite page, bottom: Both the old and new color schemes in view, 2002. TGP

Creating a Private-Mansion Feel

Greg Sligh, managing director of the Hermitage since 2002, described the renovation's goals. He said they had paid attention "to every single detail that could possibly matter to a guest—everything from the three-setting lamps to the powerful commercial-grade showerheads to the peaceful color scheme that creates a luxurious, pampered existence. We wanted a private-mansion feel, a residential rather than a commercial style."[4]

The Sixth Avenue entrance was obviously an important focal point. To enhance visitors' first impressions of the hotel, a new iron and glass canopy was installed. Through it, classical music was piped, as well as heat during cold weather. New bronze doors led to the grand staircase, which was enclosed with walls of handsome Siena marble that had been given a fresh patina.[5] On the exterior of the building facing south on Sixth Avenue, workers uncovered a five-by-six-foot plate glass window that read, "Hermitage Hotel Pharmacy." A bit of research showed that a pharmacy did operate at that location in the early 1900s.

Workers made other interesting discoveries, as well. A cavity in a restaurant wall contained some old papers, including a complete 1913 menu, which is displayed on page 34.

The interior design and architecture firm that led the restoration was ForrestPerkins LLC of Dallas and Washington, D.C. The firm, which pairs designer Deborah Lloyd Forrest, FASID, and Stephen Perkins, AIA, is known for its restoration work in landmark hotels. The architect of record was Gobbell Hays Partners of Nashville. Ron Gobbell, FAIA, served as principal, and Greg Mayo served as project architect. R. C. Mathews Contractor of Nashville was the contractor.[6] The interior painting contract was awarded to Republic, a local concern headed by Stephen W. Brown. His team repainted the interior public areas, such as the lobby, the veranda, the ballroom, the dining room, the Sixth Avenue vestibule and stairs, and some public halls. At the time, there were four layers of paint on the lobby ceiling and three on the dining room ceiling. The painting project took eighteen people approximately seven months to complete.[7]

R. C. Mathews Contractor completely renovated all of the building's systems, including electrical, sprinkler, and mechanical, even replacing the kitchen exhaust duct all the way to the roof. Work crews essentially demolished the interior of the building from the second floor up to reconfigure the bedroom suites from two room parlor/bedroom units (done in 1980) to one large bedroom and a spacious bathroom per suite.

Glory Restored

233

Craftsmanship for the Ages

ORNAMENTAL PLASTER

The grandiose nature of Beaux Arts provided the perfect opportunity for J. E. R. Carpenter to employ the use of ornamental plaster. According to Beaux Arts principles, undecorated surfaces are not to be found.

The design palette has no boundary when using ornamental plaster, allowing for a beautiful complement to the marble floor and columns. The design, molding, and sculptural intent allows the artist to create what cannot be created from wood or stone.

Fine detailing, classical designs, and symbolism are found in abundance at The Hermitage Hotel. The plaster works created a hundred years ago remain intact today, needing only minor repairs, periodic cleaning, and occasional repainting when renovation color schemes changed through the years.

Cherubs which border the lobby ceiling represent carefree angels who are laughing children forever. Swags of bundled fruit represent abundance, bounty, and the fruits of life. Scrolls symbolize knowledge and wealth. The acanthus leaf is a symbol of hospitality and vitality. Eggs typify new birth, fertility, and life, while arrows symbolize death or serious consequences; found together, these portray a place where important decisions are made. Beads represent richness, and lamb's tongues represent innocence as well as affluence.

These decorative components, while adding to the overall ambience of the hotel, also serve a functional, practical purpose, often concealing joints at corners and edges, and adding structural strength.

—*Stephen Brown and Tom Vickstrom*

Once demolition was complete, Walker Mathews, president of R. C. Mathews, stood on one of the upper floors by the windows facing Capitol Boulevard and looked across the building and out the windows facing Sixth Avenue North. He was surprised to rediscover the shell of the 1910 convention hall on the ninth floor. The vaulted ceiling was still there, along with remnants of the original wallpaper, and even a heavy brass light fixture.

Among the many changes made by R. C. Mathews were the replication/replacement of the original plaster ceiling in the Capitol Grille; the replacement of the stairway to that room with a grander one; and prefabricated plaster details on the exterior of the building. The terra cotta lions on the cornice, however, were not replaced, because to do so was prohibitively expensive.[8]

One of the most appreciated improvements was the introduction of a ventilation system that circulates fresh air throughout the hotel from a roof intake. Guests continue to comment on how clean and fresh the hotel feels. The air is heated during the winter and cooled during the summer before being circulated into the guest room floors.

The ornate painted glass ceiling also received a minor facelift. After its major renovation in the early 1980s, the ceiling needed only minor cleaning and repair. Only four panes of glass needed replacing in 2002.

The result of the months of hard and dedicated work was magnificent. The Beaux Arts style lobby was, by all accounts, breathtaking with the newly lighted original painted glass skylight, gilded moldings, freshly repainted ceilings, restored marble walls and floors, custom alabaster chandeliers, and handmade rugs.

The ballroom's wood walls were extensively cleaned and polished and the floors fitted with custom wool carpeting.[9]

Forrest said:

Lobbies have to make a statement, and also have to deliver on the profit statement. The lobby has to function as a meeting place, a business venue, and a food and drink venue, all at the same time. To be successful, design has to offset the barriers to these multiple functions—and it has to do it in a way that sets up guest expectations for the hotel and defines its images.[10]

ForrestPerkins further enhanced the lobby by building a large focal fireplace that invites guests to gather in comfortable and easily rearranged seating for informal coffee or casual meetings. Today, one can find guests enjoying afternoon tea, and champagne, brandy, or lemonade in the evenings.

Above, left and right: Painstaking restoration stripped away the old, dark finish and revealed the gleaming burled walnut in the ballroom. TGP (LEFT), JA (RIGHT)

Opposite page, top: A grand new staircase replaced the narrower old one and led to the newly redesigned Capitol Grille. MEN

Opposite page, middle: Frame outlining the previous narrow staircase. During the removal of the original stairs a pocket knife was found encased in the poured concrete since 1910. TGP

Opposite page, bottom: A framed display of fabrics, displayed on the tripod, intended for the completed project helped inspire workers and interest prospective guests during "Hardhat Tours." TGP

Historical Preservation

GRAND BALLROOM WALNUT PANELING

The restoration of the ballroom was focused on the conservation of the burled walnut panels and reliefs of the surrounding walls. The wall surfaces had become clouded and dull with the deterioration of the varnishes, which had oxidized and were full of soil and other contaminants. The varnish had also softened with age, allowing common airborne dust and grime to attach to it. A series of wood panels were tested to find a cleaning system that would work and still be cost effective and productive.

In some cases, the veneer glues had failed and had to be reattached without damaging the wood or altering the color. This delicate and daunting task included the addition of new panels and treatments to blend in with the period materials. Replacement bronze pieces were replicated by molding existing bronze units and casting them in plastic polymers that were then given an ornamental appearance.

Five people spent five months restoring and conserving the ballroom. Every square inch of wood was cleaned by hand. A wide variety of solvents and twenty pounds of cotton were used to remove the old varnish and soil from the paneled walls. Conservation adherents and techniques reattached the failed glue systems. Three coats of natural varnish were hand applied and polished to achieve the contemporary results that illuminate the historic appearance.

The richness of this room is enhanced and accentuated by the burled accents. This Russian walnut burl is extinct today for commercial purposes. This rare wood came from the valleys of the Circassion Mountains, where the soil contains minerals that lend beautiful colors to the wood. The contrasts between the long, hot summers and the freezing hard winters in these regions result in a hard wood of exceptionally fine grain, strength, and processing quality. Today, this wood is almost extinct and is no longer harvested.

—*Stephen Brown and Tom Vickstrom*

ForrestPerkins also planned and designed the changes to the guest rooms, all of which were gutted. The new bedrooms averaged four hundred seventy-five square feet of luxurious living space and were furnished with reproduction furniture, high ceilings, comfortable beds, and elegant marble bathrooms.[11] The company's intent was to redefine the Hermitage "for its second century as an essential, irreplaceable asset to the city of Nashville and to support the vision of the owners to ascend the ranks of the world's most luxurious hotels."[12]

Above: The outside of the hotel also received a facelift. The view from Union Street offers a study in contrasts with the twenty-seven story Nashville City Center in the background. TGP
Opposite page: Workers implement the new paint scheme for the plaster. TGP

Glory Restored

Illuminating the Past

PAINTED GLASS CEILING

The spacious lobby of The Hermitage Hotel is ornate and magnificent, and its centerpiece is the lighted painted glass ceiling.

The various images featured in the glass panels are based on mythology. At diagonal corners, in the symmetrical design that is a hallmark of Beaux Arts, are griffins, the winged ladies. Muses stand above them. The four stern men's faces are variations on Bacchus, the god of wine. Four round medallions are also present in the design; two are believed to represent the three-faced Janus, who symbolically looks to the past, present, and future. Pan and Mercury are depicted in the other medallions.

The hotel's decorative painted glass is different from stained glass, where different colors of glass are pieced together. In the painted glass process, clear glass is painted on one side in several steps and then fired in a kiln. The finished product allows light to pass through from the opposite side.

The four-part process begins with clear glass that is textured with tiny bubbles; the glass is painted with a black oxide paint mixed with clove oil. The dried paint is mostly scraped away, leaving what is known as the trace. Next, an oxide mixed with gum arabic coats the entire piece. This is known as the matte and is also scraped away to let light penetrate the piece. The third step involves firing the piece in a kiln for the proper time and temperature. Finally, paint is mixed with lavender oil and applied in primary colors of yellow, red, and blue, with overlapping colors producing various shades. The finished piece is fired again. It appears very dark until held up to the light, when the vibrance is evident.

All pieces were removed, cleaned, and numbered. Panes that were unable to be salvaged were replaced, and pieces that had cracked were soldered back together. Approximately three hundred panes were replaced and five hundred originals restored. The center section, which features the hotel's "HH" logo, was created new, since the original center-pieces had been destroyed. A new support system was installed to hold the heavy glass and a lighting system was installed to show the beautiful workmanship. It was upgraded in 2002.

The restoration was a complete success, returning the painted glass ceiling to its former glory and remains as a defining feature of this grand lobby.

—*Tom Vickstrom and Dennis Harmon*

When Dennis Harmon of Emmanuel Studio in Nashville was brought in on the restoration project in 1980, the hotel had been closed for a while and the glass ceiling was in terrible condition. To stop leakage, the glass had been painted over with black tar. The ornate glass could not even be recognized. In addition, a strange brown film covered the entire piece. Analysis soon showed this to be a mixture of nicotine and other contaminants.

Chapter Ten

FULL CIRCLE

The Hermitage reopened its doors on Valentine's Day, February 14, 2003. At the black-tie gala that soon followed, Nashville Mayor Bill Purcell told the crowd of VIPs, "This is a place you are all going to come back to. In fact, I think you all ought to spend the night here tonight." The mayor, who celebrated his wedding reception at the Hermitage in 1986, commented that the Hermitage was a place that had hosted or been witness to the most significant events of both the city's and his personal life.

Good Eats

As for the Capitol Grille, the most recent renovation offered handsome new furniture, restored cornice work, and wall murals depicting the Tennessee State Capitol, the War Memorial Building, and Nashville's Parthenon at Centennial Park.[1] More important for

245

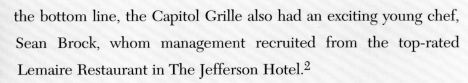

the bottom line, the Capitol Grille also had an exciting young chef, Sean Brock, whom management recruited from the top-rated Lemaire Restaurant in The Jefferson Hotel.[2]

Brock had three cardinal rules: an insistence on discipline, extended hours in the kitchen, and seasonal cooking. The dinner menu changed with each season.

High Honors

The lobby and guest rooms were not the only part of the hotel to be upgraded, however. The Hermitage Hotel's new look included top amenities such as 24-hour room and concierge service, personalized storage trunks for frequent guests, DVD players and complimentary high-speed Internet access in every room, afternoon tea in the lobby, and butler service upon request. In addition, the hotel began offering services especially for pets traveling with their owners. Dogs, which constituted 95 percent of all animals brought to the hotel by guests, could be walked by hotel staff, have treats brought to their rooms, and even dressed in specially made robes. The hotel also began offering a list of pet sitters, groomers, masseuses, and veterinarians if needs for those services arose.[3]

In June 2003, only four months after reopening its doors, the Hermitage was featured in the *Robb Report*, an upscale lifestyle magazine, as one of seven hotels worldwide in its "Best of the Best" issue. The other hotels honored were

Four Seasons Hotel George V in Paris, Four Seasons Hotel Marunouchi in Tokyo, Hotel de Russie in Rome, Grace Bay Club on the Caribbean island of Providenciales, Hotel Bel-Air in California, and WaterColor Inn & Resort in Florida. Sligh called the honor "amazing recognition, especially considering the short amount of time we have been open. This type of prestigious coverage is indicative of the exposure that the Hermitage is bringing to Nashville."[4]

The next honor, notification of which came that November, was the one the hotel's ownership had specifically aimed for back in 2000, when the Richmond group bought the property. This was the AAA's Five Diamond status for 2004. The Hermitage was one of only eighty-two properties in all of North America to hold this distinction.

David Bohan, head of Nashville-based Bohan Advertising/Marketing—which took on the hotel's account in October 2003—also had kind words. He made the point that most AAA Five Diamond properties were either in big cities or were destination resorts. The Hermitage was the only hotel in Nashville and the state of Tennessee to hold the distinction.[5] The Hermitage proved that it was delivering the same high caliber of service that guests at The Jefferson Hotel enjoyed. Hotel officials were not satisfied to rest on their

Opposite page, top: May 2009 Employee Excellence Award winners in the house-keeping department. From left to right: Maria Mora Reyes, Raquel Arevalo, Ana Reyes, Managing Director Greg Sligh, Dolores Abrego, Tammy Price, Olga Grigoreva, and Edgar Lopez. TCV
Opposite page, bottom: May 2009 Employee Excellence Award winners in guest services and the bell staff. From left to right: Managing Director Greg Sligh, David Andrews, Matthew Knott, Ryan Gibbs, Brad Naylor, and Scott Troller. TCV

The Best of the Best

HERMITAGE ACHIEVES HOSPITALITY PINNACLE

Tennessee: the Hermitage, the Madison Hotel in Memphis, and Blackberry Farm in Walland.

In November 2006, the Hermitage solidified its position among America's elite hotels by receiving Mobil's Five Star Award for 2007. This marked the first time a Tennessee hotel had received the prestigious award, and it placed the property among a group of only thirty-seven hotels, inns, and resorts throughout North America. A hotel official said, "This award is affirmation that The Hermitage Hotel's potential has not only been realized, but one of the world's finest properties now calls Nashville home. I am immensely proud of the hotel's team, without whom, none of these accolades would be possible."[7]

Managing Director Greg Sligh said, "This award confirms that it is possible, and even desirable, to combine superior service, modern amenities, and truly gracious southern hospitality."[8] The Hermitage also became one of only twenty-seven North American hotels, inns, and resorts to hold both the Mobil Five Star and the AAA Five Diamond rating awarded by the American Automobile Association. The Hermitage had held the AAA's Five Diamond rating since 2004.

Nashville Mayor Bill Purcell was elated. He said, "This award is much deserved good news for the hotel and for Nashville, further adding to the luster of our hospitality community and our reputation as a leading destination city."[9]

In 2006, there were no other Mobil Five Star or AAA Five Diamond-rated hotels in Alabama, Arkansas, Kentucky,

The Hermitage Hotel "officially" became one of the world's best places to stay when the 2004 AAA Five Diamond ratings were announced in November 2003. Another step forward occurred in October 2005 with the announcement of Mobil Travel Guide's annual rankings. That year, Mobil added nine hotels to its four-star list, and the Hermitage was among them.[6]

The next year, Conde Nast Traveller Gold List of 178 hotels and resorts across the country included three from

Mississippi, or Missouri, not to mention Indiana, Iowa, or Kansas. The closest city to Nashville with a Mobil Five Star or AAA Five Diamond-rated hotel was Atlanta to the east, Denver to the west, and Chicago to the north.[10]

In 2008, The Hermitage Hotel received Mobil's Five Star rating for the second consecutive year. Its sister properties, The Jefferson Hotel in Richmond, Virginia; and The Sanctuary at Kiawah Island Golf Resort near Charleston, South Carolina, also achieved the coveted rating. The Sanctuary for the first time. Also in 2008, the hotel was named to the *Condé Nast Traveller* Gold List; *The Robb Report's* 100 Luxury Hotels; and the *Travel + Leisure* 500. It was the only Tennessee property to make all three lists.[11]

That fall, for the sixth consecutive year, The Hermitage Hotel had once again received the AAA Five Diamond Award. Sligh said, "It is a great honor to retain this recognition. It is a tremendous credit to our staff who work hard to make the Hermitage one of the finest hotels in the world. The hotel has always been our city's premier gathering place, and is now the place for celebrities and dignitaries to stay when visiting Nashville, including during the recent Country Music Awards."[12] The 2009 Mobil Five

Star Award was next received. The awards continue to sustain the pride that so many Nashvillians have long felt for the landmark hotel. These ratings are earned anew each year on their own merits.

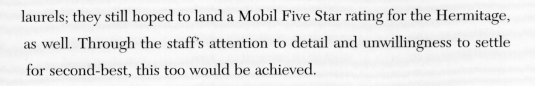

laurels; they still hoped to land a Mobil Five Star rating for the Hermitage, as well. Through the staff's attention to detail and unwillingness to settle for second-best, this too would be achieved.

Saving Room for Dessert

One example of the Hermitage returning to its place as Nashville's center of society came on April 22, 2004. Loretta Lynn, the "coal miner's daughter," was the belle of the ball at an album release party in the opulent lobby of The Hermitage Hotel. Lynn, wearing a sparkling pink ball gown, accepted well wishes from dozens of country music artists, some of the most powerful figures in the music business, and rock and roll protégés. In his introduction, rocker Jack White, called Lynn "the finest female singer-songwriter of the 20th century."

Lynn's upcoming release, *Van Lear Rose*, produced by White, was acclaimed as her richest since 1977. Among the celebrities in attendance were Crystal Gayle; Meg White, White's partner; Lorrie Morgan; Sammy Kershaw; Terri Clark; Lee Ann Womack; Joe Nichols; Chely Wright; Steve Earle; Gretchen Wilson; and Julie Roberts. In addition, several Nashville record label presidents were there, along with Doug Morris, CEO of New York-based Universal Music Group.[13]

The event was simply the latest in a rich catalogue of famous visitors in the hotel's history; others over the years included Greta Garbo, Bette Davis, Mickey Spillane, Tommy Dorsey, Willie Mays, Charlton Heston, Billy Graham, Clint Eastwood, Nancy Sinatra, Danny Glover, Tim Conway, Terry Bradshaw, Jim Varney, Steven Spielberg, Bette Midler, and more.

The spring after Lynn's extravaganza, the Hermitage received another promotional boost when *Executive Traveler* magazine's April/May 2005 edition highlighted the property as one of ten spectacular southeastern retreats.

That year, chef Sean Brock discovered in the magnificent Nashville Public Library, located just one block away, a "Hermitage Grill" menu from the summer of 1941. In the fall, he offered a ten-course menu recreating the historical menu, using the latest culinary techniques available. The menu was served in "tasting portions equal to about three mouthfuls, 'so you'll be able to save room for dessert,'" Brock said.[14]

In 2009, AAA lodging inspectors named The Hermitage Hotel as one of the top ten historic hotel properties in the United States. MEN

The Hermitage also hosted the October celebration launching the Nashville Symphony's 2005–06 season with a black-tie reception. A special guest for the occasion was Leonard Nimoy of *Star Trek* fame. The celebration also would highlight the Symphony's twenty-fifth and last season at the nearby Tennessee Performing Arts Center. The hors d'oeuvres included truffled mushroom crostini and crispy tomato, smoked trout bouchee with corn relish, and glasses of sparkling champagne. The most unusual offerings were the foie gras lollipops coated with pop rocks.[15]

Politicians had long been a mainstay of the hotel, and one contemporary political figure who appreciates the Hermitage is Harold Ford Jr. In 2006, Ford sought the U.S. Senate seat vacated by Sen. Bill Frist. Ford's campaign staff stayed at the Hermitage, and he stayed there whenever he was in Nashville. Ford quickly became a staff favorite. His opponent, Bob Corker of

Chattanooga, eventually won the election. The Tennessee Republican Party held its victory party at the Hermitage, proving the attractiveness of the hotel to both sides of the political coin.

Of Historical Significance

In October 2007, Richard Moe, president of the National Trust for Historic Preservation, and John Ueberroth, chairman and CEO of Preferred Hotel Group, announced a long-term agreement to grow and enhance the Historic Hotels of America. The plan was to add some of the most historic lodgings in the United States—including the Hermitage—to its portfolio. Such famous hotels as the Waldorf-Astoria; the Grand Hotel on Mackinac Island; the Brown Palace Hotel and Spa in Denver; the Peabody in Memphis; and the Greenbrier in White Sulphur Springs, West Virginia were already members of Historic Hotels of America. To be eligible for selection to this prestigious program, a hotel must be at least fifty years old, listed in or eligible for the National Register of Historic Places, or recognized as having historical significance.[16] The Hermitage certainly fit the bill.

In the meantime, changes had taken place in the hotel's kitchen. Chef Sean Brock left in 2006, and Tyler Brown succeeded him. Brown had two goals: to make the restaurant a more frequented destination and to make sure his diners didn't leave hungry.[17] Under Brown, the entrée choices became more reagionalized and robust. His menus usually featured upscale southern foods, as much as possible grown by Tennessee farmers. In June 2006, the Capitol Grille was the only Four Diamond restaurant in the state.

On Friday night, November 30, 2007, the epicurean Les Amis d' Escoffier Society of Nashville held its annual dinner in the 230-seat ballroom. Chef Brown and his young staff prepared an excellent five-course dinner. The California lamb loin with spaghetti squash, pumpkin seed pesto, and tomato confit was a highlight. After dinner, Managing Director Sligh, a member of the society, introduced Brown and his staff and invited the group to return in 2009. He also reminded them that there was an equally excellent hotel above their heads.

Setting the Standard

In keeping with the time, the management of The Hermitage Hotel is sensitive to the fact that, as a highly visible part of the Nashville community, the hotel has an obligation to support its home city and state. In 2008, hotel management signed a

Step into the Men's Room

A STATE-OF-THE-ART DECO MEN'S ROOM

In the summer of 2005, the staff of *Nashville Lifestyles* published a definitive list of the 101 greatest people, places, and things in Music City. The Hermitage Hotel made the list twice. One mention was for the Capitol Grille, and the other, for the hotel's famous green and black Art Deco men's room. Featuring leaded glass tiles, a shoeshine station, and authentic terrazzo floors, the room is in sharp contrast to the rest to the hotel's Beaux Arts classicism. Many say it was 1940s manager William "Bill" Caldwell who made the choice; apparently a fan of the color green, he also was credited with painting the hotel lobby walls with the shade. Over time, though the hotel went through numerous renovations and updates, the one-of-a-kind bathroom remained.

In 2008, restroom hygiene products company Cintas Facilities Services held its seventh annual Best Restroom in America Contest. Tens of thousands of people participated in the online contest, and the Hermitage space won. Its unusual charm has made it the perfect picture spot for bridal pictures and music videos, and it's believed to have been seen by more women than any other men's bathroom in the city.

partnership agreement with Land Trust for Tennessee to encourage guests to donate to the conservation organization. The hotel began collecting two dollars a night from guests for each night of their stay to benefit the trust, which protects more than 32,000 acres in the state. Though the charge is optional, few guests object. It seems appropriate that the Hermitage would be the first hotel in Tennessee to adopt the program, projected to raise $50,000 a year. That's an amount sufficient to cover the cost of preserving approximately 500 acres.[18]

None should understand better than those at The Hermitage Hotel, after all, the importance of preservation. Within the hotel, a "green" program has been implemented as well.

It's All About Our Guests

While staying at this hotel, guests enjoy a refined and genuine feeling of hospitality; a welcome sense of being at home away from home. This pleasant experience is a synergistic blend; the combined effect of dedicated efforts by all employee associates, who greet guests by name, and who carry out their chosen specialties with skill, organization, and consistency. It is the spacious, refreshing guest room and the elegance of a fabulously comfortable bed, with its six-hundred-thread-count Italian sheets, the down-filled duvet comforter, and the choice of pillows. It is the plush towels, fresh cut flowers, the freshly baked turndown treats placed on the nightstand. Special touches are everywhere, from complimentary afternoon cookies with cider or lemonade in the lobby to the lasting satisfaction of a remarkably fine culinary experience.

Full Circle

In a sense, the hotel has come full circle. Wireless Internet service today is offered where "telephone in every room" was once proudly announced.

The 1930's "radio in every room" has evolved to the Ipod docking station and music CD player. Sophisticated women business travelers stay in the very rooms where impassioned suffrage battles were waged for equal rights so many years ago. While time marches on, The Hermitage Hotel offers a place for new memories to be made; a splendid setting for events that too, shall evolve into history. For those new chapters not yet written, the Hermitage opens its doors and offers its hand in welcome.

A century ago, business leader Edward Stahlman spoke to the members of Nashville's Board of Trade and original stockholders:

It will be as handsome a structure as this part of the country can boast, and will be a credit to Nashville as well as a lasting monument and source of profit to the people who aided in making it possible. . . . Gentlemen, the clouds have broken and the sun of prosperity and success now beams upon us. . . . We were actuated by a spirit of determination which has carried us onward and upwards, and now, I repeat, the clouds have broken and the sunbeams are bathing us in rich, warm floods of light that will linger when we who are here to-night shall have passed into the great beyond.[19]

More recently, Jeff Bradford, president and CEO of PR firm The Bradford Group, said, "We were honored when The Hermitage Hotel asked our firm to assist them in creating a celebration of the hotel's centennial anniversary. . . . The more we learned about the Hermitage's storied history, as well as its present day magnificence, the more excited we got."

As The Hermitage Hotel commemorates the one hundredth anniversary of its September 17, 1910 opening, Nashvillians take enormous pride in the fact that this "Grand Old Lady" is still here—just as extravagant, just as beautiful, and just as welcoming as it was when its doors first opened. From its opulent beginnings as Nashville's first million-dollar hotel to its resurgence as Nashville's first five-star hotel, truly, The Hermitage Hotel is one of America's finest.

Appendix A

FAMOUS GUESTS OF THE HERMITAGE HOTEL

Acuff, Roy
Albright, Madeleine
Anderson, Bill
Anderson, John
Anderson, Pamela
Armstrong, Lance
Armstrong, Neil
Arnold, Eddy
Atkins, Chet
Autry, Gene
Avalon, Frankie
Baez, Joan
Bankhead, Tallulah
Barrymore, Drew
Beatty, Ned
Black, Clint
Bloom, Orlando
Bolton, Michael
Bon Jovi, John
Bono
Boy George
Bradshaw, Terry
Brokaw, Tom
Bryant, Paul "Bear"
Brynner, Yul
Burnett, T-Bone
Burnette, Smiley
Campbell, Glen
Cannon, Sarah
  (Minnie Pearl)
Capone, Al
Carlin, George

Carter, Jimmy
Carter, Lynda
Caruso, Enrico
Cash, Johnny
Catt, Carrie Chapman
Channing, Carol
Chong, Tommy
Cher
Chester, Bob
Clark, Terri
Clement, Bob
Clement, Frank G.
Clement, Lucille
Clinton, Bill
Cocker, Joe
Colter, Jessi
Conway, Tim
Cooper, Prentice
Corker, Bob
Craig, Francis
Crosby, Bing
Crow, Sheryl
Crowe, Russell
Cruise, Tom
Crump, Edward Hull
  "Boss"
Cyrus, Miley
Davis, Bette
Day, Dorothy
Day, Doris
Dempsey, Jack
Dewey, Thomas E.

Diamond Rio
Diaz, Cameron
Dillinger, John
Dixie Chicks
Dorsey, Jimmy
Dorsey, Tommy
Dudley, Ed
Duff, Hillary
Duffy, Patrick
Earle, Steve
Eastwood, Clint
Ellington, Buford
Esiason, Boomer
Fisk Jubilee Singers
Fontaine, Joan
Ford, Harold, Jr.
Foxx, Jamie
Frampton, Peter
Franklin, Aretha
Frist, Bill
Galway, Sir James
Garbo, Greta
Gates, Bill
Gatlin, Larry &
  The Gatlin Brothers
Gaul, Gilbert
Gayle, Crystal
George, Eddie
Gibson, Mel
Gleaves, Albert
Glenn, John
Glover, Danny

Goodman, Benny
Gore Sr., Albert
Gossett, Louis, Jr.
Graham, Billy
Gray, Glen
Gumbel, Bryant
Hamilton, Scott
Hayes, Helen
Hayes, Isaac
Henley, Don
Hepburn, Katharine
Herman, Woody
Heston, Charlton
Hill, Faith
Hillary, Sir Edmund
Hilton, Paris
Hines, Duncan
Hoffa, Jimmy
Hooper, Ben W.
Hudson, Kate
Jackson, Jesse
Jackson, Michael
Jennings, Waylon
Jewel
Joel, Billy
Johnson, Lyndon B.
Johnson, Magic
Johnson, Woody
Jolson, Al
Jordan, Michael
Judd, Naomi
Judd, Wynonna

Kallen, Kitty
Keith, David
Keith, Toby
Kennedy, John F.
Kennedy, Rose
Kenton, Stan
Kerry, John
Kershaw, Sammy
Kidman, Nicole
King, Don
King, Larry
King, Wayne
Krauss, Alison
Kristofferson, Kris
Lanson, Snooky
Lee, Brenda
Lindsey, George
Linkletter, Art
Lithgow, John
Loggins, Kenny
Lombardo, Guy
Long, Howie
Long, Huey
Lucas, George
Lusky, Jesse
Lynn, Loretta
MacArthur, Douglas
Maher, Bill
Mandrell, Barbara
Mandrell, Louise
Marin, Cheech
Martin, Steve

Martinelli, Giovanni
Mays, Willie
McAlister, Hill
McCord, Jim Nance
McCormick, Marie
McCullough, David
McDowell, Ronnie
McEntire, Reba
McKellar, Kenneth
McWherter, Ned Ray
Mellencamp, John
Melton, James
Messina, Jo Dee
Michaels, Al
Midler, Bette
Minnesota Fats
Moe, Richard
Montana, Joe
Montgomery, John
   Michael
Moore, Grace
Morgan, Lorrie
Morgan, Louie
Morris, Doug
Murray, Anne
Murray, Bill

Nelson, Byron
Nelson, Willie
Newhart, Bob
Nichols, Joe
Nicks, Stevie
Nimoy, Leonard
Nixon, Richard
Orman, Suze
Parker, Fess
Parton, Dolly
Parton, Stella
Paul, Les
Peay, Austin
Petty, Tom
Pines, Lily
Plant, Robert
Presley, Elvis
Presley, Lisa Marie
Rather, Dan
Richie, Lionel
Rickenbacker, Eddie
Ritter, John
Roberts, A. H.
Roberts, Julie
Rock, Kid
Romero, Cesar

Ronstadt, Linda
Roosevelt, Eleanor
Roosevelt, Franklin D.
Sanders, Deion
Sasser, Jim
Scott, Willard
Seals, Dan
Seger, Bob
Seymour, Jane
Shaw, Victoria
Shea, George Beverly
Shatner, William
Shields, Brooke
Shore, Dinah
Simmons, Gene
Simpson, Jessica
Sinatra, Nancy
Skaggs, Ricky
Skelton, Red
Smith, Alfred E.
Snow, Hank
Spacek, Sissy
Spielberg, Steven
Spillane, Mickey
Springer, Jerry
Springsteen, Bruce

Starr, Bart
Stevenson, Alexandra
Sting
Stuart, Marty
Sullivan, Steve
Swanson, Gloria
Swift, Taylor
Taft, William Howard
Talley, James
Theismann, Joe
Thomas, B.J.
Thomas, Woody
Thompson Twins
Timberlake, Justin
Tracy, Spencer
Travis, Randy
Tubb, Ernest
Tucker, Tanya
Turner, Tina
Twain, Shania
Twitty, Conway
Underwood, Carrie
Urban, Keith
Varney, Jim
Wallace, George
Walsh, Joe

White, Jack
White, Meg
Whiteman, Paul
Williams, Hank
Williams, Hank, Jr.
Williams, Paul
Williams, Robin
Williams, Vanessa
Wilson, Gretchen
Wilson, Woodrow
Winfrey, Oprah
Wiseman, Tom
Witherspoon, Reese
Womack, Lee Ann
Wonder, Stevie
Wright, Chely
Yamaguchi, Kristi
York, Alvin
Young, Neil
Zellweger, Renée
ZZ Top & Billy
   Gibbons

MANAGERS OF THE HERMITAGE HOTEL

1910–1912	Timothy Murphy		1975	Sam Bass
1912–1913	Hugh F. Galvin		1976–1977	Leroy Arnold
1914–1917	Hugh F. Galvin; Homer Wilson		1978–1980	Hotel closed
1918	Homer Wilson; Robert E. Hyde		1980–1983	Dennis E. Morgan
1919–1927	Robert E. Hyde		1983–1985	Bruce Bommarito; Allen Lonstron
1928	Joseph L. Tall		1986	Allen Lonstron; Paul Kraft
1929–1946	Howard E. Baughman		1987	Stan Ockwig; Matthew Thomas
1946–1949	William H. "Bill" Caldwell		1988	Matthew Thomas; Robert Adams III
1949–1953	Edward T. Doty		1989	Vende Morris
1953–1954	J. William Cole		1990	Ron Sedden; James Braden; Doug Vandenberg
1954	J. William Cole; George A. Scharf			
1955–1956	George A. Scharf		1991–1994	Doug Vandenberg
1956–1968	Richard R. "Dick" Hall		1994–1996	Richard Markham
1968–1969	J. Richard McGoldrick		1997	Richard Markham; Jeff Wagner
1970	John Dewey; Richard Barney; Leon Womble		1998	Jeff Wagner; Eric Smith
			1999	Eric Smith; Hugh Harper
1971	Leon Womble		2000	Hugh Harper; Teresa Silo
1972	Jack Grigsby		2001	Teresa Silo
1973	James E. Arnold; Bill Boswell		2002	Teresa Silo; Greg Sligh
1974	Bill Boswell; Russell Nichol; Sam Bass		2002–2009	Greg Sligh

SISTER PROPERTIES

The Jefferson

RICHMOND, VIRGINIA

Since 1895, The Jefferson Hotel has been recognized by travelers as one of the finest in America. Known for its genuinely friendly service, luxurious guestrooms, breathtaking architecture, and elegant décor, The Jefferson is proud to be one of the few hotels in North America to hold both the Mobil Five Star and the AAA Five Diamond awards. Guests of The Jefferson enjoy a variety of amenities and services, including two award-winning restaurants. Located in downtown Richmond, The Jefferson is just blocks from the state capital, historic Shockoe Slip, and the financial district. The Jefferson features 226 guest rooms, 36 suites, and more than 26,000 square feet of meeting space, perfect for private executive retreats or grand events.

Like The Hermitage Hotel, The Jefferson is resplendent with legendary stories throughout its rich history. The hotel opened on Halloween to host out-of-town guests attending the wedding of Miss Irene Langhorne and illustrator Dana Charles Gibson. Mrs. Gibson would later become known as The Gibson Girl. Twelve U.S. presidents have visited, along with an impressive list of celebrities, entertainers, and dignitaries. Perhaps the most renowned guests of the hotel, however, are the alligators that roamed the Palm Court lobby until 1948.

Kiawah Island Golf Resort

CHARLESTON, SOUTH CAROLINA

Just over the horizon from historic Charleston, an island of spectacular natural beauty rests between the winding Kiawah River and a pristine stretch of Atlantic Ocean beach. Kiawah Island Golf Resort welcomes you to relax in an environment enhanced by an unwavering commitment to excellence. In addition to ten miles of pristine beach, activities abound on the island, including five championship golf courses, twenty-eight tennis courts, thirty miles of paved bike trails, nature tours, and an award-winning children's program.

Lodging choices include The Sanctuary at Kiawah Island Golf Resort, an oceanfront luxury hotel and recipient of both the prestigious Mobil Five Star and AAA Five Diamond awards. The Sanctuary features two hundred forty-two spacious guest rooms and thirteen suites, distinctive dining, a Lowcountry-inspired spa, and fine shops.

Other resort accommodations include four hundred ninety-five villas and ninety private homes in ocean view, near beach and scenic settings, providing guests with all of the conveniences of home as well as the services and amenities of an award-winning resort.

The Sea Pines Resort

HILTON HEAD, SOUTH CAROLINA

The Sea Pines Resort on Hilton Head Island has welcomed guests for more than fifty years. This original Hilton Head Island resort sits on five thousand oceanfront acres and is home of the annual Verizon Heritage PGA golf tournament. Guests can enjoy unparalleled golf, award-winning tennis, world-class luxury accommodations, and gourmet restaurants.

The Sea Pines Resort offers a broad range of accommodations which cater to every taste. From The Inn at Harbour Town to luxurious vacation homes for two to twelve guests, options of virtually every shape and size are available.

Notes

Chapter One

1. "Hotel Money Is Secured," *Nashville Banner*, June 3, 1908.

2. Earlier, on November 1, 1907, realtor Claude C. Christopher had purchased for Carpenter and his associates the home of Dr. and Mrs. Henry W. Morgan at 227 Sixth Avenue North.

3. "Work to Begin on New Hotel," *Nashville Banner*, June 5, 1908.

4. "Stockholders of Hermitage Hotel," *Nashville Banner*, June 10, 1908.

5. Mrs. Huxable's undated article in the *New York Times*. Copy in the Nashville Room at the Nashville Public Library.

6. "World's Columbian Exposition," Encyclopedia of Chicago, http://www.encyclopedia.chicagohistory.org/pages/1386.html, accessed March 18, 2009.

7. Joe Sherman, *A Thousand Voices: The Story of Nashville's Union Station* (Nashville: Rutledge Hill Press, 1987), 17.

8. Jane Turner, ed., *The Dictionary of Art*, vol. 3 (New York: Oxford University Press), 464.

9. Kay Beasley, Nashville's Past, "The Old Maxwell House in Its Heyday," *Nashville Banner*, June 25, 1986.

10. Kay Beasley, Nashville's Past, "Hotel Gave Comfort Without Extravagance," *Nashville Banner*, September 23, 1987.

11. "Hotel Hermitage, Nashville, Tennessee," Travelers' Protective Association of America, *Commercial History of the State of Tennessee*, 1910, 193–4.

12. Hart Freeland Roberts, Inc., archival material.

13. Ibid.

14. Conversation, author with Walker Mathews, president, R. C. Mathews Contractor, December 18, 2007.

15. Advertisements, *The Nashville American*, September 16, 1910, and *The Nashville Tennessean*, September, 18, 1910.

16. "A Statement by the Board of Directors of the Nashville YMCA," *Nashville Banner*, February 26, 1912.

17. "Stockholders of Hermitage Hotel," *Nashville Banner*, June 10, 1908.

18. "Hotel Hermitage, Nashville, Tennessee," Travelers' Protective Association of America, *Commercial History of the State of Tennessee, 1910*, 188–89.

19. "Opening of a Great Hotel," *Nashville Banner*, September 19, 1910.

20. Ibid.

21. "Diners at the New Hotel," *The Nashville Tennessean*, September 18, 1910.

22. "Opening of a Great Hotel," *Nashville Banner*, September 19, 1910.

23. Ibid.; "Hermitage Hotel Will Open Today," *The Nashville Tennessean*, September 17, 1910.

24. Undated newspaper article, 1910. Copy in collection of the author. Two of the elevators in the lobby, across from the check-in station, were for guests, while the other two, located near the alley entrance, were for service personnel, luggage, and freight.

25. James Somerville, *The Carmack-Cooper Shooting: Tennessee Politics Turns Violent November 9, 1908* (Jefferson, N.C.: McFarland and Co., 1994), 15–16.

26. Ibid., 108, 123, 130, 132.

27. "The Hermitage Hotel History," *NASHVILLE*, February/March 2003.

28. Ibid.

29. Conversation, author with John Powers, director of engineering at the Hermitage, October 10, 2007.

30. Clara Hieronymus, "Hermitage Hotel: Fine Beaux-Arts Classicism," *The Tennessean*, August 24, 1980.

31. "The Hermitage: Days of Grandeur," *The Tennessean*, July 3, 1977.

32. The names of the managers came from the Nashville City Directories of 1913, 1914, and 1916.

J. E. R. Carpenter

1. Carroll Van West, ed., "J. Edwin R. Carpenter," in *Tennessee Encyclopedia of History and Culture* (Nashville: Rutledge Hill Press, 1998), 126.

2. "Work Is Being Pushed on J. Rosenthal's New Home," *Columbia Herald*, July 1893.

3. Van West, *Tennessee Encyclopedia*, 126.

4. Andrew Alpern, *The New York Apartment Houses of Rosario Candela and James Carpenter* (New York: Acanthus Press, 2001), 16–17.

5. Ibid., 17.

6. Ibid., 28.

7. Ibid., 20–21.

Chapter 2

1. "President Taft's Visit Like a Homecoming," *The Nashville Tennessean*, November 10, 1911.

2. A. Elizabeth Taylor, *The Woman Suffrage Movement in Tennessee* (New York: Bookman Associates, 1957), 15, 17–18.

3. Editorial, *The Nashville Tennessean*, 1911.

4. *Sadie Remembers*, remembrances of Mrs. George Augustine Frazer (1885–1974), 128–31. Copy in collection of the author.

5. "Jackson Day Is Observed in Nashville," *The Nashville Tennessean and The Nashville American*, January 10, 1911.

6. Ibid.

7. "Brilliant Ball Celebrates One Hundredth Anniversary," *The Nashville Tennessean and The Nashville American*, January 9, 1915.

8. "Cheers Greet Suffragette Procession," *The Nashville Tennessean and The Nashville American*, May 3, 1914.

9. "My First Century," reminiscences of Frances Bond Davis on the occasion of her one hundredth birthday, copy in collection of the author.

10. *Women's Protest*, vol. 9 No. 1, 13; Interview of A. Elizabeth Taylor with Josephine Pearson, February 7, 1943.

11. "Improvements at Hermitage Hotel," *Nashville Banner*, February 28, 1918.

12. "State Hotel Men Adopt Sugar Rule," *Nashville Banner,* July 10, 1918.

13. "Suffragists in Annual Session," *The Nashville Tennessean*, January 23, 1919.

14. Also in the parade were 140 Tennesseans and Alabamans from the famed "Rainbow" and "Wildcat" Divisions and the 306 trench motor battery of the 30th Division.

15. "The 114th Field Artillery Given Ovation by Grateful People," *The Nashville Tennessean*, April 1, 1919.

16. Information from Graham C. Boettcher, PhD, the William Cary Hulsey Curator of American Art, Birmingham Museum of Art.

17. "Civil War Art that Graced Local Hotel Now in Birmingham," *The Tennessean*, July 14, 2004.

18. "City Honors Distinguished Son," *Nashville Banner*, April 7, 1919.

19. Carol Lynn Yellin and Janann Sherman, *The Perfect 36: Tennessee Delivers Woman Suffrage* (Oak Ridge, Tenn.: Iris Press, 1998), 75.

20. Ibid., 77.

21. Ibid., 78–79.

22. Ibid., 83, 86–87.

23. Ibid., 81, 83, 86–87.

24. Ibid., 88.

25. Ibid., 88–89.

26. Ibid., 89.

27. "At Hotel Hermitage," *The Nashville Tennessean and The Nashville American*, October 11, 1911.

28. *All Together: A History of the Nashville YMCA 1875–1975*, 37.; "Woodrow Wilson Guest of YMCA To-day," *Nashville Banner*, February 24, 1912.

29. Nashville Public Library, Weakley Scrapbook, Box 1, 106.

30. "Program Announced for Rotary Meeting," *The Nashville Tennessean*, February 7, 1919.

31. "Architects in Annual Meeting," *Nashville Banner*, April 30, 1919.

32. Jack Norman Sr., *The Nashville I Knew* (Nashville: Rutledge Hill Press, 1984), 16.

33. Taylor, *The Woman Suffrage Movement in Tennessee*, 110.

34. Yellin and Sherman, *The Perfect 36*, 96–97.

35. Ibid., 97.

36. Ibid., 99–100.

37. Ibid., 101.

38. The word "lobbyist" was coined at the Willard Hotel in Washington, D.C. when U.S. Grant was president. Those who hoped to influence the president hung around the Willard lobby. Consequently, they became known as "lobbyists."

39. Yellin and Sherman, *The Perfect 36*, 103.

40. Ibid.

41. Hotel menu, March 1913.

42. In a February 28, 1918 article on the Hermitage Hotel in the *Nashville Banner*, the writer quoted manager Homer Wilson as saying, "Mr. Meyer operates the Hermitage." Each year, from 1914 until 1936, the Hermitage's ad in the Nashville City Directory stated that Meyer Hotels was lessee for the Hermitage.

43. "Hotel Manager Brands Story False," *Nashville Banner*, April 30, 1919.

44. Yellin and Sherman, *The Perfect 36*, 104.

45. Ibid., 106.

46. Ibid., 106–7.

47. Ibid., 107.

48. "Roberts Certifies Ratification," *Nashville Banner*, August 24, 1920.

Chapter 3

1. "On the Trail of Al Capone," *Sunday Express* newspaper (United Kingdom), Travel Section, July 22, 2007.

2. Wikipedia, the free encyclopedia, Al Capone, "Capone's Wealth and Power Grows in Chicago."

3. Jack Norman Sr., *The Nashville I Knew* (Nashville: Rutledge Hill Press, 1984), 68.

4. Conversation, author with Elizabeth Craig Proctor, July 2007.

5. Undated brochure on Nashville Hotels, vertical file, Nashville Room, Nashville Public Library.

6. Roger Biles, *Memphis In The Great Depression* (Knoxvillle, TN: University of Tennessee Press, 1986), 34.

7. William D. Miller, *Mr. Crump of Memphis* (Baton Rouge: Louisiana State University Press, 1964), 129.

8. Memories of Joel Ralph Lamphere, Atlanta, Georgia, January 2003.

9. Larry Schwartz, "Defeats Didn't Dampen Dempsey," ESPN, /sportscentury/features/00014146.html, accessed March 19, 2009.

10. Sam Davis Hotel brochure, 1932, collection of the author.

11. Hotel menu, February 27, 1923.

12. Advertisement, 1930 Nashville City Directory.

13. "The Hermitage Days of Grandeur," *The Tennessean*, July 3, 1977.

14. Rich Riebeling, "Hermitage Tenants in State of Shock," *Nashville Banner*, July 1, 1977.

15. Davidson County Deed, Book 855, 524.

16. "American Opens New Office," *Nashville Banner*, April 7, 1958.

17. Dary Matera, *John Dillinger: The Life and Death of America's First Celebrity Criminal* (New York: Carroll & Graft Publishers, 2005), 153.

18. "Child, 2, Drops Seven Floors: Saved by Fall on Pedestrian," *The Nashville Tennessean*, August 2, 1927; Rilla R. Moran, "Ninety Feet to Fame," *The Nashville Tennessean Magazine*, April 22, 1962.

19. Conversation, author with Robert A. Brandt Jr., September 20, 2007.

20. *The Nashville Tennessean*, January 16, 1936; *Nashville Banner,* January 17, 1936.

21. Reminiscences of Bob Pardue.

22. Kay Russell, "Nashville Past," *Nashville Banner*; *The Nashville Tennessean,* October 27, 1983.

23. "Huey's 'Game Wardens' to Guard Wildlife as Huey's Hordes Prepare for Nashville," *The Nashville Tennessean*, October 26, 1934.

24. "Huey's Men Nashville Bound in Six Special Railroad Trains," *The Nashville Tennessean*, October 27, 1934.

25. "Friendship for Dan McGugin and Russ Cohen Brought Huey Long and Horde from Louisiana," *The Nashville Tennessean*, October 28, 1934.

26. Joe Hatcher, *The Tennessean*, July 10, 1977; T. Harry Williams, *Huey Long* (New York: Alfred A. Knopf, 1970), 602; Miller, *Mr. Crump of Memphis*, 230.

27. Conversation, author with Peggy Henry Joyce, September 15, 2007.

28. Conversation, author with Mrs. James H. Hasson Jr., June 7, 2007.

29. David Logsdon, "History Will Kick Up Heels at Hermitage," *Nashville Banner*, January 15, 1992.

30. Written reminiscences of Herschel Robert "Bob" Pardue, 2006.

31. Ibid.

32. *The Nashville Tennessean*, June 1938.

33. Conversation, author with Peggy Henry Joyce, September 15, 2007

34. Pat Welch, "No Darn Use to Quit Tears Now," *The Nashville Tennessean*, October 20, 1966.

35. Written remembrances of Bob Pardue, 2006.

36. Ibid.

37. Ibid.

38. John M. Burns, "Howes Likens Roosevelt Administration to Jackson's; 'No Retreat' on Principles," *The Nashville Tennessean*, January 8, 1939.

39. "Rickenbacker Urges New Air Routes Here," *Nashville Banner*, March 21, 1939.

40. Miller, *Mr. Crump*, 278.

41. Peter Mikelbank, "What a Bellman Knew," *Nashville* Magazine, September 1986.

Francis Craig

1. Robert W. Ikard, *Near You: Francis Craig, Dean of Southern Maestros* (Franklin, TN: Hillsboro Press, 1999), 1, 5, 16.

NOTES

2. Ibid., 18, 21.

3. Ibid., 30.

4. Powell Stamper, *The National Life Story* (New York: Appleton-Century-Crofts, 1968), 122.

5. Ibid., 120–22.

6. "Beasley Smith's Orchestra to Play," *Nashville Banner*, October 4, 1925; "Francis Craig's Orchestra to Play for WSM Opening," *Nashville Banner*, October 4, 1925.

7. Craig Havighurst, *Air Castle of the South: WSM and the Making of Music City* (University of Illinois Press, Urbana and Chicago, 2007), 16.

8. Stamper, *The National Life Story*, 123.

9. Ikard, *Near You*, 41.

10. Ibid., 49, 55, 57, 61.

11. Ibid., 61, 65–66.

12. "'Pee Wee' Is Engaged by Craig's Orchestra Here," *Nashville Banner or The Nashville Tennessean*, undated, collection of Donia Craig Dickerson, Nashville.

13. Ikard, *Near You*, 143.

14. Ibid., 144.

15. "Melton Welcomed by Many Friends; Praises Teacher," *Nashville Banner*, November 26, 1935.

16. Conversation, author with Jane Graham McKay, September 16, 2007.

17. Ikard, *Near You*, 71.

18. Ibid., 72.

19. "Season's First Debut Ball Attended by Out-of-Town Guests," *Nashville Banner*, December 28, 1938.

20. "Brilliant Debut Ball Is Given for Miss Fort," *Nashville Banner*, December 30, 1938.

21. Ikard, *Near You*, 84.

22. "Whiteman Sees Horses; No Purchase Yet," *Nashville Banner*, March 27, 1946.

23. "Francis Craig's New Tune, 'Near You' Sensational Nation-wide Hit," *The Ragland Reporter*, October 1947.

24. "Craig Tops Hit List Parade with 'Near You,'" C. A. "Neil" Craig II, collection of Donia Craig Dickerson, Nashville.

25. Ikard, *Near You*, 119, 121, 124.

Chapter 4

1. "'Community Concerts,' New Drive Opens," *Nashville Banner*, March 3, 1942.

2. Ridley Wills II, *Yours to Count On* (Nashville: Vanderbilt University, 2007), 28.

3. Letter, John B. Nixon to the author, September 5, 2008.

4. "Bing's Personality Puts Bond Auction Over with a Bang," *Nashville Banner*, June 2, 1943.

5. Conversation, author with Lynne Wallman, March 26, 2008.

6. Pete Wills was assistant manager of the Hermitage in 1943. One of his responsibilities was to make arrangements when dance bands stayed at the hotel.

7. Conversation, author with Patti Hardison Geltz, Monteagle, Tennessee, summer 2006.

8. Interview, Tom Vickstrom with Horace Bornstein, Stone Mountain, Georgia, September 2005.

9. "Food Expert Hines Finds Ladies Skills on Upgrade," *Nashville Banner*, September 16, 1953.

10. "Improvements Slated for Hotel," *The Nashville Tennessean*, April 25, 1946.

11. "Hotel Man Named Honorary Colonel," *Nashville Banner*, April 26, 1946.

12. Margaret L. Phillips, *The Governors of Tennessee* (Gretna, LA: Pelican Publishing Co., 1978), 158; "State and County Give Democrats Big Majorities," *Nashville Banner*, November 3, 1948.

13. Craig Havighurst, *Air Castle of the South*, 142.

14. "Reception to be Given January 25 at Hermitage for Nashville Civic Music Association Members," *The Nashville Tennessean*, January 2, 1947.

15. "Named to Staff of Hermitage Hotel," *Nashville Banner*, December 30, 1948.

16. "W. H. 'Bill' Caldwell Quits Hermitage Hotel," *The Nashville Tennessean*, October 25, 1949.

17. Reminiscences of Bob Pardue.

18. Conversation, author with Robert P. Banniza, September 2, 2007.

19. Conversation, author with Thomas Wiseman Jr., November 20, 2007.

20. Conversation, author with Peggy Henry Joyce, February 4, 2008.

21. Amy Lynch, *Service Above Self: A History of Nashville Rotary* (Springfield, IL: Phillips Brothers, 1995), 143.

22. "Hermitage Hotel to Refinish Front," *The Nashville Tennessean*, October 31, 1951.

23. "Hermitage Building Ready by Feb. 15," *The Nashville Tennessean*, March 15, 1952.

24. Written reminiscences of Bob Pardue, 2006.

25. Marie Bankhead Owen, *The Story of Alabama: A History of the State* (New York: Lewis Historical Pub. Co., 1949), 1282.

26. "Nixon Predicts 'Democratic' Bolt," *The Nashville Tennessean*, September 28, 1952.

27. Conversation, Hermitage Controller Tom Vickstrom with Lannie Neal, July 7, 2005.

28. Mrs. Donna S. Sepull, of Edgewater, Maryland, found the picture in a thrift shop in Williamsburg, Virginia. Having stayed at the Hermitage in 1971, she felt that it should be returned to the hotel, and did so in 2007.

29. "J. William Cole New Manager of Hermitage Hotel," *Nashville Banner*, January 14, 1953.

30. Remembrances of Bob Pardue, 2006.

31. Ibid.

32. Conversation, Tom Vickstrom with the Davenports, October 26, 2008.

33. Conversation, author with Judge Thomas A. Wiseman Jr., November 20, 2007.

34. Phillips, *The Governors of Tennessee* (Gretna, LA: Pelican Publishing Co., 1978), 165; Lee Seifert Greene, *Lead Me On, Frank G. Clement and Tennessee Politics* (Knoxville: Univ. of Tennessee Press, 1982), 62.

35. Mark Newman, "The Catholic Church in Tennessee and Desegregation, 1954–1973," *Tennessee Historical Quarterly*, Vol. 66, Summer 2007, 148.

36. "Burton Takes Hermitage Post," *The Nashville Tennessean*, October 3, 1956.

37. "Meeting Called on Hotel Sale," *The Nashville Tennessean*, October 6, 1955.

38. "Hermitage Hotel Building for Sale," *Nashville Banner*, October 14, 1955.

39. Davidson County Deed 362, 454.

40. Ross Fitzgerald, "Hermitage Hotel $2 Million Sale Thursday Due," *Nashville Banner*, May 29, 1956.

41. "Hotel Sale to Alsonett Completed," *Nashville Banner*, June 1, 1956.

42. Ross Fitzgerald, "Hall Leaves Maxwell House to Take Hermitage Post," *Nashville Banner*, June 5, 1956.

43. Dr. Michael Birdwell, "Alvin Cullum York," SgtYork.Org, accessed March 19, 2009.

44. John Perry, *Sgt. York His Life, Legacy & Legend* (Nashville: Broadman and Holman Publishers, 1997), 96–97.

45. Ibid., 108–12.

46. "Sergt. York Home, His Girl Says Yes," *New York Times*, May 31, 1919.

47. "Wedding Bells for Sergt. York," *Nashville Banner*, June 7, 1919.

48. "York Returns to Pall Mall," *Nashville Banner*, June 12, 1919.

49. Perry, *Sgt. York*, 265–66.

50. "York Picture, York Avenue. York Day Feature Fair, Preview Here," *The Nashville Tennessean*, September 19, 1942.

51. Perry, *Sgt. York*, 278, 283.

52. Ibid., 284.

Chapter 5

1. Reminiscences by Grace Ward Hall, August 20, 2007.

2. "Mae Boren Axton," Oklahoma Music Hall of Fame, http://oklahoma musichalloffame.com/news/Inductees/MaeBorenAxton-2-1.html, accessed March 19, 2009.

3. "American Opens New Office," *Nashville Banner*, April 7, 1958.

4. 1959 Map of Downtown Nashville, Freeman Webb Co. Realtors.

5. "Flames Damage Hermitage Hotel Manager Suite," *Nashville Banner*, November 20, 1957.

6. "Boy, 3, Loses Clothes in Hermitage Blaze," *The Nashville Tennessean*, November 21, 1957.

7. Conversation, author with Peggy Henry Joyce, September 15, 2007.

8. Neil Cunningham, "Thousands Jam Hotel for Ellington HQ Opening," *Nashville Banner*, May 2, 1958.

9. Neil Cunningham, "First Governor Here for Parley," *The Nashville Tennessean*, September 25, 1961; "World Crisis in Governor's Spotlight," *Nashville Banner*, September 25, 1961.

10. "Nashville Business Day," *Nashville Banner*, July 8, 1958.

11. "Governor, Wife, Serenade Jockeys," *The Nashville Tennessean*, November 9, 1958.

12. Joe Hatcher, "Voices in Old Hotels," *The Tennessean*, July 10, 1977.

13. "Rubbing Elbows with Presidents," *The Tennessean*, July 5, 1987.

14. Conversation, author with Robert P. Banniza, September 3, 2007.

15. David Halberstam, "Tells Tennessee GOP Unaware of Future," *The Nashville Tennessean*, September 22, 1960; Julie Hollabaugh, "Senator's Mom Charms Nashville," *The Nashville Tennessean*, October 6, 1960.

16. "Buys Champion," *Nashville Banner*, December 10, 1960.

17. Marshall Morgan, "Culinary Architect Whips Up Sugary, Tiny Village, Gingerbread Houses," *Nashville Banner*, December 11, 1956.

18. Reminiscences by Grace Ward Hall, August 20, 2007.

19. "Big Brothers Bids Garner $24,122 for Poor," *The Nashville Tennessean*, December 12, 1961.

20. "Negroes Try Entry Into Hotels Here," *Nashville Banner*, February 1, 1962.

21. "Attempt to Integrate Hotel Here Fails," *Nashville Banner*, February 15, 1962.

22. Reminiscences of Jeanne and Bob Dudley Smith. Copy in collection of the author.

23. "ETC Winter Dance," *Nashville Banner*, December 14, 1962.

24. "Allen Headquarters Will Open Monday," *The Nashville Tennessean*, August 25, 1962.

25. "Plush Hotel Roof Club Eyed for Nashville," *Nashville Banner*, October 6, 1962.

26. Dolph Honicker, "Hillary Blasts Myth of Yeti," *The Nashville Tennessean*, October 31, 1962.

27. Conversation, author with Robert P. Banniza, September 3, 2007.

28. "Personnel Notes," October 10, 1962.

29. Grace and Dick Hall would have a daughter, Wendy, born in 1966, and a son, Rhoads, born in 1970.

30. "Hotel Life with Dad," *The Nashville Tennessean*, June 20, 1965.

31. Conversation, author with Alex Joyce, August 7, 2007.

32. "City Club to Build Lounge in Hotel," *The Nashville Tennessean*, January 2, 1964.

33. Reminiscences by Grace Ward Hall, August 20, 2007.

34. John Hemphill, "Memorial Square Speech at Noon," *Nashville Banner*, September 21, 1964.

35. "Thousands to Greet President," *The Nashville Tennessean*, October 9, 1964.

36. Reminiscences by Grace Ward Hall, August 20, 2007.

37. "Tall Man Surprises Reporters' Luncheon," *The Nashville Tennessean*, October 10, 1964.

38. Conversations, author with Brooks Katzman and Irwin Kuhn, August 5, 2007.

39. "Hermitage Hotel Is Now Long Way from the Capitol," *Nashville Banner*, February 23, 1965.

40. Julie Hollabaugh, "Rudolph, TV Star Holiday Pals," *The Nashville Tennessean*, December 24, 1964.

41. Dick Battle, "Hermitage Hotel, Club Breaking Laws: Metro," *Nashville Banner*, December 22, 1966.

42. "Guests Recall Anxious Hour," *The Nashville Tennessean*, March 20, 1968.

43. Jerry Thompson, "Firemen Quickly Douse Hermitage Hotel Flames," *The Nashville Tennessean*, March 20, 1968.

44. "McGoldrick Manager of Hermitage Hotel," *Nashville Banner*, June 5, 1968.

45. "Miss Baumgartner Resigns Sales Post," *The Nashville Tennessean*, May 7, 1969.

46. "Hermitage Hotel Joins 'Telemax' Reservations System," *Nashville Banner*, December 1, 1971.

47. Conversation, author with Mr. and Mrs. James F. Gallivan, September 26, 2007.

48. "Andrew Jackson Hotel Leveled in 9 Seconds," *The Nashville Tennessean*, June 14, 1971.

Chapter 6

1. "Womble Will Manage The Hermitage Hotel," *Nashville Banner*, October 23, 1970.

2. "A Line on Everything," *The Nashville Tennessean*, July 28, 1971.

3. "State Offices Slated Here by Democrats," *The Nashville Tennessean*, September 22, 1973.

4. Conversation, author with Van T. Irwin Jr., March 3, 2008.

5. Clara Hieronymus, "Museum Makes Part Move," *The Nashville Tennessean*, June 1, 1974.

6. Allen Green, "Metro Closes Hermitage Hotel Kitchen," *Nashville Banner*, September 27, 1974.

7. Allen Green, "Two Clubs Still Meeting at Hermitage, Cater Food," *Nashville Banner*, October 1, 1974.

8. "Hotel Reopens Dining Room," *Nashville Banner*, November 15, 1974.

9. Conversation, author with Rob Stallings, September 18, 2007.

10. Interview, author with Paul Carlisle, February 25, 2008.

11. David Fox, "Ready for Restoration," *Nashville Banner*, March 25, 1976.

12. Larry Brinton, "Hermitage Hotel Renovation Off," *Nashville Banner*, June 7, 1977.

13. Notes and National Register of Historic Places nomination form, Hermitage Hotel file, Metropolitan Historical Commission.

14. Email, May Dean Eberling to the author, October 28, 2007.

15. Rich Riebeling, "Health Hazards Force Hermitage Hotel Closing," *Nashville Banner*, July 1, 1977.

16. "15 Businesses Must Close with Hotel," *The Nashville Tennessean*, July 2, 1977.

17. Rich Riebeling, "Hermitage Tenants in State of Shock," *Nashville Banner*, July 1, 1977.

18. Ibid.

19. At some point, Dick Hall and Harry Banniza were co-owners of the liquor store.

20. Rich Riebeling, "Hotel Vendor Seeks Carter's Help," *Nashville Banner*, July 8, 1977.

21. Frances Meeker, "Preserve Historic Sites, Pleads Businessman," *Nashville Banner*, November 3, 1977.

22. Clara Hieronymus, "Nashville Beaux Arts," *The Tennessean*, August 14, 1977.

23. "Hermitage Tenants to Get 30 Days Extension," *Nashville Banner*, July 23, 1977.

24. Marsha Vande Berg, "Hotel Owner Told to Fix Up or Close Up," *The Nashville Tennessean*, August 27, 1977.

25. "Empty, But No Vacancies," *Nashville Banner*, August 1, 1977.

26. Rich Riebeling, "Hermitage Hotel Renovation Planned," *Nashville Banner*, September 2, 1977; Frank Gibson, "'Grand' Hermitage Hotel Eyed," *The Nashville Tennessean*, September 2, 1977.

27. Pete Bird, "Funding Key in Hermitage Renovation," *Nashville Banner*, October 13, 1977.

Chapter 7

1. Albert Cason, "Office Use for Hermitage Hotel Possible," *The Tennessean*, February 16, 1979.

2. Pete Bird, "Office Building at Hermitage Hotel to Begin," *Nashville Banner*, February 16, 1979.

3. Susan Thomas, "Hermitage Hotel Project Hangs on Codes," *The Tennessean*, February 18, 1979.

4. Ken Renner, "Revamp Bond for Hermitage Hotel Approved," *Nashville Banner*, March 15, 1979.

5. *The Tennessean*, February 28, 1979.

6. "Andrew Johnson Building Attracting Buyers," *Knoxville News-Sentinel*, October 27, 1991.

7. Pete Bird, "HAI May Move to Hermitage Hotel," *Nashville Banner*, April 10, 1979.

8. Albert Cason, "Restored Hermitage May House Luxury Restaurant," *The Tennessean*, May 10, 1979.

9. Albert Cason, "Hermitage Hotel, With Elegance of Old, To Serve as HAI's Home," *The Tennessean*, May 27, 1979.

10. Ibid.

11. Albert Cason, "Hermitage Hotel Rebirth to Have Mark of Luxury," *The Tennessean*, September 9, 1979.

12. "Hermitage Hotel Plan Snagged," *Nashville Banner*, December 4, 1979.

13. *The Tennessean*, January 7, 1980.

14. "List Request Stalls Hotel Plane," *The Tennessean*, January 9, 1980.

15. "Public Hearing Set on Plans for Hotel," *The Tennessean*, December 31, 1979.

16. *Nashville Banner*, July 17, 1980.

17. "Old Hermitage Hotel Project Gains Support," *Nashville Banner*, June 12, 1980.

18. *Nashville Banner*, June 22, 1980.

19. Ronnie Hatcher also worked on the bond issue for J. C. Bradford. Murray Hatcher told the author on April 14, 2008 that the bonds were sold "retail," meaning they were purchased by private individuals.

20. "Hotel Work Papers Inked," *The Tennessean*, June 25, 1980.

21. Clara Hieronymus, "Hermitage Hotel Returns to its Youthful Beauty," *The Tennessean*, June 29, 1980.

22. "Hermitage Hotel Girds for Sales," *Nashville Banner*, October 16; "Hermitage Sales Office Now Open," November 5, 1980.

23. "Dennis Morgan Named Hermitage Manager," *Nashville Banner*, November 27, 1980.

24. "No Thanks," *The Tennessean*, April 10, 1981.

25. "People," *Nashville Banner*, December 2, 1980.

26. Pete Bird, "Hermitage Hotel Set for Grand Reopening," *Nashville Banner*, January 9, 1981.

27. "Refurbished Hotel to be Open Feb. 1," *The Tennessean*, January 4, 1981.

28. Pete Bird, "Hermitage Hotel Set For Grand Reopening," *Nashville Banner*, January 9, 1981.

29. Ibid.

30. "Hermitage Hotel Plans Gala Opening," *The Tennessean*, January 23, 1981.

31. Conversation, author with Cherrie Hall, October 2007.

32. Caroline McNeilly, "New Hermitage Hotel is Artist's Masterpiece," *Nashville Banner*, February 3, 1981.

33. "The Hermitage: An Aging Beauty Recovers Status," *The Tennessean*, February 4, 1981.

34. "Hermitage Hotel Looking for China," *The Tennessean*, March 5, 1981.

35. "Hermitage Hotel Plans Gala Opening," *The Tennessean*, January 23, 1981.

36. *The Tennessean*, April 8, 1981.

37. "Hermitage Hotel to Open, Tossing Key to the Winds," *Nashville Banner*, April 10, 1981.

38. *Nashville Banner*, June 19, 1981.

39. "Hermitage Hotel to Open, Tossing Key to the Winds," *Nashville Banner*, April 10, 1981.

40. *Nashville Banner*, June 18, 1981.

41. "Memories of Francis Craig Still Linger," *The Tennessean*, June 26, 1981.

Minnesota Fats

1. "Hotel Gives Table to Minnesota Fats," *The Tennessean*, October 11, 1985.

2. Minnesota Fats with Tom Fox, *The Bank Shot and Other Great Robberies* (Guilford, CT: The Lyons Press, 2006), 8.

3. Ibid., 53.

4. Ibid., 133.

5. Fats, *The Bank Shot*, xiii.

6. Interview, author with Semra Triplett, September 14, 2007. Triplett also sold custom-made ties to her customers at the Hermitage.

7. Interview, author with Patrick Franzone, October 2, 2007.

8. Ibid.

9. Reminiscences of Alton Kelley, August 27, 2007.

10. *Nashville Banner*, May 15, 1997

11. Conversation, author with Stan Ockwig, March 26, 2008.

12. Interview, author with Theresa Bell, September 21, 2007.

Chapter 8

1. Joan Dew, "Sentimental Journey," *Nashville Magazine*, July 1981.

2. Joan Dew, "Hermitage Holiday," *Nashville Magazine*, December 1981.

3. "Hermitage is One Hotel Restaurant Worth Attention," *Nashville Banner*, December 10, 1981.

4. "Hotel Doormen, An Open-and-Shut Job? Not Anymore," *Nashville Banner*, October 19, 1981.

5. Ibid.

6. *Nashville Banner*, December 1981.

7. "People in the News," *Nashville Banner*, March 19 and May 7, 1982.

8. Interview, author with Patrick Franzone, October 2, 2007.

9. "Holiday Spirit Reigns at Hotel," *The Tennessean*, December 15, 1983.

10. "A Holiday of Good Will," *The Tennessean*, December 29, 1983.

11. "Hermitage Hotel Has Anniversary," *Nashville Banner*, March 15, 1984.

12. Interview, author with Patrick Franzone, October 2, 2007.

13. James H. Jesse, "Save Room for Dessert When Eating at the Hermitage," *The Tennessean*, April 1, 1984.

14. Interview, author with Patrick Franzone, October 2, 2007.

15. "5 Hotels Here Win AAA Quality Award," *The Tennessean*, March 12, 1985.

16. "Hotel Man Makes City the Gainer," *The Tennessean*, October 27, 1985.

17. Clarke Canfield, "Hermitage Hotel Is for Sale," *Nashville Banner*, April 23, 1986.

18. Ibid.

19. Max York, "Hermitage Hotel Still Grand Lady," *The Tennessean*, November 9, 1986.

20. Ibid.

21. Interview, author with Stan Ockwig, January 2008.

22. Interview, author with Theresa Bell, September 21, 2007.

23. Interview, author with Patrick Franzone, October 2, 2007.

24. Cathy Schultze, "A Brighter Future Forecast for Historic Hermitage Hotel," *Nashville Banner*, January 2, 1987.

25. Chris Rodell, "Couple's 50th Anniversary Spurs Reunion," *Nashville Banner*, September 3, 1986.

26. Jane Taylor, "At Hermitage Hotel, It's 'Back to Basics' to Revive 'Grand' Image, Offset Money Woes," *The Tennessean*, February 24, 1987.

27. "Hotel Stay a New Twist," *The Tennessean*, March 20, 1987.

28. "Hermitage Hotel Gives Cabbies Lunch," *The Tennessean*, July 1, 1987.

29. Cindy Roland, "Water Main Means Tricks, Not Treat for Flooded Hotel," *The Tennessean*, November 1, 1987.

30. Program for the VIPPS dinner, January 19, 1988, VIPPS Archives.

31. "Hotel Owner's Suit Charges Embezzlement," *The Tennessean*, May 29, 1988.

32. Conversation, author with James Braden, October 31, 2007.

33. "Restaurant Review," *Nashville Scene*, December 21, 1988.

34. *Nashville Scene*, June 8, 1989; "Hermitage Hotel Soon to Become Embassy Suites," *Nashville Banner*, June 7, 1989.

35. Conversation, author with Doug Vandenberg, October 29, 2007.

36. Tim Tanton, "3rd National Is Suing Hermitage Operator," *Nashville Banner*, July 17, 1991.

37. "Third National Seeks $5 Million in Hermitage Hotel Bond Default," *The Tennessean*, July 18, 1991.

38. "History Will Kick Up Heels at Hermitage," *Nashville Banner*, January 15, 1992.

39. Conversation, author with Doug Vandenberg, October 29, 2007.

40. "Music City's Grand Hotel Gets a Facelift," *The Tennessean*, April 4, 1992.

41. Christine Kreyling, "Architecture Crimes: The Case of the Crumbling Cornice," *Nashville Scene*, July 2, 1992.

42. *Nashville Banner*, December 16, 1992.

43. Robert Sherborne, "Hotel's Debts Prompt Lawsuit," *The Tennessean*, December 17, 1992.

44. Tim Tanton, "Receiver Handling Hotel," *Nashville Banner,* January 14, 1993.

45. Conversation, author with Robert Waldschmidt, September 24, 2007.

46. Bill Carey, "Hermitage Hotel Sale Approved by Judge," *The Tennessean*, November 18, 1993.

47. Ibid.

48. Bill Carey, "Hermitage Hotel Renovation Set," *The Tennessean*, April 13, 1994.

49. Conversation, author with Doug Vandenberg, October 29, 2007.

50. "Hotel Turns to Veteran Manager," *Nashville Banner*, April 26, 1994.

51. "The Hermitage Suite Hotel Where Elegance Lives Again," a four-page advertising piece produced by The Hermitage Suite Hotel in 1995.

52. "Renovation Gets Hermitage Hotel Ready for Future," *Nashville Banner*, April 1995.

53. Conversation, author with Rudolph Gomez, March 26, 2008.

54. "Say 'Wow' Renovation Gets Hermitage Ready for Future," *Nashville Banner*, May 10, 1995.

55. Christine Kreyling, "Regilding the Lily," *Site* Magazine, March 13, 2003.

56. "The Hermitage Suite Hotel Where Elegance Lives Again," a four-page advertising piece produced by The Hermitage Suite Hotel in 1995.

57. Kay West, "Glory Days Again at Capitol Grille," *Nashville Scene*, October 5, 1995.

58. Will Pinkston, "Hermitage Hotel Is Sold," *The Tennessean*, March 12, 1997.

59. Cree Lawson, "Hermitage Suite Changes Hands for $15.85 Million," *Nashville Banner*, March 12, 1997.

60. Ibid.

61. Will Pinkston, "Hermitage Joins Hotel Chain," *The Tennessean*, December 4, 1997.

62. Lisa Benavides, "Starwood Renovates City Hotels," *The Tennessean*, April 22, 1999.

Chapter 9

1. Richard Lawson, "New Owners Have Big Plans for Hermitage," *The Tennessean*, June 17, 2000.

2. Rose French, "A Grand Revival," *The Tennessean*, August 6, 2002.

3. Carrie Ferguson, "Sale Seekers Hit Hermitage Hotel," *The Tennessean*, April 2, 2002.

4. Interview, author with Greg Sligh, December 5, 2007.

5. Ibid.

6. Press Release, ForrestPerkins LLC, February 24, 2003.

7. Interview, author with Stephen W. Brown, January 15, 2008.

8. Conversation, author with Walker Mathews, December 18, 2007.

9. Press Release, ForrestPerkins LLC, February 24, 2003.

10. Ibid.

11. Ibid.

12. Ibid.

Chapter 10

1. *Nashville Lifestyles*, February/March 2003.

2. Alexa Hinton, "Tyler Brown, Executive Chef at Capitol Grille," *The City Paper*, March 20, 2007.

3. "A Dog's Life at The Hermitage Hotel," *Nashville Today*, January 8, 2004.

4. "Hermitage Hotel called 'Best of the Best' by The Robb Report," Hermitage Hotel press release, June 2003.

5. Craig Boerner, "Hermitage Hotel Earns AAA Five Diamonds," *The City Paper*, November 18, 2003.

6. *The Wall Street Journal*, October 26, 2006.

7. "The Hermitage Hotel Receives Mobil Five Star Award," Hermitage Hotel press release, November 9, 2006.

8. Ibid.

9. Ibid.

10. Ibid.

11. Marketing email released by hotel, July 22, 2008.

12. Marketing email released by hotel, November 14, 2008.

13. "Loretta Back in Spotlight," *The Tennessean*, April 23, 2004.

14. "Back to the Future," *Nashville Lifestyles*, September 2005.

15. Hermitage Hotel banquet event order, September 7, 2005.

16. "Historic Hotels of America Joins Preferred Hotel Group Brand," Preferred Hotel Group press release, October 25, 2007.

17. "Everyday Opulence," *Nashville Lifestyle*, September 2006.

18. "Hermitage Hotel partners with Land Trust," *The Tennessean*, July 12, 2008.

19. "Hotel Money Is Secured," *Nashville Banner*, June 3, 1908.

Selected Bibliography

Alpern, Andrew. *The New York Apartment Houses of Rosario Candela and James Carpenter*. New York: Acanthus Press, 2001.

Biles, Roger. *Memphis in the Great Depression*. Knoxville: University of Tennessee Press, 1986.

Cochran, Bess White. *All Together: A History of the Nashville YMCA 1875–1975*. Nashville: Rich Printing Co., 1975.

Connors, Thomas. *Meet Me in the Bar*. New York: Stewart, Tabori & Change, 2001.

Fats, Minnesota with Tom Fox. *The Bank Shot and Other Great Robberies*. Guilford, CT: The Lyon Press, 2006.

Graham, Eleanor, ed. *Nashville: A Short History of Selected Buildings*, Historical Commission of Metropolitan Nashville–Davidson County, 1974.

Greene, Lee Seifert. *Lead Me On, Frank G. Clement and Tennessee Politics*. Knoxville: University of Tennessee Press, 1982.

Havighurst, Craig. *Art Castle of the South, WSM and the Making of Music City*. Chicago: University of Illinois Press, 2007.

Ikard, Robert W. *Near You: Francis Craig, Dean of Southern Maestros*. Franklin, TN: Hillsboro Press, 1999.

Lynch, Amy. *Service Above Self: A History of Nashville Rotary*. Springfield, IL: Phillips Brothers, 1995.

Matera, Dary. *John Dillinger: The Life and Death of America's First Celebrity Criminal*. New York: Carroll & Graft Publishers, 2005.

Miller, William D. *Mr. Crump of Memphis*. Baton Rouge: Louisiana State University Press, 1964.

Morehouse, Ward, III. *Inside the Plaza*. New York: Applause Books, 2001.

Norman, Jack, Sr. *The Nashville I Knew*. Nashville: Rutledge Hill Press, 1984.

Owen, Marie Bankhead. *The Story of Alabama: A History of the State*. New York: Lewis Historical Pub. Co., 1949.

Perry, John. *Sgt. York His Life, Legacy & Legend*. Nashville: Broadman and Homan Publishers, 1997.

Phillips, Margaret L. *The Governers of Tennessee*. Greta, LA: Pelican Publishing Co., 1978.

Sandoval-Strausz, Andrew K. *Hotel, An American History*. New Haven, CT: Yale University Press, 2007.

Sherman, Joe. *A Thousand Voices: The Story of Nashville's Union Station*. Nashville: Rutledge Hill Press, 1987.

Somerville, James. *The Carmack-Cooper Shooting: Tennessee Politics Turns Violent November 9, 1908*. Jefferson, NC: McFarland and Co., 1994.

Stamper, Powell. *The National Life Story*. New York: Appleton-Century-Crofts, 1968.

Taylor, A. Elizabeth. *The Woman Suffrage Movement in Tennessee*. New York: Bookman Associates, 1957.

Thompson, E. D. *The Nashville Nostalgia Years*. Nashville: Westview Publishing Co., 2005.

Travelers' Protective Association of America, Commercial History of the State of Tennessee, 1910.

Turner, Jane, ed. *The Dictionary of Art*, vol. 3. New York: Oxford University Press, 2003.

White, Marjorie L., ed. Downtown Birmingham Architectural and Historical Walking Tour Guide, Birmingham Historical Society and the First National Bank of Birmingham, 1977.

Wills, Ridley, II. *Yours to Count On*. Nashville: Vanderbilt University, 2007.

Yellin, Carol Lynn and Janann Sherman. *The Perfect 36: Tennessee Delivers Woman Suffrage*. Oak Ridge, TN: Iris Press, 1998.

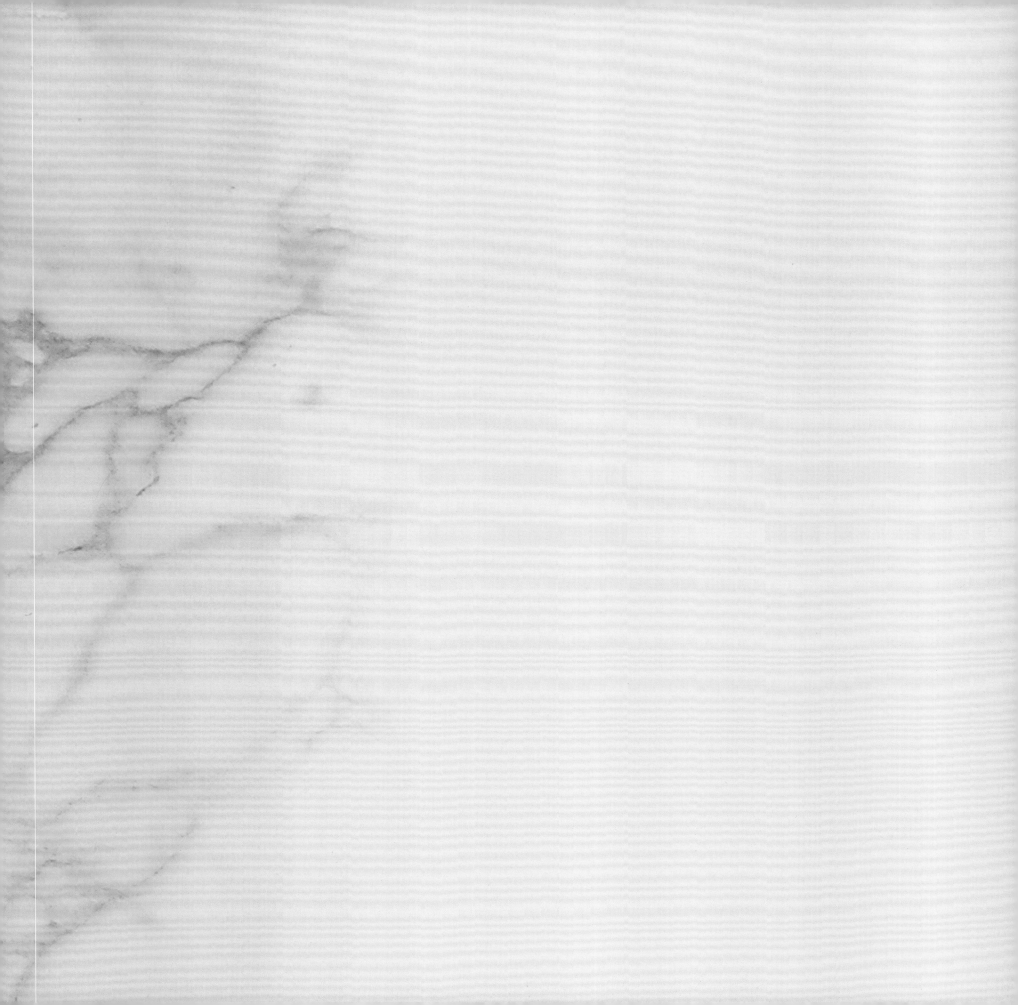

List of Abbreviations

AA—Andrew Alpern from his book *The New York Apartment Houses of Rosario Candela and James Carpenter*
AL—Alan LeQuire
AR—*Architechtural Record*, July 1911
DCD—Donia Craig Dickerson Collection
EWF—Edgar W. Foster Collection
FP—ForrestPerkins
GH—Grace Hall
HH—Hermitage Hotel Collection; image on p. 196 compliments of Buddy Potts

HRP—Herschel Robert Pardue Collection
HSS—Henry Schofield Studio
JA—Jerry Atnip
JJH—Janet and James Hasson Jr.
KRS—© 1988, Kevin C. Rose/ Rose Studio, Inc.
LC—Library of Congress
LM—LeAnna Massingille
MA—Metropolitan Government Archives of Nashville and Davidson County Tennessee
MC—Mark Couturiér
MEN—Mary E. Nichols

MOP—Martin O'Conner Photography
MW—Marvin Wiles
MWS—Marion Ward Studio
NB—*Nashville Banner*
NPL-SC—Nashville Public Library, Special Collections; image on p. 11 donated by Hart Freeland Roberts
NT—*The Nashville Tennessean*
PP—Prakash Patel
RML—Randal McGavock Lea Collection
RWII—Ridley Wills II Collection

TBW—From the collection of Theresa Bell Wanderone
TCV—Tom C. Vickstrom
TGP—Tom Gatlin Photography
TN—*The Tennessean*
TSLA—Tennessee State Library and Archives
WOODS—From the collection of Frank A. and Jayne Ann Owens Woods

Photo Credits

The following is a list of credits for images not otherwise identified.
The number at the left of the column indicates on which page the image is found.

v, *left*, David Wright Photography
v, *center*, David Wright Photography
v, *right*, a 1938 meeting of the United Daughters of the Confederacy, Nashville Public Library, Special Collections
vi, *background*, Nashville Public Library, Special Collections
x, Hermitage Hotel Collection
xii, *left*, *Nashville Banner*, September 17, 1910
xii, *center*, *The Nashville Tennessean*, September 18, 1910
xii, *right*, *Nashville Banner*, September 17, 1910
xiii, *left*, *The Nashville Tennessean*, April 6, 1919

xiii, *center*, *The Nashville Tennessean*, September 18, 1910
xiii, *right*, *The Nashville Tennessean*, September 18, 1910
xiv, *left*, *The Nashville American*, September 16, 1910
xiv, *center*, *Nashville Banner*, September 16, 1910
xiv, *right*, *The Nashville American*, September 16, 1910
2, David Wright Photography
3, Jerry Atnip
4, Jerry Atnip
8, Nashville Public Library, Special Collections
9, *top*, Nashville Public Library, Special Collections

9, *bottom*, Nashville Public Library, Special Collections
20, Nashville Public Library, Special Collections
21, *newspaper*, Tennessee State Library and Archives
21, *photo of statue*, Tennessee State Library and Archives
26, Kermit C. Stengal Jr.
27, Jerry Atnip
28, *Architectural Forum*, 1932
30, *top*, Lincoln Building, New York Public Library
30, *bottom*, 812 Park Avenue lobby, Andrew Alpern
31, *top*, Ridley Wills II
31, *middle*, New York Public Library

31, *bottom*, Ridley Wills II
32, Mary E. Nichols
33, Hermitage Hotel Collection
36, Jerry Atnip
38, Tennessee State Library and Archives
39, *left*, Ace Photography
39, *right*, *The Nashville Tennessean*, January 10, 1915
44, *Leaving Home*, Birmingham Museum of Art; Gift of John Meyer
45, *top*, *Holding the Line at All Hazards*, Birmingham Museum of Art; Gift of John Meyer
45, *bottom*, *Glorious Fighting*, Birmingham Museum of Art; Gift of John Meyer

Index

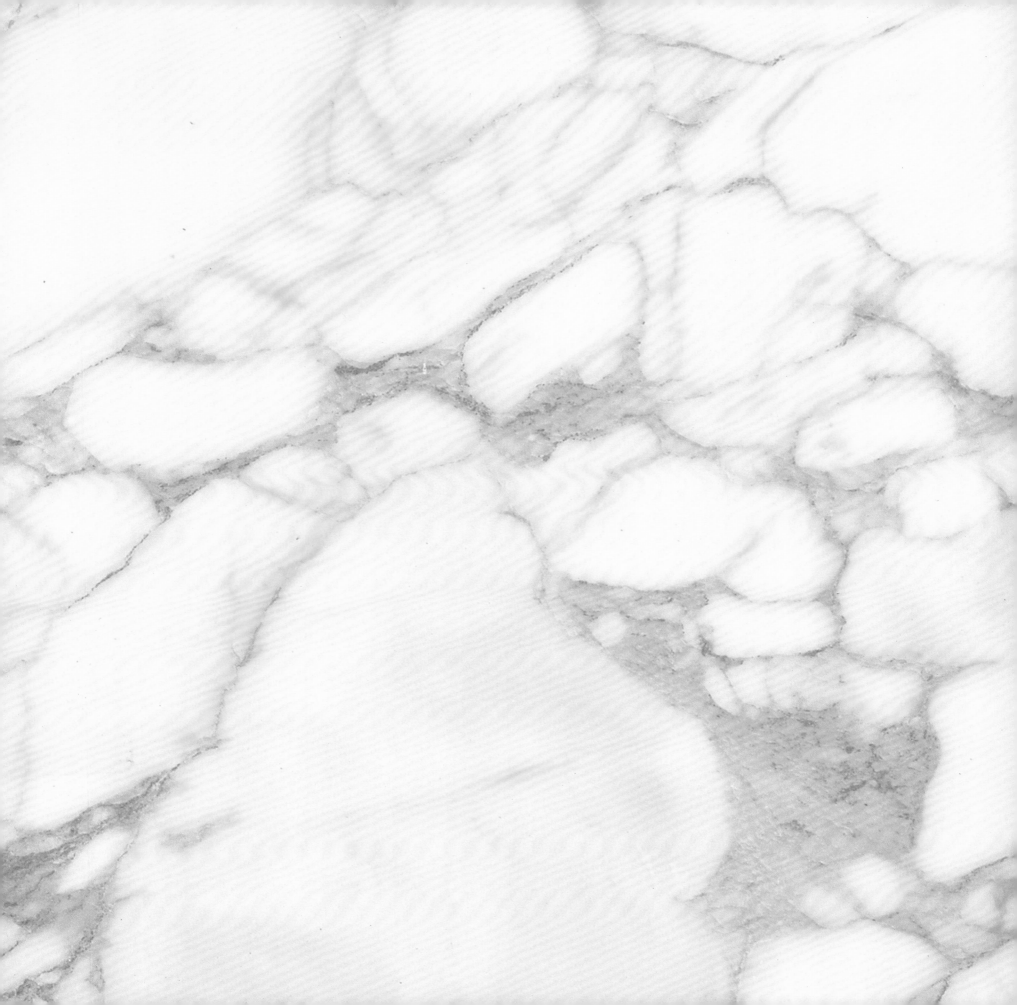